21st Century Socialism

21st Century Socialism

Reinventing the Project

Edited by

Henry Veltmeyer

Merlin Press

Editing: Jean Wilson
Cover Design: John van der Woude

First published in Canada by Fernwood Publishing, 2011
Published in the UK in 2011 by
The Merlin Press
6 Crane Street Chambers
Crane Street
Pontypool
NP4 6ND

ISBN. 978-0-85036-657-0

Printed in the UK by Imprint Digital, Exeter

Contents

Preface

The collapse of socialism as actualized in the Soviet Union in the late 1980s and early 1990s led to a triumphalist declaration of the end of history, the forces of economic freedom (capitalism and democracy) having vanquished the forces of evil that were intent on overthrowing capitalism and replacing it with socialism. Socialism in this context was generally understood as the abolition of private property and state-led control over the forces of production and the distribution of the social product in the public interest. As for capitalism, at the time it was advanced and took the form of neoliberal globalization—structural adjustment to the dictates of capital and the new world order, a system in which the forces of economic freedom (competitive individualism, greed, private capital, the free market) were liberated from the regulatory constraints of the welfare development state. From this perspective and these optics, the defeat of socialism was seen as the superiority of free market capitalism over both state-led or regulated capitalism and socialist development, giving free reign to the quest for maximum private profit.

Fast forward to the future in the present: a system in crisis, a growing polarization of society between the rich and powerful and the poor and powerless, and a yawning social and development divide that has given rise in diverse contexts to an urgent political question: barbarism or socialism? It was Rosa Luxemburg who first famously confronted and formulated this question in conditions of free market capitalist development close to a hundred years ago in the second decade of the twentieth century, on the eve of the Russian Revolution.

In October 2009, a group of socialists concerned with how possibly or best to confront this dilemma in the conditions of a new millennium met in Halifax, Nova Scotia, to consider how best or possibly respond to the challenge of combatting the barbarism of capitalist development today. The agenda of this meeting was to consider and debate how socialists all over the world can contribute to the process of rebuilding socialism—to move towards the socialism of the twenty-first century. At issue in the resulting discussions was not only the meaning of socialism and the form taken by socialism in the twentieth century, but also the different forms of socialist politics—and the thinking behind it: Marxism itself, or the way that Marxism was understood and acted upon. This volume is a product of these discussions and subsequent reflections. It is published as a modest contribution to an emerging debate.

James Petras sets the stage and defines some of the terms of this debate in an introductory essay on twentieth-century socialism and a brief review of several political projects in Latin America to bring about or concerned with the socialism of the twenty-first century. In the concluding essay Petras and Henry Veltmeyer reflect on the fundamental problematic of our times: barbarism or socialism? At issue, as they see it, is whether the forces of change generated in conditions of a multidimensional systemic crisis, and discussed by the other contributors to this volume, are organized and mobilized by the Left or the Right. The world, they add, is at the crossroads of substantive social change. The question is: will it result in a new form of socialism or in a new form of capitalism? The answer to this question is by no means evident, but it does mean a critical re-examination of socialist thought and practice and, at the very least, some action on the ideas advanced by the contributors to this volume.

Reinventing Socialism

Mike Lebowitz, in Chapter 2, addresses the problem identified by Petras and Veltmeyer (of barbarism or socialism?) in an essay that problematizes both traditional Marxist thought and socialism practice, and the need to both "reinvent socialism" and to "recover Marx," a theme picked up on by Hugo Radice in Chapter 9. Subsequent essays in this section reflect on different problems involved in Marxist thought and twentieth-century socialist practice—and in rebuilding socialism in the current conjuncture of capitalist development. Errol Sharpe in this connection argues that socialists should re-examine their fundamental received ideas about socialism as well as the political practice related to these ideas. Socialists, he argues, should break the self-imposed habit of so many socialist intellectuals to "cloister criticism" of socialist practice and to break away from self-imposed bonds on socialist thought and practice. Thom Workman in the same connection reconstructs the ideological broadsides directed against Marxism from the ideological ramparts of "modernisms." From the perspective of this attack on Marx and Marxism, and thus socialism, the project of reinventing socialism hinges on a "recovery of Marx" from the weight of an ideology designed to bury Marx and infect Marxism with counter-productive ideas in a ideological struggle to undermine the search for a genuine socialist alternative to capitalism.

Organization and Strategy

The project of reinventing or building socialism in part is a matter of understanding better the forces at play, and, as Hugo Radice argues, to revisit concepts of class and capital, and rethink the form that socialism might and should take—to reimagine the socialist project. But of equal importance in the project of rebuilding socialism is the question of how best to organize and mobilize the forces of social transformation, a matter of organization and political strategy so as to determine, as Lenin had it, "what needs to be done." In the legacy of Marxist-Leninist thought, twentieth-century socialist practice by and large was based on the agency and use of the communist or socialist party as a political instrument for socialist transformation. Marta Harnecker in one context (developments in Latin America), and Mario Casadio and Luciano Vasapollo in another (Italy), problematize the political party as an instrument of socialist transformation (or at least in its Marxist-Leninist traditional form), posing the problem of socialist transformation as a matter of "people's power," which more often than not in diverse contexts has been manifest in the organizational form of a social movement rather than a political party. In her reflections on this problematic—spontaneity vs. organization? the political party vs. a social movement? the state as an agency of socialist transformation?—Harnecker advances a series of propositions that socialists might use as points of reference to inform their political practice. Casadio and Vasapollo complement this analysis with several reflections and lessons drawn from the organizational experience of their Communist Network. The focus of these reflections is on the instrumentality and organizational form of the political party and a network-based social movement rather than the state. On the state as an instrument of socialist transformation—another critical issue of socialist thought and practice—the essay by Jeffery Webber is particularly relevant. As for Murray Smith and Josh Dumont, they locate the issue of how to organize for socialist transformation in the context of adverse debates on this question within the socialist movement in the twentieth century. The reflections and arguments advanced in these three essays constitute a useful repertoire of ideas in the project of rebuilding socialism in the twenty-first century.

Prospects and Limitations

In his contribution to the debate on how to bring about socialism in the changed conditions of the twenty-first-century ideology Hugo Radice argues that the mistakes in socialist practice made in the twentieth century hinge on a misapprehension by socialists of the fundamental dynamics of capitalism, or Marx's understanding of it. In a critique of twentieth-century socialism, i.e., of the ways in which the goal of building a socialist society was pursued, he points towards the need to re-examine alternative forms of socialist politics submerged by the dominant forces of social democracy and communism.

William Carroll in his chapter argues that humanity's prospects in the twenty-first century hinge on the creation of a counter-hegemonic historical bloc within which practices and social visions capable of fashioning a postcapitalist economic democracy begin to flourish. The organic crisis of neoliberal capitalism creates openings for such a breakthrough; the deepening ecological crisis renders such a breakthrough an urgent necessity. The analytical challenge pursued here is to discern, in the contemporary conjuncture, elements of practice that might weld the present to an alternative future.

How can new movement practices and sensibilities be pulled into a historical bloc—an ensemble of social relations and human agency for democratic socialism? How might that bloc move on the terrain of civil society, and vis-à-vis states, opening spaces for practices that prefigure a postcapitalist world? The aim of the chapter is to show how a Gramscian problematic furnishes us with an analytical and strategic lens that can illuminate practical answers.

Jeffrey Webber for his contribution to the debate reviews in some detail Hugo Chávez's project of a Bolivarian revolution and the ongoing efforts to bring about the socialism of the twenty-first century in Venezuela. This is at the moment the most important, if not only serious, worldwide effort and experiment designed explicitly to bring about the socialism of the twenty-first century. The close analysis that Webber provides of the forces at play in this process, and an assessment of the prospects for bringing about socialism in the conditions generated by these forces, makes an important contribution to our understanding and the project of reinventing and rebuilding socialism in the twenty-first century.

1

Latin America's Twenty-First Century Socialism

James Petras

The electoral victory of centre-left regimes in the first decade of the new millennium in a swath of Latin American countries (Venezuela, Argentina, Brazil, Bolivia, Ecuador, Paraguay, Uruguay) and the search for a new ideological identity to justify their rule, led ideologues and incumbent presidents to embrace the notion that they represent a new twenty-first-century version of socialism (21cs). Prominent writers, academics and regime spokespeople celebrated a totally new variant of socialism as completely at odds with what they dubbed as the failed twentieth-century, Soviet-style socialism. The claims of the advocates and publicists of the 21cs of a novel political-economic model rest on what they ascribe as a radical break with both the free market neoliberal regimes that have dominated the political landscape, and the statist version of socialism embodied by the former Soviet Union as well as China and Cuba.

This chapter examines the variety of critiques put forth both by 21cs neoliberalism and twentieth-century socialism (20cs), the authenticity of their claims of a novelty and originality, and a critical analysis of their actual performance.

21cs Critique of Neoliberalism

The rise of 21cs regimes grew out of the crises and demise of neoliberal regimes that pervaded Latin America from the mid-1970s to the end of the 1990s. Their demise was hastened by a string of popular uprisings that propelled the ascent of centre-left regimes based on their rejection of neoliberal socioeconomic doctrines and promise of basic changes favouring the great majorities. While there are important programmatic differences among the 21cs regimes, they all shared a common critique of six features of neoliberal policies.

1.   They rejected the idea that the market should have precedence and

dominance over the state, by which they meant that the logic of capitalist class profit maximization should exclusively shape public policy. The collapse of market-driven capitalism in the recession of 2000 and mass impoverishment discredited the doctrine of "rational markets" as banks and business bankruptcies skyrocketed, the middle class lost their savings and the streets and plazas filled with unemployed workers and peasants.

2. The 21cs regimes condemned deregulation of the economy that led to the rise of speculators over and above productive capitalism. Under the aegis of neoliberal rulers, regulatory legislation in place since the Great Depression was abrogated and in its place the policies of capital controls and financial oversight were suspended in favour of a "self-regulated" regime in which market players established their own rules, thus leading, according to their critics, to speculation, financial swindles and the pillage of public and private treasuries.

3. The predominance of finance over production was the centrepiece of the anti-capitalist discourse of the 21cs regimes. Implicit was a differentiation between "bad" capitalism that earned wealth without producing goods and services over "good" capitalism, which presumably did produce value of social utility.

4. Related to its overall critique of neoliberalism was a specific critique of the lowering of tariff barriers, the privatization of public enterprises at below their true market value, the denationalization of ownership of strategic resources and the massive growth of inequality.

5. The 21cs regimes argued that neoliberal regimes surrendered the economic levers of the economy to private and foreign bankers (such as the IMF) which imposed deflationary measures instead of reflating the economy through infusions of stale spending. Political leaders of the centre-left used this critique of neoliberalism and the implicit future promise to break decisively with neoliberal capitalism, without committing themselves to a specific break with capitalism of another variety.

6. While the centre-left critique of neoliberal capitalism appealed to the popular classes, their rejection of 20cs was directed at the middle class and to reassure the productive classes (business class) that they would not encroach on private ownership as a whole.

Critique of Twentieth-Century Socialism

In a kind of political balancing act to their opposition to neoliberalism, 21cs advocates have also put distance to what they dub "twentieth-century socialism." Partly as a political tactic to disarm or neutralize the numerous and powerful critics of past socialist regimes and partly to further claims of a novel, up-to-date variant socialism in tune with the times, the 21cs advocates make the following critique and highlight their differences with twentieth-century socialism.

1. Past socialism was dominated by a heavy-handed bureaucracy that misallocated resources and stifled innovation and personal choices.
2. The old socialism was profoundly undemocratic both in the way it ruled, the organization of elections and the one-part state. The denial of civil rights and the abolition of all market activity figure large in the 21cs narrative.
3. The 21cs advocates conflate democracy as a system with the electoral road to power or regime change. Changes of government resulting from armed struggle, especially guerilla movements, are condemned, though all three 21cs governments came to power via elections that followed popular upheavals.
4. A key argument put forth by 21cs regimes is that in the past socialists failed to take account of the specifications of each country. Concretely they emphasize differences in racial, ethnic, geographic, cultural, historical traditions and political practices, which are now considered as defining 21cs.
5. Related to the previous point, 21cs advocates emphasize the new global configuration of power in the twenty-first century which shapes the policies and potentialities of 21cs. Among the new factors, they cite the disappearance of the former U.S.S.R. and China's conversion to capitalism; the rise and relative decline of a U.S.-centred global economy; the rise of Asia, especially China; the emergence of Venezuelan promoted regional initiatives; the rise of "centre-left" regimes throughout Latin America; and diversified markets, in Asia and within Latin America, the Middle East and elsewhere.
6. The 21cs regimes claim that the "new configuration of society and state" is not a "copy" of any other past or present socialist state. It is almost as if every measure, policy, or institution is the design of the contemporary 21cs regime. Originality or novelty is an argument to enhance the legitimacy of the regime before external and internal critics from the anti-communist Right and to dismiss substantive criticism from the Left.
7. The 21cs regimes make a point of emphasizing the fact that the leadership has no links past or present with Communism and in the case of Bolivia and Ecuador openly rejects Marxism both as a tool of analysis or as a basis for policy prescription. The exception is President Chávez, whose ideology is a blend of Marxism and nationalism linked to the thought of Simon Bolivar. Both Correa (Ecuador) and Morales (Bolivia) eschew class divisions, counterpoising a "citizen's revolution" against a

corrupt party oligarchy, in the case of the former, and a culturally oppressed Andean Indian community against an "European oligarchy."

Critique of Twenty-First Century Socialist Regimes

While 21cs regimes have more or less clearly stated what they are not and what they reject in the past both on the Left and the Right, and have in general terms stated what they are, their practices, policies and institutional configurations have raised serious doubts about their revolutionary claims, their originality and their capacity to meet the expectations of their popular electorate.

While a number of ideologues, political leaders and commentators refer to themselves as 21cs, there is a great variety of differences in theory and practice between them. A critical examination of the country experiences will highlight both the differences between the regimes and the validity of their claims of originality.

Venezuela: The Birthplace of 21cs

President Chávez was the first and foremost advocate and practitioner of 21cs. Though the following presidents and publicists in Latin America, North America and Europe have jumped on the bandwagon, there is no uniform practice to match the public rhetoric. In many ways President Chávez's discourse and the Venezuelan government's policies define the radical outer limits of 21cs both in terms of its foreign policy challenging Washington's war policies and in terms of domestic socioeconomic reforms. Nevertheless, while there are innovative and novel features to the Venezuelan model of 21cs, there are strong resemblances to previous radical populist–nationalist regimes in Latin America and European welfare state reforms.

The most striking novelty and original feature of Venezuelan versions of 21cs is the strong blend of "historical" Bolivarian nationalism, twentieth-century Marxism and Latin American populism. Chávez's conception of 21cs is informed and legitimated by his close reading of the writings, speeches and actions of Simon Bolivar, the nineteenth-century founding father of Venezuela independence. His conception of a deep rupture with imperial powers, and reliance on mass support against untrustworthy domestic elites capable of selling out the country to defend their privileges are deeply embedded in his readings of the rise and fall of Simon Bolivar. Although Chávez makes no pretext of identifying Bolivar with Marxism, he does make a strong case for the endogenous, national roots of his ideology and practice. While supporting the Cuban revolution and maintaining a close relation with Fidel Castro, he clearly makes no effort to assimilate or copy the Cuban model even as he adapts to Venezuelan realities certain features of mass organization.

Chávez's economic practice includes extensive nationalization and expropriation (with compensation) of large sectors of the petrol industry, selective nationalization of key enterprises based on pragmatic political considerations including capital-labour conflict (steel, cement, telecoms) and in pursuit of greater food security (land reform). His political agenda includes the formation of a mass competitive socialist party within the framework of a multi-party system and the convoking of free and open referendums to secure constitutional reforms. The novelty is found in his encouraging of local self-government through the formation of non-sectarian communal councils based in the neighbourhoods to bypass the dead hand of an inefficient, hostile and corrupt bureaucracy. Chávez's goal appears, at times, to be the replacement of "representative" electoral politics run by the professional political class by a system of direct democracy based on self-management, in factories and neighbourhoods. In terms of social policy Chávez has funded a plethora of programs designed to raise living standards of 60 percent of the population that includes the working class, self-employed, poor, peasants and female heads of households. These reforms include universal free medical care and education, up to and including university enrolment. The contracting of over 20,000 Cuban doctors, dentists and technicians and a massive program encompassing the building of clinics, hospitals and mobile units crisscross the entire countryside, with a priority to low income neighbourhoods ignored by previous capitalist regimes and private medical staffers. The Chávez regime has built and financed a large network of publicly run supermarkets that sell food and related household items at subsidized prices to low-income families. In foreign policy Chávez has consistently opposed U.S. wars in the Middle East and South Asia, and the entire rationale for imperial wars embedded in the "War on Terror" doctrine.

How Novel is Venezuela's 21cs?

Several questions arise regarding the Venezuelan version of 21cs: (1) Is it really "socialist" or, better still, does it represent a break with twentieth-century socialism in all of its variants? (2) What is the "balance" between past and existing capitalist features of the economy and the socialist reforms introduced during the Chávez decade? (3) To what degree have the social changes reduced inequalities and provided greater security for the mass of the people in this transition period?

Venezuela today is a mixed economy, with the private sector still predominant in the banking, agricultural, commercial, foreign trade sector. Government ownership has grown and national social priorities have dictated the allocation of oil resources. While the mixed economy of Venezuela resembles the early post-World War II social democratic configurations in Europe, there is one key difference: the state owns the most lucrative export sector and is the principal earner of foreign exchange.

While the government has vastly increased social expenditures comparable or even exceeding spending in some of the earlier social democratic governments, it has not reduced the great concentrations of wealth and income of the upper classes via steep progressive tax rates as in Scandinavia and elsewhere. Inequalities are still far greater than existed under twentieth-century socialist societies and comparable to existing Latin American societies. Moreover, the upper and upper middle levels of the state bureaucracy, especially in oil and related industries, have levels of remuneration that are comparable to their capitalist counterparts, as was the case in nationalized industries in England and France.

Self-management of public enterprises, a relatively new idea in Venezuela, has moved beyond the limits of German social democratic co-participation schemes but is confined to less than a half-dozen major enterprises — a far cry from the extensive, nationwide networks found in socialist Yugoslavia between the 1940s and the 1980s.

The agrarian reform proposals of the Chávez regime, though radical in intent and forcibly promoted by Chávez, have failed to change the relationship between farm workers, peasants and large landowners. Where inroads have been made in land distribution, the government bureaucracy has failed to provide the extension services, financing, infrastructure and security to land reform beneficiaries.

The National Guard has by commission or omission failed to end landlord assassinations of leaders and supporters of land reform by the hired guns of landlords. Over 200 unsolved killings of peasants were on the books by the end of 2009.

While publicists of 21cs have emphasized the government's nationalizations of oil enterprises from existing owners, they have failed to take account of the growing number of new joint ventures with multinational corporations from China, Russia, Iran and the European Union. In other words while the role of some U.S. multinationals has declined, foreign capital investment in mineral and petrol fields has actually increased, especially in the vast Orinoco tar fields. While the shift of investment partners in oil reduces Venezuela's strategic vulnerability to U.S. pressure, it does not enhance the socialist character of the economy. Joint ventures do add weight to the argument that Venezuela's mixed public-private economy approximates the social democratic model of the mid-twentieth century.

The most questionable aspect of Venezuela's claim to socialism is its continued dependence on a single commodity (oil) for 70 percent of its export earnings and its dependence on a single market, the United States, an openly hostile and destabilizing trading partner. The Chávez regime's efforts to diversify trading partners has taken on greater urgency with Obama's military pact with Columbian President Alviro Uribe, to occupy seven military bases.

Equally threatening to the mass base of the Chávez road to socialism is the skyrocketing crime rate based on the growth of a lumpenproletariat and its links to Columbian drug traffickers and civilian and military officials. In many popular barrios the lumpen compete with the leaders of the communal councils for hegemony, using unrest and violence to exercise dominance. The ineffectiveness of the Ministry of Interior and the police and their lack of a close working relation with neighbourhood organizations represent a serious weakness in mobilizing civil society and mark a limitation in the effectiveness of the communal council movement.

The remarkable reforms instituted by the Chávez government and the original synthesis of Bolivarian emancipatory anti-colonialism with Marxism and anti-imperialism mark a rupture with the predominant neoliberal practice pervasive in Latin America over the previous quarter century and still operative under numerous contemporary regimes, who claim otherwise.

What is doubtful, however, is whether all the changes amount to a new version of socialism given the predominance of capitalist property relations in strategic sectors of the economy and the continuing class inequalities in both the private and public sector. Yet one should keep in mind that socialism is not a static concept, but an ongoing process, and the bulk of recent measures are tending to extend popular power in factories and neighbourhoods.

Ecuador

In Ecuador, President Correa has adopted the rhetoric of 21cs and it has gained credibility in association with several foreign policy initiatives. These include termination of the U.S. military base lease in Manta; the questioning of parts of the foreign debt incurred by previous regimes; the critique of Columbia's border incursions and military assault of a clandestine Columbian guerilla camp; Corea's criticism of U.S. free trade policies and support of Venezuela's regional integration program (ALBA). President Correa has been identified as part of the "new wave of leftist Presidents" by the mass media, including the *NY Times, The Financial Times* and numerous Leftist journalists, North and South.

In terms of domestic policy issues, Correa's claim to be a founding member of 21cs rests on his critique of the traditional Rightist parties and the oligarchy. In other words, his socialism is defined by what and who he opposes, rather than by any social structural changes.

His main domestic achievements revolve around his denunciation of the major electoral parties; his support for and leadership of a "citizens movement"; and its success in overthrowing the Rightist U.S.-backed authoritarian electoral regime of Lucio Gutiérrez; the convoking of a constitutional assembly; and the writing of a new constitution. These legal and political transformations define the outer limits of Correa's radicalism and provide the substantive bases for his claim of being a 21cs. While these foreign policy and domestic political changes, especially when understood in the context of increased social expenditures during his first three years of office, warrant his being included as a "centre-leftist" they hardly suffice or add up to a socialist agenda, especially if they are seen in the context of the large socioeconomic structural matrix.

The most striking departure of any credible claim to socialism is the persistence and expansion of foreign private capitalist ownership of the strategic mining and energy resources: 57 percent of oil is produced by overseas petroleum multinationals. Large-scale, long-term mining contracts have been signed and renewed giving foreign-owned mineral companies majority control over the principal foreign exchange and export-earning sectors. Worse, Correa has violently repressed and rejected the long-standing claims of the Amazonian and Andean indigenous communities living and working on the lands signed off to the mineral multinationals. In rejecting negotiations, Correa dismissed the four major indigenous movements and their allies in the ecology movements as little more than a "handful of backward elements" or worse. The contamination of waters, air and land leading to serious illnesses and deaths by the foreign oil companies has been demonstrated in U.S. courts where Texaco faces a billion dollar lawsuit. Despite adverse court rulings, Correa has vigorously pursued his push to make foreign-led mineral exploitation the centrepiece of his "development strategy."

While Correa has vigorously attacked the coastal financial agro-commercial capitalist class, centred in Guayaquil, he has vigorously supported and subsidized the Quito (Andean-based) capitalist class. His "anti-oligarchy" rhetoric is certainly not anti-capitalist—as his embrace of 21cs would imply.

President Correa's success in building a mass citizen electoral movement is measured by his impressive electoral victories, securing presidential majorities under multi-party competition, and over 70 percent in the constitutional elections. Despite his popularity, Correa's popular backing is largely based on short-term concessions, in the form of wage and salary increases and credit concessions to small business, measures that are not sustainable with the onset of the world recession. His granting of telecommunication monopolies to private firms, his opposition to land reform, and the restrictions of trade union strikes, while not provoking systemic challenges, have led to an increasing number of strikes and protests. More important, the strengthening of capitalist, especially foreign ownership, control of strategic banking, commercial export and mineral sectors, reduces the claims of 21cs to a merely symbolic, rhetorical exercise. What is apparent is that the basis for 21cs is rooted in foreign policy pronouncements (which are subject to reversal) rather than in changes in class relations, property ownership and popular power. "21cs socialism," in the case of Ecuador, appears to be a convenient way of combining innovative foreign policy measures with neoliberal "modernization" development strategies. Moreover, initial radical measures do not preclude subsequent conservative backsliding as is evidenced in the questioning of the foreign debt (which caused premature Leftist ejaculations of glee) and subsequent return to full debt payments.

Bolivian Socialism: White Capital, Indigenous Labour

The greatest contrast between twentieth- and twenty-first-century "socialism" is found between the current regime of Evo Morales (2005–) and the short-lived presidency of J.J. Torres (1970–71).

While the former has openly and publicly invited mineral and extractive multinational companies from five continents to exploit gas, oil, copper, iron, lithium, zinc, tin, gold, silver and a long list of other minerals, under the twentieth-century Torres regime, foreign and local capitalist firms were nationalized and expropriated. While billions of profits have been repatriated both during and after the commodity boom; under Torres, state control over capital flows and foreign trade limited the decapitalization of the country. While Evo Morales provides hundreds of millions in loans, export subsidies and tax incentives to the wealthiest agro exporters and expels landless indigenous squatters from large estates, under President Torres land takeovers were encouraged as furthering the regime's agrarian reform policies. There is an abundance of socioeconomic data demonstrating that the socialist polices undertaken during President Torres' term of office stand in polar opposition to the social liberal policies practised by the Morales regime. In the following sections I will outline the major social and liberal policies of the Morales regime in order to assess the true meaning of the self-declared 21cs politics in Bolivia.

Social Changes

Numerous social changes have been implemented by the Morales regime during its first five years in power (2005–09). The question is whether these changes add up to any of the most generous definitions of socialism or even to transitional measures pointing to socialism in the near or even distant future, given the scope and depth of the liberal economic policies adopted.

Morales has implemented socio-political changes in nine policy areas. The most significant domestic change is in the area of political/cultural/legal rights for indigenous people. The regime has granted local governance rights for Indian municipalities, recognized and promoted bilingualism for carrying out local affairs and education, given national importance to Indian religious and holiday celebrations and promoted prosecution of those who violate or persecute Indian civil rights.

Under Morales the state has slightly increased its share of revenues in its joint ventures with multinational corporations, and increased the price of gas sold to Brazil and Argentina, while increasing the share going to the national government over and against provincial governments. Given the record prices received by Bolivia's agro-mineral exports between 2005 and 2008, local municipalities increased their revenue flow, though actually investments in productive and service sectors lagged behind because of bureaucratic bottlenecks.

Morales allowed for incremental increases in the minimum wage, salaries and wages, thus marginally improving living conditions. The increases, however, were far below Morales' electoral promise to double the minimum wage and certainly not commensurate with the large-scale windfall profits resulting from the commodity boom.

Morales' prosecution of local officials and the provincial governor of Pando province and Rightist terrorists for the assault and murder of Indian activists put an end to impunity for assaults on citizens of indigenous complexion and culture.

The regime's biggest boast was the accumulation of foreign reserves from $2 billion to $6 billion dollars, fiscal discipline and strict control over social spending and the favourable balance of payments. In this regard, Morales' practices were more in line with the IMF than anything remotely resembling the expansive economic practices of socialist and social democratic regimes.

Tripling hard currency reserves in the face of continuing brutal poverty levels affecting at least 60 percent of the mostly rural indigenous population is a novel policy for any regime claiming socialist credentials. Even contemporary capitalist North American and E.U. regimes have not been as orthodox as Evo Morales' left of-centre national populist or popular nationalist, and self-proclaimed revolutionary, regime.

Morales has promoted trade union organizations and by and large has avoided repression of miners and peasant movements, but at the same time he has co-opted their leaders, thus lessening the number of strikes and independent class action, despite the widespread and deep social inequalities that characterize and afflict Bolivian society. De facto greater tolerance is matched by the increased "corporatist" relation between the regime and the social movements in the popular sector, a relation mediated by "civil society"—the complex of nongovernmental organizations that the World Bank and many other international development "associations" have brought into play in the global war on poverty waged by these organizations in the name of "international development."

Morales' economic strategy is based on a triple alliance between the agro-mineral multinationals, small- and medium-sized capitalists and the social movements, mostly indigenous. The MAS government has poured millions of dollars in the form of subsidies into so-called "co-operatives," which in reality are private small- and medium-size mine owners who exploit wage labour at or below standard wages of miners in larger operations.

The principal changes made by the Morales regime are in its foreign policy and rhetoric. Evo Morales has aligned with Venezuela in supporting Cuba, joining ALBA, forming ties with Iran, and above all, opposing U.S. policy in important areas of international relations. Bolivia opposes the U.S. embargo against Cuba, the seven military bases in Columbia, the coup in Honduras and the lifting of tariff preferences. Of equal importance, Bolivia has terminated the presence of the DEA and curtailed some activities of USAID in subsidizing right-wing socio-political organizations and activities designed to undermine and destabilize the regime. Morales has spoken out forcefully against the U.S. war in Afghanistan and Iraq, condemned Israel's assaults against the Palestinians and been a consistent supporter of non-intervention, except in the case of Haiti, where Bolivia continues to dispatch troops.

21cs in Bolivia

The most striking aspect of Bolivia's economic policy is the increased size and scope of foreign-owned multinational corporate extractive capital investments. Twenty-nine major foreign multinationals, close to a hundred in total, are currently exploiting Bolivia's mineral and energy resources under very favourable conditions, including low wages, weak environmental regulations, and an enhanced royalty- and tax-rate regime. Moreover, in a speech in Madrid (September 2009) Morales told an audience of elite bankers and investors that they were welcome to invest as long as they did not intervene in politics and agreed to a joint ownership regime. Whatever the merits of Bolivia's foreign capital driven mineral export strategy (and the historical record is not encouraging), it puts a peculiar twist on "21cs": replacing proletarian and peasants with overseas CEOs and local technocrats: a novel way to practise "socialism" in any century and more fittingly associated with free market capitalism.

In line with Morales' "open door" policy toward extractive capital, he has strengthened and provided generous subsidies and low-interest loans to the agribusiness sector, even in those provinces like the "media luna" where "big agro" has backed extreme right-wing politicians bent on destabilizing his regime. His willingness to compromise with the political opposition in Santa Cruz, overlook the political hostility of the agribusiness elite and to finance their expansion are clear indications of the priority which the government gives to orthodox capitalist growth, over and above any concern with developing an alternative and socialist-oriented form of development built on the social base of peasants, landless rural workers and indigenous communities.

My on-site visits to different rural areas and peri-urban conglomerations such as El Alto reinforce anecdotal evidence and published reports as to the persistence of class and other social inequalities. The super-rich 100 families of Santa Cruz still own over 80 percent of the fertile lands in the lowlands while over 80 percent of the peasant households and the rural indigenous population are below the poverty line. Ownership of the means of production in mines, retail and wholesale trade, banking and credit continues to be concentrated in an oligarchy that in recent years has diversified its asset portfolio across economic sectors, resulting in a more integrated ruling class with greater links to global capital.

Morales has fulfilled his promise to protect and secure the traditional multi-sector economic elite, but he has also added and promoted new private and bureaucratic entrants to the ruling class, mainly foreign CEOs and high-paid functionaries directing public private partnership. While most socialists (of any century) would agree that big landowners are hardly the building blocks of a socialist transition, the Morales-Garcia MAS (Towards Socialism) regime in fact has depended upon and promoted agroexport production over family farming for local food production. With the re-election of the MAS regime in 2009, the vice-minister for land and agriculture, a proponent of community-owned and -based co-operative enterprises, arguably a proto-socialist form of production, was replaced with a representative of the indigenous peasantry but an advocate of individual land-holding.

The "agrarian revolution" declared in 2006, with reference to a law that authorized the government to expropriate any and all land that was not in productive use or having a social function, is stillborn. In subsequent years the government has indeed given land title to several thousand small landholders, but the land in question was part of the commons or publicly owned; not one big landlord has had his land expropriated. Even worse, the conditions of farm workers on these landholdings have barely improved, if at all. In extreme cases, into the sixth year of Morales' administration, several thousand "indios" are reported to be exploited in the form not of wage labour, which is bad enough, but of slave labour.

Reports have been filed by a Dutch TV media company and the United Nations of slave labour in the landed estates and operations of both foreign companies and private companies in Bolivia as well as Argentina and Brazil. But it would seem that to the regime the harsh super-exploitation of farm workers is of far less concern than productivity growth and generation of export revenues. While labour legislation facilitating labour activity has been approved, it has not been enforced in the countryside, especially in the "media luna" provinces, where, by numerous accounts, labour inspectors avoid confrontations with well-entrenched landowner associations. The few land occupations engineered by the landless rural workers have been denounced by the government. Grassroots movements pressing for land reform in extensive under-cultivated estates have been strongly opposed by the government, violating its own norms—and indeed the agrarian reform law enacted in 2007—that only cultivated farms would not be expropriated.

Given the regime's emphasis on the "cultural and political" aspects of its version of 21cs it is not surprising that it has spent more time and funds celebrating indigenous fiestas, song and dances than it has in expropriating and distributing fertile lands to the malnourished mass of indigenous.

The regime's effort to deflect attention from agrarian reform by settling landless Indians on public lands in distant tropics was a disaster. This "colonization plan" organized by the so-called agrarian reform institute, dumped highland Indians in disease-ridden lands which were not cleared, without farm tools, seeds, fertilizers or even living quarters. Needless to say in less than two weeks the Indians demanded bus transportation back to their impoverished villages, an improvement over these remote malaria-ridden ill-planned settlements. To compensate for the lack of any comprehensive land redistribution program, Evo Morales occasionally organizes, with pomp, ceremony and much publicity, "gifts" of tractors to middle- and small-scale farmers, more a political patronage opportunity rather than an integral part of a social transformation.

The two most striking aspects of the government's economic and political strategies are the emphasis on traditional extractive mineral exports and construction of a typical corporatist patronage-based electoral machine.

Into the sixth year of Morales' regime and administration the joint ventures signed with foreign multinational corporations have extracted and exported raw materials with little of value added. To an astonishing degree there has been a minimal degree of industrialization and final product manufacture that would generate greater industrial employment. The same story is true of agricultural exports; grains and other agricultural products are not processed in Bolivia, which would provide thousands of jobs for the poverty-stricken mass of landless indigenous. To attract foreign direct investment and gain the confidence of investors the regime has accumulated huge hard currency reserves, but it has failed to finance or foment local industry to substitute for imports of capital and intermediate and durable consumer imports.

The government's political strategy closely resembles that adopted by the Nationalist Revolutionary Movement (MNR) a half century ago, in which trade unions and especially peasant movements were incorporated into the dominant party-state regime. In the absence of any significant socioeconomic changes, the government has relied on public patronage, channeled through trade union and peasant and indigenous leaders, which trickles down in the form of local favours for party loyalists. This clientelism is reinforced by symbolic gestures that reaffirm both the ethnic identity of indigenous groups and nations and relations of "solidarity" between the giver and recipient of political patronage.

The 21cs of Morales' political practice is far less innovative and "socialist" and far closer in political style to twentieth-century corporatist predecessors. Observers with little knowledge of Bolivia's past, impressionable journalists enamoured by symbolic politics and financial writers who pin the "socialist label" indiscriminately on politicians who even rhetorically question the free market doctrine have reinforced the "radical" or 21cs image of the Morales regime. Given what I have described about the real practices of the 21cs regimes it is useful to place them in a broader historical-comparative framework to make sense of their possible impact on Latin American society.

Comparative Historical Analyses of Three Cases of 21cs

Despite claims by regime publicists, the most striking aspect of 21cs regimes is what is not novel or special about their policies. Their adoption of a mixed economy and playing politics according to the institutional rules of a liberal capitalist state differs little from the practices of European social democratic parties of the late 1940s to the mid-1970s. To the degree that the 21cs pursue nationalist politics (and I should note that nationalization means expropriation and public ownership) they are a pale reflection of the measures taken between the 1930s and the mid-1970s. With the exception of the Chávez regime, the rest of what passes as 21cs has at best nationalized bankrupt private firms, increased shares in joint ventures and raised taxes on agro-mineral exporters.

The "indigenismo" most forcefully expressed by two Andean regimes, Bolivia and Ecuador, resonated with the rhetoric of the "indo-americanismo" of the 1930s. This was forcefully pronounced by Peruvian Marxist writer Mariatagui and APRA political leader Haya de la Torre, as well as the Chilean Socialist Party, a number of Bolivian and Mexican writers, Augusto Sandino, the Nicaraguan guerilla leader, and the revolutionary El Salvadorean leader Farabundo Marti. In striking contrast to the 21cs indigenistas, their predecessors in Central America pursued profound agrarian reforms, including the restoration of millions of acres of confiscated fertile lands and a profound rejection of the agro-business export model. The earlier version of indigenismo combined symbolic identification with deep substantive changes in contrast to the contemporary indigenistas, who rely mostly on symbolic gestures and identity politics.

The current policies relying on joint ventures resonate with the reformist alternatives to the Cuban revolution, which found expression in J.F. Kennedy's Alliance for Progress, which was taken up by the Christian and Social Democratic counter-insurgency regimes of the 1960s. In opposition to the twentieth-century socialists and communists who favoured the socialization of the economy, the Chilean Christian Democratic government (1964–70) promoted an alternative "Chileanization," which resembles Evo Morales and Correa's "joint ventures." In other words, the economic model of 21cs is far closer to the anti-socialist U.S.-backed reformist model of the 1960s than to any socialist variant of the past.

21cs and Twentieth-Century Social Democracy

While the scope and depth of socio-economic changes pursued by 21cs does not approximate the structural changes of 20cs regime, how do they measure up to the reformist or social democratic variant? Three cases of social democratic regimes based on electoral politics come to mind: the Arbenz regime in Guatemala (1952–54); the Goulart regime in Brazil (1962–64) and the Allende regime in Chile (1970–73). All past social democratic regimes pursued agrarian reforms of greater impact, with thousands of peasant beneficiaries, than contemporary 21cs. More substantial real nationalizations of foreign firms took place than in two of the three contemporary 21cs social democratic regimes (Venezuela has expropriated a comparable number of firms).

In terms of foreign policy pronouncements and practices the anti-imperialist political rhetoric is similar, but the earlier social democrats were more likely to expropriate foreign capital. For example, Arbenz expropriated land from United Fruit, Goulart nationalized ITT and Allende expropriated Anaconda Copper. In contrast, our 21cs have promoted and invited foreign agro-businesses and MNC mining corporations to exploit land and mineral resources. The different foreign economic policies correspond to the different internal class composition and economic alignments between twentieth- and twenty-first-century social democracy. In contrast to conventional misconceptions, the 21cs have consummated pacts between regime technocrats, the multinationals and domestic agro-mineral elites which weigh far heavier in decisionmaking centres, than the mass electoral base of Indians and workers. In contrast, the peasant and worker movements had greater representation and independence of action within and without the twentieth-century social democratic regimes.

21cs: A New Historical Configuration
or a Cyclical Political Process?

Examination of Latin American's past sixty years of history reveals a cyclical pattern of alternating Left and Right "waves" of political regimes. The underlying "constant" has been the struggle between, on the one hand, U.S. imperialist projections of power either through direct intervention, military dictatorships and client civilian regimes and, on the other hand, popular democratic and socialist movements and regimes. The question of whether the latest wave of "centre-left" regimes is simply the latest expression of this cyclical pattern or whether basic alterations in the underlying internal and external structural relations are operating to provide a more sustainable process. I will outline the past cyclical pattern of Left/Right politics in the past and follow with a discussion of some key contemporary global and regional changes that might lead to greater sustainability for Left political hegemony.

Post-World War II, Latin American history has experienced roughly five cycles of Left/Right predominance. The immediate period after World War II, following the defeat of fascism, witnessed the worldwide advance of democracy, anti-colonialism and socialist revolutions. Latin America was no exception. Centre-left social democratic, nationalist populist, popular front governments took power in Chile, Argentina, Venezuela, Costa Rica, Guatemala, Brazil and Bolivia between 1945 and 1952. Juan and Eva Perón nationalized the railroads, legislated one of the most advanced welfare programs and elaborated a regional "third way" foreign policy, independent of the U.S. A coalition of socialists, communists and radicals won the 1947 election in Chile on the promise of extensive labour and social reforms. In Costa Rica a political upheaval dismantled the national army. In Venezuela a social democratic party (Acción Democratica) promised to extend public control over petroleum resources and increase tax revenues. In Guatemala, newly elected President Arbenz expropriated uncultivated fields of the United Fruit Company, implemented far-reaching labour legislation promoting the growth of unionization and ended debt peonage of Indians.

In Bolivia a social revolution resulted in nationalization of the tin mines, a profound agrarian reform, destruction of the army and the formation of workers and peasant militia. In Brazil, Getulio Vargas promoted state ownership, a mixed economy and national industrialization.

The launching of the Truman doctrine in the late 1940s, the U.S. invasion of Korea (1950) and the aggressive pursuit of the Cold War entailed vigorous U.S. intervention against democratic Left of centre and nationalist regimes in Latin America. Given the green light in Washington, the Latin American oligarchies and U.S. corporate interests backed a series of military coups and dictatorships throughout the 1950s. In Peru, General Odria seized power; Perez Jimenez seized power in Venezuela; General Castillo Armas was put in power by the CIA in Guatemala; elected President Peron was overthrown by the Argentine military in 1955; Brazilian President Vargas was driven to suicide. The U.S. succeeded in forcing the break-up of the popular front and the outlawing of the Communist Party in Chile. The U.S.-backed Batista's coup in Cuba, the Duvalier and Trujillo dictatorships in Haiti and the Dominican Republic, the rise of the extreme Right, the overthrow of centre-left regimes and the bloody repression of trade unions and peasant movements secured U.S. hegemony, assured conformity with U.S. Cold war policies and opened the door wide for a corporate economic invasion.

By the end of the 1950s the very extremities of U.S. domination and exploitation, the brutal repression of all democratic social movements and Left parties and the oligarchies' pillage of the public treasury led to popular upheavals and the return of Leftist hegemony. From 1959 through 1976, Leftist regimes ruled or challenged for power throughout the continent with varying degrees of success and duration. The social revolution in Cuba in 1959 and a political revolution in Venezuela in 1958 were followed by the election of the nationalist populist regimes of Jango Goulart in Brazil (1962–64), Juan Bosch (1963) reinstated for a brief moment in (1965), Salvador Allende in Chile (1970–73) and Peron in Argentina (1973–75). Progressive nationalist-populist military rulers took power in Peru (Velasco), 1968, Rodriquez in Ecuador (1970), Ovando (1968) and J.J. Torrs (1970) in Bolivia and Torrijos in Panama. All challenged U.S. hegemony to one degree or another. All were backed by mass popular movements, clamoring for radical socio-economic reforms. Some regimes nationalized strategic economic sectors and implemented far-reaching anti-capitalist measures.

However, all but the Cuban revolution had short lifespans. Even in the midst of the Left turn of the 1960s and 70s, the U.S. and its military clients intervened vigorously to avoid the prospect of progressive social changes. Brazil's Goulart fell to a U.S.-backed military coup (1964), which was preceded by a coup against Juan Bosch in the Dominican Republic (1963) and followed by the U.S. military invasion against the restorationist revolution of 1965/66; a U.S.-backed military coup in Bolivia overthrew Torres in 1971; Chile's Allende was overthrown by a joint CIA–military coup in 1973; followed by Peru's Velasco (1974) and Argentina's Perón (1976). The promising and deep-going Leftist wave was over for most of the duration of the twentieth century.

From 1976 to 2000, with the notable exception of the victory of the Sandinista revolution in 1979, the Right was ascendant, its long rule secure through the worst continent-wide repression in the history of Latin America. The military regimes and subsequent authoritarian neoliberal civilian electoral regimes dismantled all tariffs and capital controls in a wild plunge into the most extreme and damaging free-market, imperial-centred economic policies. Between 1976 and 2000 over 5,000 public firms were privatized and most were taken over by foreign multinationals; over a trillion and a half dollars were transferred overseas via profits, royalties, interest payments, pillage of public treasuries, tax evasion and money laundering. However, the "golden era" for U.S .capital during the 1990s was a period of economic stagnation, social polarization and growing vulnerability to crisis. The stage was set for the popular revolts of the early years of the new millennium and rise of the latest wave of centre-left regimes in the region, which brings us back to the question of the sustainability of this new wave of Leftist regimes.

Some World-Historical Structural Changes

A key factor reversing past Leftist waves in Latin America was the economic power and interventionary capacity of the U.S. There is strong evidence that U.S. power has suffered a relative decline on both counts. The U.S. is no longer a creditor country; it is no longer the leading trading partner with Brazil, Chile, Peru and Argentina and is losing ground in the rest of Latin America, except for Mexico. Washington has lost influence even in its "patio," the Caribbean and Central America, where several countries have signed up for the Venezuelan-subsidized petroleum agreement (Petrocaribe). Washington, as if to compensate for its loss of economic leverage (highlighted by the rejection of its proposed Latin American Free Trade Agreement), has increased its military presence by expanding seven military bases in Columbia, backing a coup in Honduras against a social liberal president and increasing the presence of the Fourth Fleet off Latin America's coast. Despite the projection of military power, circumstances outside Latin America have weakened U.S. interventionist capacity, namely the prolonged costly unending wars in Iraq, Afghanistan, Pakistan and the military confrontation with Iran. The already high levels of public exhaustion and opposition make it difficult for Washington to launch a fourth war in Latin America. Therefore it relies on and finances local client military–civilian power configurations to destabilize and overthrow centre-left adversaries. The increase in global markets, especially in Asia, has allowed Latin American regimes to diversify their markets and investment partners, which limits the role of U.S. multinationals and limits their possible political role as purveyors of State Department policies. The financialization of the U.S. economy has eroded the U.S. industrial base and limited its demand for agro-mineral export products from Latin America, shifting the latter's dependence on new emerging powers. Moreover, having suffered the consequence of financial crises, Latin regimes have imposed some regulations on capital movements, which limits the operation of U.S. investment bank speculators, prime movers in the U.S. economy. While Washington talks "free markets," its application of protectionist measures (on overseas leading) and subsidies to agriculture (sugar, ethanol) have antagonized key Latin American countries like Brazil. As the leading exponent of failed free market neoliberal doctrine, the U.S. has suffered a major loss of ideological influence in the region as a consequence of the global recession of 2007–10.

For these reasons, one major actor (U.S. imperialism) responsible for the cyclical rise and fall of Leftist regimes has been structurally weakened, improving the chances for longer duration. Yet the U.S. is still a major factor acting with potent resources based on its close ties with major Rightist military and economic forces in the region. Second, by the very nature of the development strategies chosen by the "centre-left regimes," they are very vulnerable to crises, namely the agro-mineral export policies based on foreign and domestic economic elites and fluctuating world demand. Third, the centre-left regimes have failed to resolve basic regional imbalances, to significantly lessen social inequalities and to recapture ownership and control of strategic economic sectors. These considerations call into question the middle-term durability of contemporary centre-left regimes.

There are few internal changes in the nature of the state apparatus and class structure that could prevent a reversion to neoliberal policies. The basic question of whether current 21cs regimes are stepping stones toward further socialization or simply transitory regimes opening the way for a restoration of neoliberal pro-U.S. regions is still open to dispute, even as evidence is accumulating that the latter outcome is more likely than the former.

Conclusion

The question of whether 21cs is better or worse than 20cs depends on what versions of each we choose to compare and what political dimensions we select in our comparative evaluation. First and foremost there is no single "model" of 20cs despite the facile equation of it with the Soviet variant. There were essentially four radically different types of 20cs regimes, which in turn were internally varied.

- Revolutionary single party regimes, which includes Cuba, North Korea, China, Vietnam and the U.S.S.R. The first four combined socialist and national liberation struggles and were consummated independently of the U.S.S.R. and exhibited at different times greater and lesser degree of openness to debate and individual freedoms. The "four" all fought U.S. invasions and were all subject to embargos and under intense destabilization campaigns requiring a high level of security measures.
- Electoral revolutionary socialist regimes include Chile (1970–73), Grenada (1981–33), Guyana (1950s), Bolivia (1970–71) and Nicaragua (1979–89). Multi-party competition and the four freedoms were encouraged even at the expense of national security. All were subject to successful U.S.-backed military intervention, military coups and economic embargos.
- Self-managed socialism was put in practice in Yugoslavia factories from the late 1940s to the mid-1980s and was briefly experimented with in Algeria between 1963 and 1964. U.S. and European-promoted separatist movements dissolved the Yugoslavian state, and a military coup ended the Algerian experiment.
- Social democracy based on a large-scale, long-term social welfare

program linked to state management of macroeconomic policy was implemented in the Scandinavian countries, especially Sweden.

The stereotype of the Soviet model of externally imposed authoritarian socialism was applicable only to Eastern Europe; even that was subject to changes and democratic moments such as 1968 in Czechoslovakia and Hungary in the 1980s. Likewise there are significant variations among 21cs and socialists. First, Venezuela has nationalized major foreign and nationally-owned enterprises (oil, steel, cement, banking, telecoms) expropriated large tracts of farmland and settled over 100,000 families, financed universal public health and educational programs and encouraged community councils and worker self-management in a few instances. Second, Bolivia has expropriated few if any major firms. Instead Morales has promoted and signed public-private joint ventures, opened the door to dozens of foreign mining consortiums, supported political reform enhancing and extending civil rights to Indians and increased social expenditures for housing, infrastructure and poverty alleviation. No agrarian reform has taken place and none is foreseen. The third and most conservative variant of 21cs is found in Ecuador, where major concessions to mining and petroleum companies is accompanied by the privatization of telecom concessions and subsidies to regional business elites. Rather than land reform, Correa has transferred indigenous lands to mining companies for exploitation. Major claims to socialism are found in increased levels of social expenditures, the revoking of U.S. use of a military base in Manta and a general criticism of U.S. military and free trade policies. Correa retained the dollarized economy, limiting any expansionary fiscal policies.

By drawing on commonly agreed criteria for evaluating the socialist nature of both twentieth- and twenty-first -century socialism we can form an informed judgment on their performance in achieving greater economic independence, social justice and political freedom.

Public Ownership

All variants of twentieth-century socialism, with the exception of the Scandinavian model, achieved greater public control over the commanding heights of the economy than their twenty-first-century counterparts. Venezuela is the closest approximation of the twentieth-century experience. The comparative performance of the public, public-private and private models varies: in terms of growth and productivity, the public enterprises in the twentieth century have a mixed record of high growth tailing off to stagnation; the mixed enterprises are subject to the vagaries of the market and world demand, alternating between high growth in times of boom and depressed output in times of low commodity prices.

In terms of social relations, the social benefits and work conditions in the public sector socialism are generally more generous than in mixed and privately owned industries, though wage remuneration may be higher in the latter.

Agrarian Reform
The 20cs were far more successful in redistributing land and breaking the power of the landlord class than any measures applied by the 21cs. The redistributive reforms of the 20cs contrast with the agro-export strategies by most contemporary "21cs" that have actually promoted greater concentration of land ownership and inequality between agro-business elites and peasants and rural landless workers. The agrarian reforms, however, were poorly managed, especially in the case of Cuba and China and led to a second transformation, redistributing state farms to family farmers and co-operatives.

On the whole, twentieth-century socialists were much more successful in reducing inequalities of income (but not eliminating them) than their contemporary counterparts. Because twenty-first-century capitalists, especially big mine owners, agribusiness capitalists and bankers, still control the commanding heights of the economies, the historic inequalities between the top 5 percent and the bottom 60 percent remain unchanged.

In terms of social welfare, twenty-first-century socialists have increased social spending and raised the minimum wage, but with the notable exception of Venezuela, do not match the universal free public health and educational programs financed by twentieth-century socialism.

While there were regional imbalances between the countryside and the city under twentieth-century socialism; free medical care, social security and basic health care was available to the rural poor under 20cs and is still lacking in most 21cs regimes.

In terms of anti-imperialist struggles, the record of 20cs is far superior to that of the 21cs. For example, Cuba sent troops and military aid to southern Africa (especially Angola) to repel an invasion by the racist South African regime. China sent troops in solidarity with Korea and secured the northern half from the U.S. invading army. The U.S.S.R. provided essential arms and air defence missiles in support of the Vietnamese national liberation struggle and provided Cuba with almost a half decade of economic subsidies and military aid allowing it to survive the U.S. embargo.

Today's 21cs with the partial exception of Venezuela have provided no material support for ongoing liberation struggles. On the contrary, Brazil, Bolivia, Chile and Argentina continue to provide military forces in support of the U.S.-sponsored occupation of Haiti. At best the 21cs condemn the U.S.-backed coup in Honduras (2009), Venezuela (2002) and military bases in Ecuador and Columbia and reject a U.S.-centred free trade agreement.

The one area in which the 21cs have an apparent advantage is in the promotion of greater individual freedoms and electoral processes. There is greater tolerance of public debate, competitive elections and political parties than was allowed in some variants of 21cs. Nonetheless, economic democracy, or workers' power, was far more advanced in twentieth-century Chilean socialism and Yugoslavian self-management than is the case of 21cs parliamentary elections. Moreover, in the past there was greater concern for workers' opinions in making policy even in the authoritarian systems than takes place in current agro-mineral 21cs states. The greater openness of 21cs is related to the fact that they face less high-intensity military threats. In part this is because they have not altered the basically capitalist nature of their economics.

In comparison with 20cs, 21cs is generally more conservative, works closer with the multinationals, is less consistently anti-imperialist and is based on multi-class coalitions that span the class hierarchy, linking the impoverished poor sectors of the middle class to the very powerful agro-mineral elites. Although 21cs may occasionally make reference to class analysis, in times of crisis their operative concepts obscure class divisions through the use vague non-specific "populist" categories.

Perhaps the radical image of 21cs results from the contrast with the preceding extremist right-wing regimes that ruled during the previous quarter century. The socialist or radical populist label pinned by Washington and the Western media on a number of Latin American regimes that have emerged in the new millennium represents nostalgia for a past of unfettered political submission, unregulated economic pillage and robust repression of popular movements rather than a careful analysis of their policies.

Although 21cs in its diverse forms is less radical and perhaps departs from commonly accepted definitions of socialist politics, it nevertheless draws the line against imperialism, opposes U.S. militarism and interventionism and seeks to limit and regulate, and put a cap on, foreign control over natural resources and capitalist exploitation and profitmaking, and it also provides greater tolerance for the organization of social movements and thus the possible maturation of the latent forces of socialist transformation.

2

Reinventing Socialism and Recovering Marx

Michael A. Lebowitz

What is socialism? For many people schooled in the texts of the twentieth century, the following propositions essentially hold:

1. Socialism is the first stage after capitalism and is succeeded by the higher stage, communism.
2. Development of the productive forces is the condition for communism.
3. The principle of distribution appropriate to socialism and the development of productive forces is in accordance with one's contribution.

In short, socialism in this received doctrine is the stage in which you develop productive forces and thereby prepare the way for the higher stage. Further, an important characteristic of the socialist stage is the place of material incentive, the application of the "socialist principle" of "From each according to his ability, to each according to his work."

To a significant extent, these propositions can be traced back to Lenin. It is well-known, too, that these propositions were accepted as the theoretical foundations for attempts as disparate as the Soviet model and Yugoslav self-management to build socialism in the twentieth century—attempts, we know, that ended in a miserable fit of the blues. The question I pose, then, is whether we don't have to *reject* these propositions—not only based on the fate of these historical experiments but also as a distortion of Marx.

Key Link

"We have to re-invent socialism." This was the statement with which Hugo Chávez electrified activists in his closing speech at the January 2005 World Social Forum in Porto Alegre, Brazil. "It can't be the kind of socialism that we saw in the Soviet Union," he stressed, "but it will emerge as we develop new systems that are built on co-operation, not competition. If we are ever

going to end the poverty of the majority of the world, capitalism must be transcended," Chávez argued. "But we cannot resort to state capitalism, which would be the same perversion of the Soviet Union. We must reclaim socialism as a thesis, a project and a path, but a new type of socialism, a humanist one, which puts humans and not machines or the state ahead of everything" (Lebowitz 2006: 109).

In short, neither expansion of the means of production nor direction by the state should define the new socialist society; rather, human beings must be at its centre. *This is the spectre that is haunting capitalism—the spectre of socialism for the twenty-first century.* At its core is the "key link" of human development and practice—a concept that can be seen clearly in the Bolivarian Constitution of Venezuela, adopted in 1999.

In its explicit recognition in Article 299 that the goal of a human society must be that of "ensuring overall human development," in the declaration of Article 20 that "everyone has the right to the free development of his or her own personality" and the focus of Article 102 upon "developing the creative potential of every human being and the full exercise of his or her personality in a democratic society"—the theme of human development pervades the Bolivarian Constitution.

But there is more. This Constitution also focuses upon the question of *how* people develop their capacities and capabilities—that is, *how* overall human development occurs. Article 62 of the Constitution declares that participation by people in "forming, carrying out and controlling the management of public affairs is the necessary way of achieving the involvement to ensure their complete development, both individual and collective." The *necessary* way. The same emphasis upon a democratic, participatory and protagonistic society is also present in the economic sphere, which is why Article 70 stresses "self-management, co-management, co-operatives in all forms" and why Article 102's goal of "developing the creative potential of every human being" emphasizes "active, conscious and joint participation" (Lebowitz 2006: 72, 89–90).

This key link—this focus upon human development and upon practice and protagonism as the "necessary way"—was at the core of Marx's perspective. The young Marx, for example, envisioned a "rich human being"—one who has developed his capacities and capabilities to the point where he is able "to take gratification in a many-sided way"— "the *rich* man *profoundly endowed with all the senses*" (Marx 1844: 302). "In place of the *wealth* and *poverty* of political economy," he proposed, "come the *rich human being* and rich *human need*" (ibid.: 304).

But it was not only a young, romantic, so-called pre-Marxist Marx who spoke so eloquently about rich human beings. In the *Grundrisse*, Marx returned explicitly to this conception of human wealth—to a rich human being "as rich as possible in needs, because rich in qualities and relations." Real wealth, he understood, is the development of human capacity—the "development of the rich individuality which is as all-sided in its production as in its consumption" (Marx 1973: 325). Indeed, what is wealth, he asked, "other than the universality of individual needs, capacities, pleasures, productive forces, etc." (ibid.: 488).

In short, Marx looked to a society where each individual is able to develop his full potential—i.e., to the "absolute working-out of his creative potentialities," the "complete working out of the human content,' the 'development of all human powers as such the end in itself" (ibid.: 488, 541, 708). Could anything be clearer? This is what Marx's conception of socialism was all about—the creation of a society which removes all obstacles to the full development of human beings.

But how are rich human beings produced? Marx was always clear that people develop through their own activity. This was his concept of "revolutionary practice"— "the coincidence of the changing of circumstances and human activity or self-change" (Marx 1845). People don't develop by giving them gifts from above. That was the essence of the utopian socialism that Marx rejected—the belief that if we change the circumstances for people (for example, by creating new structures, new communities and the like and then insert people into these), they will be themselves different people.

In contrast, Marx's concept of revolutionary practice is the red thread that runs throughout his work. He talked, for example, of how people develop through their own struggles—how this is the only way the working class can "succeed in ridding itself of the muck of ages and become fitted to found society anew." And he told workers that they would have to go through as much as fifty years of struggle "not only to bring about a change in society but also to change yourselves, and prepare yourselves for the exercise of political power" (Lebowitz 2003: 179–84).

Joint Products

Always the same point: we change ourselves through our activity. And this is true of *all* activities of people. Every process of activity has *two* products: the change in circumstances and the change in the actor; every labour process creates a joint product, a particular human product. As Marx commented in the *Grundrisse*, in production "the producers change, too, in that they bring out new qualities in themselves, develop themselves in production, transform themselves, develop new powers and ideas… new needs and new language" (Marx 1973: 494). Here, indeed, is the essence of the co-operative society based upon common ownership of the means of production—"when the worker co-operates in a planned way with others, he strips off the fetters of his individuality, and develops the capabilities of his species" (Marx 1977: 447).

But what about human activity under capitalist relations of production? What is the joint product that develops alongside the commodities containing surplus value that emerges from this particular labour process? How are the capacities of producers shaped by the social relations characteristic of capitalism?

Within capitalist relations of production, people are subjected to "the powerful will of a being outside them, who subjects their activity to his purpose." The creative power of the worker's labour here "establishes itself as the power of capital, as an *alien power* confronting him" (ibid.: 450; 1973: 453, 307). Thus, fixed capital, machinery, technology, all "the general productive forces of the social brain" appear as attributes of capital and as independent of workers (Marx 1973: 694; 1977: 1053–54, 1058). Workers produce products that are the property of capital, which are turned against them and dominate them as capital. The world of wealth, Marx commented, faces the worker "as an alien world dominating him."

And that alien world dominates the worker more and more because capital constantly creates new needs to consume as the result of its requirement to realize the surplus value contained in commodities (Lebowitz 2003: 37–39). For workers, producing within this relationship is a process of a "complete emptying-out," "total alienation," the "sacrifice of the human end-in-itself to an entirely external end" (Marx 1973: 488). How else but with money, the true need that capitalism creates, can we fill the vacuum? We fill the vacuum of our lives with *things*—we are driven to consume.

But consumerism is only one way that capitalism deforms people. In *Capital*, Marx described the mutilation, the impoverishment, the "crippling of body and mind" of the worker "bound hand and foot for life to a single specialized operation" that occurs in the division of labour characteristic of the capitalist process of manufacturing. Did the development of machinery rescue workers under capitalism? Certainly, the potential to permit workers to develop their capabilities was there; however, you can detect the horror with which Marx explained how machinery provided a technical basis for the capitalist "inversion"—how it *completed* the "separation of the intellectual faculties of the production process from manual labour" (Marx 1977: 482–84, 548, 607–08, 614).

In this situation, head and hand become separate and hostile, "every atom of freedom, both in bodily and in intellectual activity" is lost. "All means for the development of production undergo a dialectical inversion," Marx indicated; "they distort the worker into a fragment of a man," they degrade him and "alienate from him the intellectual potentialities of the labour process" (ibid. 1977: 548, 643, 799). In short, in addition to producing commodities and capital itself, the joint product of capitalist production that Marx identified in *Capital* is the fragmented, crippled human being, whose enjoyment consists in possessing and consuming things—a *poor* human being.

The Spectre Haunting Marx's *Capital*

Once we understand Marx's consistent focus upon human development, it is clear that the very *premise* of his *Capital* is the concept of a society in which the development of all human powers is an end in itself. The "society of free individuality, based on the universal development of individuals and on the subordination of their communal, social productivity as their social wealth" is the spectre that haunts Marx's *Capital* (Marx 1973: 158).

Can we doubt at all the presence of this other world from *Capital's* opening sentence? We are immediately introduced there to the horror of a society in which wealth appears *not* as real human wealth but, rather, as "an immense collection of commodities" (Marx 1977: 125). In contrast to the society propelled by the capitalist's impulse to increase the value of his capital (and which looks upon human beings and nature as mere means), Marx explicitly evoked in *Capital* "the inverse situation in which objective wealth is there to satisfy the worker's own need for development" (ibid.: 772).

What "inverse situation"? In fact, that "inverse situation" oriented to human development is the perspective from which Marx persistently critiques capitalism. After all, he describes the fact that in capitalism means of production employ workers as "this inversion, indeed this distortion, which is peculiar to and characteristic of capitalist production" (ibid.: 425). Read *Capital* with the purpose of identifying the inversions and distortions in capitalism that produce truncated human beings and we can get a sense of Marx's idea of the alternative necessary to produce rich human beings. We understand what is "peculiar to and characteristic of" production in Marx's conception of socialism by inverting the capitalist inversion.

Given Marx's description of the crippling of the body and mind of the worker, of how all means for the development of capitalist production "undergo a dialectical inversion" and alienate from the worker "the intellectual potentialities of the labour process," it is no accident that he indicated in *Capital* that the "revolutionary ferments whose goal is the abolition of the old division of labour stand in diametrical contradiction with the capitalist form of production" (ibid.: 619). To develop their capacities and potential, the producers must put an end to (what Marx called in his *Critique of the Gotha Programme*) "the enslaving subordination of the individual to the division of labour, and therewith also the antithesis between mental and physical labour" (Marx 1962: 24).

Indeed, expanding the capabilities of people requires the uniting of mental and manual activity. Not only does the combination of education with productive labour make it possible to increase the efficiency of production;

this is also, as Marx pointed out in *Capital*, "the only method of producing fully developed human beings" (Marx 1977: 614). The answer to truncation and crippling of people is "variation of labour, fluidity of functions, and mobility of the worker in all directions"—this is what is meant by the development of human capacity. The partially developed individual, Marx argued, "must be replaced by the totally developed individual, for whom the different social functions are different modes of activity he takes up in turn" (ibid.: 617–18).

In short, there can be little surprise that Marx looked forward to the *re-combining* of head and hand, the uniting of mental and physical labour—i.e., to a time when the individual worker can call "his own muscles into play under the control of his own brain." Here, then, is the way to ensure (in the words of the *Gotha Critique*) that "the productive forces have also increased with the all-around development of the individual, and all the springs of co-operative wealth flow more abundantly" (Marx 1962: 24).

What kind of productive relations can provide the conditions for the full development of human capacities? Only those in which there is conscious co-operation among associated producers; only those in which the goal of production is that of the workers themselves. Clearly, though, this requires more than worker management in individual workplaces. They must be the goals of workers in society, workers in their workplaces and communities.

Implicit in the emphasis upon this key link of human development and practice is our need to be able to develop through democratic, participatory and protagonistic activity in every aspect of our lives. Through revolutionary practice in our communities, our workplaces and in all our social institutions, we produce ourselves as "rich human beings"—rich in capacities and needs—in contrast to the impoverished and crippled human beings that capitalism produces. This concept is one of democracy in *practice*, democracy *as* practice, *democracy as protagonism*. Democracy in this sense—protagonistic democracy in the workplace, protagonistic democracy in neighbourhoods, communities, communes is the democracy of people who are transforming themselves into revolutionary subjects.

Socialism for the Twenty-First Century

I am describing here one element in the concept of socialism for the twenty-first century—a concept of socialism as a particular organic system of production, distribution and consumption. *Social production organized by workers* is essential for developing the capacities of producers and building new relations—relations of co-operation and solidarity. If workers don't make decisions in their workplaces and communities and develop their capacities, we can be certain that *someone else will*. In short, protagonistic democracy in all our workplaces is an essential condition for the full development of the producers

But there are other elements in this socialist combination, which I explore in *The Socialist Alternative: Real Human Development* (Lebowitz 2010a). The society we want to build is one that recognizes that "the free development of each is the condition for the free development of all" (Marx and Engels 1848: 506). But how can we ensure that our communal, social productivity is directed to the free development of *all* rather than used to satisfy the private goals of capitalists, groups of individuals or state bureaucrats? A second side of what Chávez in January 2007 called the "elementary triangle of socialism" concerns the distribution of the means of production. *Social ownership of the means of production* is that second side. Of course, it is essential to understand that social ownership is not the same as state ownership. Social ownership implies a profound democracy—one in which people function as subjects, both as producers and as members of society, in determining the use of the results of our social labour.

However, are common ownership of the means of production and co-operation in the process of production sufficient for "ensuring overall human development"? What kind of people are produced when we relate to others through an exchange relation and try to get the best deal possible for ourselves? This brings us to the third side of the triangle: *satisfaction of communal needs and communal purposes*. Here, the focus is upon the importance of basing our productive activity upon the recognition of our common humanity and our needs as members of the human family. In short, the premise is the development of a solidarian society—one in which we go beyond self-interest and where, through our activity, we both build solidarity among people and at the same time produce ourselves differently.

These three sides of the "socialist triangle" form members of a whole; they are parts of a "structure in which all the elements coexist simultaneously and support one another" (Marx 1847: 167). Its premises are results of the system; and its products are social ownership of the means of production, social production organized by workers and a solidarian orientation to communal needs and purposes. Yet the very interdependence of these three specific elements suggests that realization of each element depends upon the existence of the other two. In socialism as an organic system, "every economic relation presupposes every other in its [socialist] economic form, and everything posited is thus also a presupposition; this is the case with every organic system" (Marx 1973: 278).

Of course, an organic system does not drop from the sky. A new system never produces its own premises at the outset. Rather, when it emerges, it necessarily *inherits* premises from the old. Its premises and presuppositions are "historic" ones, premises which are produced outside the system. Thus, every new system as it emerges is inevitably defective: it is "in every respect, economically, morally and intellectually, still stamped with the birth marks of the old society." Recognizing the difference between the being and the becoming of an organic system is at the core of a dialectical perspective.

As Hegel put it, the "new world is perfectly realized as little as the new-born child"; it realizes its potential "when those previous shapes and forms… are developed anew again, but developed and shaped within this new medium, and with the meaning they have thereby acquired" (Hegel 1967: 75–76, 81). Marx understood such development as the process of *becoming*— "the process of becoming this totality forms a moment of its process, of its development." And, how does this development occur? "Its development to its totality consists precisely in subordinating all elements of society to itself, or in creating out of it the organs which it still lacks. This is historically how it becomes a totality" (Marx 1973: 278).

The First Reject

This brings us to the first proposition in the received doctrine that must be rejected. Reading Marx's distinction between the new society as it initially emerges and that society once it has produced its own foundations, Lenin in *State and Revolution* interpreted this difference as two separate stages, social- ism and communism. But was this conception of two stages (which he called "stages of economic ripeness") consistent with Marx's view?

In his *Critique of the Gotha Programme*, Marx did indeed distinguish between a communist society "as it has *developed* on its own foundations" and one "just as it *emerges* from capitalist society; which is thus in every respect, economically, morally and intellectually, still stamped with the birthmarks of the old society from whose womb it emerges." Further, he explicitly recognized that it was "inevitable" that this new society "when it has just emerged after prolonged birth pangs from capitalist society" would be characterized by "defects"— defects such as the orientation toward an exchange of equivalents (where "the same amount of labour which he has given to society in one form he receives back in another form").

But this conception of two separate stages *distorts* Marx's perspective. How was what Marx said any different from his general description of a single organic system and his description of the development of capitalism—that a new system necessarily develops on the basis of inherited, historic premises and that its further development requires it to transform those premises into ones it produces itself? As capitalism did in its process of becoming, socialism must go beyond what it has inherited to produce its own premises; it has to generate premises in their socialist economic form.

And, once socialism *does* produce its own premises, then we can say that the system "has developed on its own foundations." Again, this process of development is the process of becoming the organic system of socialism: *"its development to a totality consists precisely in subordinating all elements of society to itself, or in creating out of it the organs it still lacks.* This is historically how it becomes a totality" (Marx 1973: 278 emphasis added).

As I argue in *The Socialist Alternative*, "We will never understand Marx's conception of socialism or what he had to say about economic systems in general if we don't grasp the essential distinction between the 'becoming' of a system and its 'being'—between the historical emergence of a particular form of society and the nature of that society *once it has developed upon its own foundations*" (Lebowitz 2010a: Ch. 4).

Should we accept that Marx abandoned his dialectical perspective and substituted for it a concept of discrete stages with differing principles?

In fact, there is no basis for this substitution. But does it *matter*? Does it make a difference whether we think about a single organic system in the process of becoming or whether we consider this as two separate stages? Well, yes, it does. Because the concept of separate stages is only the first step in Lenin's interpretation that became the received doctrine for all twentieth-century attempts to build socialism. It creates the theoretical space for the concept of a distinct "socialist principle," distribution in accordance with contribution, and for the place assigned to the development of productive forces in the transition from lower to higher stage.

The Second Reject

Consider the latter first. Recall that the central question Lenin was asking in State and Revolution was the character of the state after capitalism. His answer was that it varied: a state would be unnecessary in the higher stage of communism. However, a state *would* clearly be required within socialism. Why? Because until such time as it was possible to distribute products in accordance with needs and until such time as it was possible to allow people to choose whatever activities they wished, a state was necessary. And what would determine that time? The state would be needed to regulate "the quantity of products to be received by each" and this would continue until the socialist stage brought about "an enormous development of productive forces." The latter would be the "economic basis for the complete withering away of the state" and the development of communism. Distribution in accordance with needs would be possible for people only "when their labour becomes so productive that they will voluntarily work *according to their ability*" (Lenin 1965: 114–15).

Everything, in short, would depend upon the development of productive forces to move you to the higher stage of "economic ripeness." No question is posed, though, about the *nature* of those productive forces and the organic link between the character of the relations of production and the productive forces developed within them. But that ignores everything that Marx had to say about this in Volume I of *Capital*! The productive forces developed under capitalism flow from and reflect the particular set of relations of production characteristic of capitalism.

After all, the specifically capitalist mode of production was developed as capital proceeded to subordinate all elements of society *to itself* and to create the organs that *it* still lacked. This was "the historical reshaping of the traditional, inherited means of labour into a form adequate to capital" (Marx 1973: 694, 699). *Those new productive forces, in short, were not neutral.* "Peculiar to and characteristic" of the productive forces that capital develops, Marx explained, is that "they distort the worker into a fragment of a man, they degrade him to the level of an appendage of a machine, they destroy the actual content of his labour by turning it into a torment; they alienate from him the intellectual potentialities of the labour process…they deform the conditions under which he works." Indeed, "within the capitalist system," Marx concluded, "all methods for raising the social productivity of labour are put into effect at the cost of the individual worker" (Marx, 1977: 799).

Of course, a*ll new productive forces are not like that.* Rather than dividing, crippling or otherwise harming producers, would not the productive forces introduced by associated producers be oriented toward the development of rich human beings? Just as capital develops productive forces which serve its goals, the specific productive forces developed in a society of associated producers would reflect that "inverse situation in which objective wealth is there to satisfy the worker's own need for development." This inversion of the capitalist inversion necessarily involves the protagonistic democracy in the workplace that breaks down the division between thinking and doing; it involves a change in the economic structure of society that allows productive forces to increase "with the all-round development of the individual."

Ignore the link between productive relations and the particular productive forces developed within them, and all that matters is the expansion of productive forces without regard for the particular joint product. Ignore the character of productive relations and their effect upon the development of human capacities, and you are led logically to the introduction of Taylorism and the capitalist factory. The protagonism in the workplace which is an investment in human capacities then becomes a matter for the *higher* stage. Meanwhile, the production process does the job of producing alienated and emptied-out workers who must possess more and more alien commodities.

The Third Reject

Third, it is necessary to reject the proposition that distribution in accordance with contribution is "the socialist principle." This was a serious misinterpretation (and misapplication) of Marx's *Critique of the Gotha Programme.* The inevitable "defect" Marx identified in socialism as it emerges was transformed from a defect into a *principle.* Rather than a distribution relationship that had to be reinforced, for Marx this defect was a historical premise that had to be *subordinated*.

The precise nature of that premise was the continued existence of an exchange relation—an exchange not of commodities but, rather, of one's labour with society: "the same amount of labour which he has given to society in one form he gets back in another." It was an exchange between an *owner* (the owner of what Marx referred to as "the personal condition of production, of labour power") and the one who owns the use-values he desires. And, Marx noted here that "the same principle prevails as in the exchange of commodity-equivalents: a given amount of labour in one form is exchanged for an equal amount of labour in another form."

"Give me that which I want, and you shall have this which you want," is the principle of exchange of equivalents; and, it, of course, implies its *opposite*: if I *don't* get the equivalent, you shall not have what *you* want. If members of society relate to each other as owners of their labour-power, each seeks to maximize income for a given quantity of labour (or to minimize labour for a given income).

This continuation of "bourgeois Right," of course, immediately reveals that solidarity is not the bond between members of society. The only thing that matters in such a social relation is how much labour an individual has contributed. Because of the inequality in the capacities owned by the individual producers, this exchange relation is necessarily marked by inequality in distribution.

Marx unequivocally *condemned* this relation as an entirely one-sided perspective. He pointed out that it "tacitly recognizes unequal individual endowment and thus productive capacity as natural privileges." By this standard, those who own greater productive capacity are *entitled* to get more. Nothing else matters. Individuals unequal in their capacities are considered, Marx noted, "from one *definite* side only, for instance, in the present case, are regarded *only as workers* and nothing more is seen in them, everything else being ignored" (Marx 1962: 23–24).

This sounds familiar—*just like the political economy that Marx criticized in his earliest writings*, this conception of distribution according to contribution looks at the producer "only as a *worker*.... It does not consider him when he is not working, as a human being" (Marx 1844: 241). Everything else is ignored except that they are owners. Indeed, Marx's critique of this particular exchange relation in socialism as it first emerges mirrors his earliest critique of the political economy of capital, which begins from the premise that we are *separate*, that the community of human beings is at its core a relationship of separate property owners. It "starts out from the *relation of man to man* as that of *property owner to property owner*" (Marx 1844a: 217).

The relation of exchange, Marx wrote in the *Grundrisse*, is one that presumes that despite "the all-round dependence of the producers on one another," those producers are separate and isolated—and that what exists is "the total isolation of their private interests from one another" (Marx,1973: 156–58). We engage in exchange out of our own self-interest. But what kinds of people are produced in this relationship that begins from "the separation of man from man"? Very clearly, people who *remain* alienated from each other, from our activity and from our own products.

Consider, on the other hand, the alternative that Marx envisioned—the "association of man with man," where there is "*communal* activity and *communal* enjoyment—i.e., activity and enjoyment which are manifested and affirmed in *actual* direct *association* with other men." As Marx indicated in the *Grundrisse,* "a communal production, communality, is presupposed as the basis of production. The labour of the individual is posited from the outset as social labour" (ibid.: 172). In this relation, the "communal character," the "*social character,*" of our activity is presupposed, and thus there is an exchange not of exchange values but of "activities, determined by communal needs and communal purposes" (ibid.: 171–72).

What is so obvious here is the joint product characteristic of this relation—in consciously developing communal relations and producing directly for others, we not only satisfy the needs of others but we also produce ourselves as rich human beings. The process of developing socialism as an organic system is the process of developing this communality. How could we ever think that socialism would develop based upon a principle that views members of this society "*only as workers* and nothing more is seen in them, everything else being ignored!" This one-sided conception, Marx recognized, does not look upon producers as human beings. It stands in contrast to a *different* relation—what a person is entitled to "in his capacity as a member of society." The new principle of distribution which socialism introduces, the *true* socialist principle, expands "*that which is intended for the common satisfaction of needs... in proportion as the new society develops*" (Marx 1962: 23–24).

The point we need to draw from the *Critique of the Gotha Programme* is, of course, that socialism inevitably emerges with defects that it inherits from capitalism. But it does not develop by *building* upon those defects. Rather, its development into an organic system "consists precisely in subordinating all elements of society to itself, or in creating out of it the organs which it still lacks." It develops by changing the economic structure that subordinates individuals and prevents their all-round development.

The Market Self-Management Model of Yugoslavia

What happens, though, if instead of consciously attempting to subordinate the defect of self-interest by building solidarity among members of society, you instead attempt to build upon the defect? Consider in this context the experience with Yugoslav self-management. Looking at the Soviet model, in 1949 the Yugoslav leadership described it as state capitalism and bureaucratic despotism; and they argued that the bureaucracy in the Soviet Union had become a new class. State ownership, they declared, was only a *precondition* of socialism. For socialism, you need socialist relations of production—i.e., self-management. Without worker management, they argued, there is no socialism.

Accordingly, a process was begun to develop worker-managed enterprises based upon social ownership of the means of production. Certainly, the extreme alienation characteristic of the Soviet workplace was not to be found. But something went wrong. In the end, there was neither social production organized by workers nor social ownership of the means of production.

What had happened? For one, in the absence of a sustained effort to educate workers in the workplace as to how to run their enterprises, the distinction between thinking and doing remained. Although they had the *power* to decide upon critical questions like investments, marketing and production, the workers councils did not feel that they had the competence to make these decisions—compared with the managers and technical experts. Thus, they tended to rubber-stamp proposals that came from management.

Why weren't the workers real self-managers? A very important part of the problem is the context in which these self-managed enterprises existed: they functioned in the market and were driven by one thing—*self-interest*. When maximizing income per worker rather than the development of human capacity is the goal, the Yugoslav experience shows that it may be logical to rely upon experts who promise to take workers to that goal; the result is to undermine worker management and to ensure that workers do not develop their potential.

Further, the emphasis upon self-interest necessarily affects solidarity. If the goal of worker management is co-operation among a specific group of producers for their self-interest, then *who is the Other?* Other groups of workers who are competing, producers who are selling required inputs, members of society who are your market or who assert a claim upon your means of production or upon the results of your labour, those who would tax you, the State—indeed, *everyone else*. How do you build solidarity within society on this basis?

The focus upon self-interest also infected the concept of social property. While these enterprises were legally property of the state and were viewed as social property, there was differential access to the means of production. Some workers possessed much better means of production than others, and the unemployed (a growing portion because of machine-intensive investments) obviously had access to *no* means of production.[1] Growing inequality was the product of monopoly—the ability to exclude others from particular means of production. Rather than social property, what existed was *group property*.

Despite measures and constitutional changes introduced to strengthen workers against what was described as a "techno-bureaucracy" ruling over expanded reproduction, those measures did not challenge the entrenched power of the group property relation—a relation that only on its surface was one of worker management. After all, it was the managers and technical experts in these enterprises who understood about marketing and selling commodities; it was the managers and technical experts who knew about investments, about placing the funds of the enterprises in banks and establishing links with other enterprises, creating mergers, and so forth. Workers didn't know these things; they knew that they were dependent upon the experts.

The Yugoslavian case demonstrates that even with state ownership of the means of production and the institution of workers' councils for the purpose of worker management, an overwhelming emphasis upon self-interest undermines the development of socialism as an organic system. *Self-orientation infects all sides of the socialist triangle.*

Should we be surprised at this development? It is precisely the point made by Che Guevara in his *Man and Socialism in Cuba*:

> The pipedream that socialism can be achieved with the help of the dull instruments left to us by capitalism (the commodity as the economic cell, individual material interest as the lever, etc.) can lead into a blind alley. And you wind up there after having travelled a long distance with many crossroads, and it is hard to figure out just where you took the wrong turn. (Tablada, 1989: 92)

The Spectre of Socialism for the Twenty-First Century

The concept of socialism for the twenty-first century as an organic system points to the need to build all sides of the socialist triangle. Obviously, differing concrete circumstances means that it will not be possible to build all sides at the same pace or for all countries to follow the same steps. There is no single model. However, what this concept fosters is the recognition of the *interdependence* of these elements.

The failure to develop one side of this combination does not mean that socialism is as yet incomplete. Rather, it means that it is *infected*. After all, these defects are only defects from the perspective of the new society; in actual fact, they are integral parts of the *old* society. Private ownership of the means of production, despotism in the workplace and self-interest as the goal of production all point backward to the old organic system and infect the elements alien to them. In contrast to a concept of stages in which you can put aside some questions until a later stage, the concept of socialism as an organic system theoretically posits what the experience of the twentieth century has demonstrated: *the continued presence of elements which not only tend toward the reproduction of capitalism but which, sooner or later, open the door to its restoration.*

But is socialism for the twenty-first century only a concept, only a spectre? There is definitely an attempt to make this spectre real in Venezuela at this time. Although it is attempting to advance all three sides of the socialist triangle (and most excitingly with the development of the communal councils which Chávez has called the cells or the embryo of a new socialist state), that spectre is far from being realized and the obstacles (both internal and external) are immense (Lebowitz 2006: Ch. 7; Lebowitz 2007).

Nevertheless, that spectre of socialism for the twenty-first century has far more substance than the spectre Marx wrote about in the Communist Manifesto in the mid-nineteenth century. The spectre of socialism for the twenty-first century is a spectre, but one which is capable of becoming a material force; it is capable of grasping the minds of masses precisely because it puts human development and practice at its core. Socialism for the twenty-first century offers a vision that both reinvents socialism and recovers Marx. And, in this world of capitalist crisis, ecological disaster and the spectre of barbarism, we desperately need that vision. The choice before us is socialism or barbarism.

Note

1.   See a discussion of the general problem of differential access to the means of production in Michael A. Lebowitz (2003a).

3

Cloistering Criticism or Breaking Bonds?

Errol Sharpe

The university has long been held up as an institution that protects and encourages freedom of thought. It is in the university, we are told, that individual and on occasion groups of individual researchers and scholars seek to analyze and explain society or do independent scientific research. The university in most Western countries is heavily funded from the public coffers. Individual professors from universities are often called upon to be expert witnesses at court trials and to speak as experts on many social and political issues. The university is seen to be a place of knowledge, knowledge that is independently gained through a rigorous scientific process. Indeed university professors are among the only individuals in society who are paid what is a comparatively good wage or salary to think and do independent research. The vast majority of non-university-based researchers are hired by private organizations to do specific research that is directed by and serves the objectives and interests of the organization that employs them.

One mechanism that is held up as a safeguard to individual freedom of thought and research is the tenure system, whereby once a person has proven their capability and demonstrated basic knowledge of their chosen discipline they are given, or awarded in academic terms, a tenured position. A tenured position is a virtual guarantee of a job as long as the person wants to pursue their career. For the most part it also affords the individual professor the right and opportunity to pursue their desired area of study within, and even outside, the particular academic discipline, where they first were awarded their tenure.

On the surface it would then appear that the university would hold the possibility for many individuals to pursue research and writing careers that would address the concerns and needs of the society at large. This would only seem just given the core public financing of universities. Here I will focus on the area of study that falls under the rubric of social science. The latter is where the operations, functions and the dynamic relations of society are studied and analyzed and thus come under scrutiny. It is here that relations

48

of class, gender, race, ethnicity and the dynamics of power are revealed.

The institution professes to protect, even champion, freedom of thought. However it assures through various mechanisms that critical thought, scholarship that challenges the status quo, is muted by being forced to follow predictable mainstream formulas. It occupies a position of authority in society, yet what goes on inside is a mystery for most people. For this reason it is often called the ivory tower because much like the castles of medieval times it exists in our cities and towns and occupies a prominent space. Occasionally the local media might report on a visiting lecturer but for the most part, and here I am focusing on the social sciences, learned discussions, lectures by visiting professors and the work of students remain cloistered in the institution. When professors do emerge from its walls they are greeted with respect and honour on the one hand but often with derision on the other. News reporters quite often call on a professor to offer an opinion on some political event or some societal incident. Most of the time those who emerge are academics who support the status quo and are called on to offer evidence, which serves to legitimize and promote reactionary social, political and economic actions.

When deemed necessary or appropriate, token Leftists, who are critical of the institution itself or broader social structures, are paraded forth and legitimize the institution's claim to be a supporter of freedom of thought. More often such professors are hidden away and have little impact on society as a whole. In this chapter I want to first of all briefly outline how critical thought and expression is silenced and to argue that the critical "Left" in academia needs to find ways to break out of the cloister and to become more active both in supporting and lending "Left critical analysis and discourse" to struggles for social justice and social change. Second, I will offer some comment on what I see the direction and content of this "Left critical analyses and discourse."

In my capacities as a part-time contract professor and as a publisher, I have been exposed to and have acquired a firsthand knowledge of the academic world. Our publishing company carries the moniker "Critical Books for Critical Thinkers" and it has been this genre of books that I have published and promoted to professors for use in their university courses and have used in the courses that I have taught. It is largely out of these experiences, and in particular my experience as a publisher, that I have come to see how the university operates and manipulates people on the critical Left to serve the interests of the dominant groups in society.

What appears below is an analysis of how progressive, critical and even radical thinking in the university is both cloistered and shielded from the general public and indeed, as stated above, often used to legitimize the claim by academia to being a protector of freedom of thought. I will argue that universities do not so much protect as stifle freedom of political and social thought.

When they can serve to legitimize the institution, token Leftists and critical thinkers are occasionally brought out to say their piece. This serves the purpose of creating the impression that the university is a democratic context where a broad range of thinking takes place. Furthermore, it can be done safely because such token expressions of opinion easily get lost in the din of mediocrity that characterizes the public media in general. The sad truth is that once safely domesticated, politically erstwhile Leftist academics can be trusted to take part in public debate because they will not challenge the status quo. As such they have an impact on society which belies their critical demeanour.

While critical thinkers and Leftists are used as legitimizing tokens, it is important to understand that the overwhelming majority of academic endeavours favour the status quo and support and promote reactionary social, political and economic actions. Because their voices and opinions resonate with mainstream discourse, they strengthen its message and provide a different kind of legitimization. Rather than legitimizing the university's claim to freedom of thought, they invoke its prestige as a centre of knowledge to add legitimacy to mainstream thought and shore up the existing order. In this way, they and the university work against effective social change and help maintain existing power structures that assure the continuance of capitalist accumulation that is necessary to keep the existing oppressive socioeconomic system in place.

This role of erstwhile Leftists must be linked in turn to other things. Central to getting a handle on the problem is understanding how critical thought and expression are silenced. Those who comprise the critical Left in academia need to find ways to break the silence and become active in both supporting and lending critical analysis to struggles for social justice and social change. The critical Left, particularly critical Left academics, must break free of the hegemonic agenda of the Right, reconstruct and advocate socialism and set the agenda for radical social change.

.   There has been much analysis done, especially in media studies, about how a framework is set up within which all topics get discussed. Gramsci's concept of "cultural hegemony" helps us to understand how the dominant/ruling groups in society establish control over subordinate groups not necessarily or most effectively by use of force or coercion but by engineering the conditions whereby the ideology of the ruling class is seen to be the norm. In modern society, the dominant class has been most successful in exerting control by setting the agenda within which most discourse is conducted. To paraphrase Noam Chomsky, "If you can control how people think, you know how they will act."

It is seemingly inexplicable that, in spite of copious radical rhetoric, much exposé "Left" journalism and many efforts to rally people against the program of the bourgeoisie, things do not change in favour of the oppressed members of our society. The bourgeoisie, it seems, can allow apparently oppositional voices, journalistic essays and academic discourse to be expressed in confidence that they will not upset their apple cart. On top of that, the bourgeoisie, as stated above, often points to such expressions of opposition to justify their claim that we live in a free and democratic society.

This apparently contradictory phenomenon is the crowning success of the liberal capitalist society. It is far more effective in exercising social control than outright coercion, enabling the canceling of progressive programs and the implementation of more oppressive laws. We see this happening today in Canada with the Harper government.

It is clear from the plethora of daily press and television reports of people getting shot, killed and maimed that such reporting engenders a climate of fear — a climate that has the psychological effect of creating a sort of bunker mentality and a belief that there is nothing that can be done except maybe "look after number one." I picked up a well-known progressive Left journal, and as I read the headlines and scanned through it I realized that, while the content was different, the reporting was cast within the same genre. So this, I thought, might explain the growing sense of emptiness and despair that I had been feeling when I read so much of the Left literature. What characterizes both mainstream and much Left journalism is the lack of hope, the lack of suggestion or vision as to what might be done to bring about positive social change. While one does not expect that from the mainstream media, since it is largely the mouthpiece of the ruling class, one should expect more of the press, which situates itself as oppositional, critical and progressive.

It is within this context that one should talk about how universities are able to allow critical research and critical thinking without being overly concerned that such activity will effectively challenge the status quo. As indicated earlier, I am thinking here largely of the social sciences.

In the many years that I have been associated with universities, both as a publisher and as a teacher, I have watched as many progressive ideas, progressive programs and progressive people have been absorbed into the bowels of the institution and effectively muted if not turned into agency for the dominant forces of oppression in our society.

Part of the problem is language. In academia every discipline and every system of thought has its own language. If an individual is to be successful in their chosen field they have to learn to converse in that language. Once they have learned the language they effectively shut themselves out from meaningful dialogue with anyone except others in their discipline. In this way even radical and oppositional discourse can be allowed because it remains cloistered within the discipline or system of thought. To take one example, there have been thousands of papers written and thousands of courses taught about social inequality, but in spite of this output, social inequality is more pronounced today than it was thirty years ago. In academia we have seen a plethora of theories advanced to explain social inequality. However, most of them are couched in a language and a cultural milieu that limits understanding and relegates them to just another academic discourse. While the public has paid for all of this activity, the vast majority of citizens has neither access to the research findings nor reap any benefits from them. Little or no effort has been made to transform this accumulation of knowledge into a language that can be used in social action for social change, and so, as pointed out above, such discourse serves the function of appearing to be critical, even transformative, while at the same time legitimizing the institution and the particular discipline.

Canada's current prime minister, a conservative politician and a neo-liberal ideologue—more reactionary if possible than George W. Bush and certainly in bed with the most reactionary elements of the capitalist class—has been agitating for more programs in universities that would serve the interest of the corporate sector. There have been suggestions that social science courses are not useful and that resources going to them should be channeled into programs such as those offered in faculties of commerce.

While I think that government's primary goal is to shift the cost of corporate training from the private sector to the public sector, rather than to mount an ideological attack on the social sciences, it does have the effect of setting up a dichotomy that effectively does not exist. When the critical discourse that is effectively cloistered and rendered ineffective is positioned as oppositional, a false dichotomy is created. In this way the dominant class in society, and its spokespersons in the universities, are able to make it appear that there is a real division. The bad social sciences, if you will, against the good corporate sector. It is a social/educational version of the good cop–bad cop scenario that is so effectively employed in the administration of injustice. The two sides of the imagined dichotomy, while both effectively serving the interests of the dominant class, appear to be opposites. As long as we continue to think within this hegemonic framework there is little room for any real or lasting opposition to emerge. Our energy is dissipated in a false fight and the ruling elite goes marching on.

While language is one way that critical discourse is muted, the other is the form in which knowledge is presented. In my role as a publisher I have struggled many times with manuscripts that have been written or modeled on the thesis format. The vast majority of them follow a prescribed pattern. The work normally begins with an introductory chapter, which outlines the scope of the thesis topic and often presents a hypothesis that is later to be proven. A section or chapter on methodology and another on the theoretical framework follow the introduction. While this structure may well serve the purposes of the academy, when presented to anyone, including the introductory university student, who is not conversant with the theories being presented, it will most likely confuse rather than enlighten. In some theses, empirical evidence or narrative is sort of hung on the theory; in others the theory is largely forgotten. It is as if, once the thesis author has proven that they have read and have a passing abstract knowledge of the theory, they have no further obligation to show how it might apply in reality.

This, I want to assure you, is not an argument against theory. It is because theory is so important that it must be taken out of the abstract and explained within the context of an empirical narrative. All theories were initially developed in an empirical context. They didn't come from the sky. When we learn to root theory in practice and in an analysis of concrete situations, people who are not abstract theoreticians will learn how theories can help to understand not only the topic to hand but provide guidance when applied to other situations.

The university has both a teaching and a research component. As a publicly funded institution and as the only institution in society where people are paid to think and do independent research, we might expect that the research that goes on would be in the public interest. However, as outlined above, even when research and research findings appear to be in the public interest, they seldom actually serve the public. It is the responsibility of those employed in the university to work toward changing this situation. This, I would suggest, is a particular responsibility of those who consider themselves Leftists or socialists.

So how do progressive, even radical, people get caught in this web? First, on the personal level, there are many appealing things about academic life. The remuneration is lucrative, far above that of the average citizen. For those who successfully navigate the many hoops and achieve tenure, their job is virtually guaranteed, as is an above-average pension. There are few other positions in society that allow a person the freedom to pursue their own intellectual interests. Unlike the average working-class person, even relatively well-paid assembly line tradespeople, there is ample opportunity for advancement on both the organizational and intellectual planes. In short, it is a career worth pursuing.

Second, on the intellectual level, pursuit of this career is largely an individual endeavour. Along the road to tenure, individual scholars are subjected to a series of grueling examinations; their ideas are challenged, their research questioned and their intelligence viewed under a fine microscope. By the time they achieve tenure, they have been carefully honed to speak, act and think within a defined framework. They have, as in Gramsci's analysis of groups in society at large, consented to the practices of the dominant group. In the process of controlling what they think, the institution in large part can predict what they will do.

Before going on to talk about the content of Left critical analysis and discourse I will advance a few ideas that might help Left academics break out of this cloister and use their position and their learning to more effectively work toward a just and rewarding society for all.

I want to make it clear that I do not think that progressives can change institutions created to protect and further the interests of the ruling class. Progressive people get involved in electoral politics thinking that they can change the state and the way that we are governed. If their party is the governing party, they soon get tied up in a process that exists to defend and advance the interests of the dominant class and assure the maintenance of and, when necessary, create the conditions for capitalism to thrive. Whether in the governing party or not they get caught up in the discipline of a political party that exists mainly to get elected. In the end it is they who change and not the state or the governing process. Much the same thing happens in the university. If the university as it exists were to radically change it would not be allowed to exist. So our efforts need to be directed elsewhere.

Leftist intellectuals must see society, the places where ordinary people live and work, not the institution, as the workplace. This means that we—I include myself in this group—need to become personally and directly active in engaging with working people, including working people in the university, and social action groups. By so doing we will unlearn much of the language and form that isolates us from the masses. We must unlearn our abstract way of thinking, our conformity to language and forms that limit the utility of what we do in terms of fomenting social justice and social change. And lest we forget, we must learn to work and act collectively. This means unlearning our individual approach to solving problems and dealing with issues. It means using what we have learned to serve the people who paid for our learning. So what does serving the people mean?

It is crucial that we come to understand that we need to build new institutions that serve the interest of the people we work with. Reform or revolution has been a question that has divided the Left for over one hundred years. It was this question that divided the Social Democrats in Germany in the early twentieth century. It was the centre of the divide between Eduard Bernstein, a leading social democratic theorist, and Rosa Luxemburg. In the end Bernstein's position, which supported reform, reform without any vision for a new society, an alternative to capitalism, as well as the social democratic participation in the World War I, led to the fulfillment of Luxemburg's prediction that the alternative to socialism would be barbarism. This was "confirmed by the Stalinisation of the Soviet Union, the rise of fascism across Europe and the catastrophic scale of World War II" (Luxemburg in La Blanc and Scott 2010: 29).

Following the war, the trade union leaders of the working class in North America reached a compact with capital, a compact that stabilized the struggle between workers and bosses. The great compact assured that workers would be bound to the terms of state-run labour legislation. In return the labour elite, those workers who were members of the big industrial unions and part of the 30 percent or so of the working class that was organized, received what amounted to guaranteed work and relatively high wages. This led to a muting of the workers' struggle for a new society and relegated the struggle to an economic one. The once vaunted militancy of labour was traded for the bureaucratic control of the union leaders and the "right" to participate in the capitalist consumer society. The struggle was now between paid union leaders who represented the workers and the boss's representatives. As union leaders wages approached those of the corporate executives they negotiated with, workers lost their agency and found themselves dependent on the professional unions' leaders for their economic gains.

This was brought home to me recently in the context of a role play that was presented to an academic session at the spring 2010 session of the Society for Socialist Studies at Concordia University in Montréal. I was cast in the role of the worker who was brought before the boss, who accused me of being late for work. A union educator was instructing the union representative, who was called in to plead my case, on how to confront the boss. In the role play I, the aggrieved worker, just sat and watched. I felt helpless to intervene. My fate was in the hands of others.

To further illustrate this point, I recall that in the sixties and early seventies when I was an active participant in a radical, if seriously sectarian, organization, we constantly talked of workers control. This theme was part of the discourse in those days, as it had been for many years before. Today, talk of workers' control, far from being part of union negotiations or even most Left discourse, is simply off the table.

While it is true that discussions around issues such as "reform or revolution" and "workers' control" are as old as the struggle for socialism itself, it is also true that today such discussions have been muted. Strikes, when they happen, are more often than not over wages. Occasionally issues such as safety enter the discussion but even then there is no talk of working people controlling their own workplace. Workers, indeed all of us, are led to believe that incremental material gains are all that we can expect.

So what needs to be done?

One thing is clear. The historical socialist message is not getting through. The powerful corporate media control the social discourse and the Left seems unable to mount any sort of effective challenge. And when the message does get through, as it did in 2003 when millions upon millions of people around the world, two million in London, England, alone, rose in protest against the Iraq war, the United States of America, the United Kingdom and their often coerced allies attacked Iraq anyway. The massive protests posed little threat because the masses were devoid of tools to take control and prevent the war. They had hoped that their presence in the streets would persuade "their governments" not to go to war. If the end result proves anything, it proves that the governments are not the governments of the people and that governments will do what is in the interests of global capitalism.

All of this makes it clear that we are at a new juncture in the struggle for a better world. While the historical Left debates can and must be informative in building a new movement, they must be tempered by a "made in the present" vision that is rooted in the reality of what some might call the postneoliberal world. We need a new Left discourse that has a forward look and speaks to our present conditions.

Thom Workman in personal correspondence summed it up for me when he said, "We need a specific type of Left discourse that must reach out and illustrate the connections between class power, public policy and oppressive experience. It does not seek to 'raise consciousness' but rather locate the 'critical consciousness of the oppressed 'within a context that connects dots." Working people and other oppressed groups do not need intellectuals to tell them that they are oppressed or the nature of their oppression. But progressive intellectuals can build bridges and make connections. As Workman writes: connect the dots.

The Academic Left, the Economic Crisis and Some Thoughts about the Future

Since the advent of neoliberalism the intellectual Left, including academics, has not, for the most part, connected the dots. In this failure, they have let the working class down. The Left has allowed the neoliberal agenda to dominate discussions and the intellectual discourse. This is most evident in the recent analysis of the latest crisis of neoliberal capitalism.

Discussions on the Left have primarily centred on an analysis of the causes of the crisis. These debates simply bow to the dominant debate being conducted by mainstream economists. Contributors to this debate come from many groups and individuals identified as being on the Left. In Canada this would include groups like the Council of Canadians, the Canadian Centre for Policy Alternatives and the New Democratic Party to name three of the more prominent. Those who engage in this set of debates are really only proposing that they could manage the economics and the political economy of the existing capitalist system better then those managing it now. Some, the CCPA for one, are critical of existing governments for not spending enough of the public's money to bail out the capitalists who caused the problem in the first place. This set of debates is dominated by those on the Left who for over forty years have called for a return to Keynesianism by advocating a return to the welfare state of the 1960s and early 1970s.

Those engaged in this debate further legitimize capitalism, suggesting that with some reforms and greater attention to social welfare concerns such as health and education, capitalism can work for the common citizen. These reformers, we need to be reminded, seem to forget that the historic compact between capital and labour demilitarized the working class and ceded to the capitalists the right to manage the workplace while relegating the working class struggle, managed as it is by trade unions, to a largely economist one and that conducted within the laws of the capitalist state. For them it is simply a question of reform, for reform's sake, not a struggle for revolutionary change. The debates about workers' control, as we have seen, have all but disappeared from the agenda. All too often the unions, rather than organizing workers' resistance, meekly surrender, hoping to save their own skin. Witness the collapse, during the latest capitalist crisis, of the autoworkers' unions both in Canada and the United States. In Canada alone the work force in the auto industry was reduced by 70 percent as the Canadian Autoworkers Union bowed to the demands of the corporations and the Canadian state.

We also need to be reminded that "The history of capitalism and the history of nation-state sovereignty are closely intertwined" (Workman 2009a: 138). This fact seems to have been forgotten by those who think that somehow the nation-state can be a more human state that responds to the needs of its citizens and the environment in which we live. It is not by chance that the history of the nation-state and that of capitalism are so closely intertwined. One does not and cannot exist without the other.

To suggest that the nation-state is anything other than a defender of capitalism and a body that creates the conditions for capitalism to survive and expand denies the historical record. Yet the mantra of so many progressives and so many identified with the Left that the leaders of the nation-state and capitalist corporations can somehow be persuaded to act morally and enact policies that would serve the interest of people rattles on. They fail to see, as pointed out years ago by Karl Marx and others, that the driving force behind capitalism, in fact its very ethos, is growth and accumulation. It is only by chance, and it is a fat chance, that capitalist accumulation ever corresponds with the interests and welfare of the citizens of the nation. Appeals to morality and justice fall on deaf ears. The enduring appeal to some ethical response on the part of the state does little more than delude people into thinking that there is some hope that the barons of capitalism will somehow someday have a change of heart. They cannot because to do so would be the death knell of capitalism.

Those of us who seek meaningful social change and particularly those of us on the Left who want to distinguish ourselves from the reformers and social democrats who have become identified as "the Left" must break the bonds that tie people to the belief that our existing political, economic and business leaders will bring relief from the ravages of capitalism and save our world. We must build an alternative movement, an alternative vision that is built on community and the morality of the common good.

A second category of debates has centred around an analysis that posits that this latest crisis is but the most recent crisis of capitalism and advances some tentative suggestions for both reviving the teachings of our past and forging new directions for the future (among others Smith 2010; Shutt 2010; Panitch and Guindin 2004; McNally 2011). These and other works provide very persuasive arguments analyzing the state of capitalism and show that the capitalist system is fraught with crisis. In fact, particularly in the latest neoliberal stage (see also McBride and Whiteside 2011), it lurches from one crisis to another with each crisis putting new pressures on working people and relying on the public purse to bail out the capitalists. These recent writings dealing with the endemic crisis point to the need for an alternative social and economic system. While such calls are not new in the annals of socialist discourse, they are a welcomed respite from the morass of the Left's pining over the past thirty years or so for the good old days of the Keynesian welfare state.

Leo Panitch and Sam Gindin enter this debate when, in writing about the American empire, they conclude that:

> The need to sustain intervention abroad by mobilizing support and limiting opposition through instilling fear and repression at home raises the prospect that the American state may become more authoritarian internally as part of its becoming more blatantly aggressive externally. But the attractiveness of an empire that is no longer concealed in its coercive nature at home as well as abroad suggests that anti-imperialist struggles—even in the rich capitalist states at the heart of the empire as well as in the poor ones at its extremities—will have growing mass appeal and force. (Panitch and Gindin 2004: 76)

Indeed, there are new rumblings of such in many parts of the world, particularly in Latin America in countries such as Venezuela, Bolivia, Argentina, Brazil and Costa Rico where anti-imperialist struggles are growing. Progressive governments have been elected by a more and more restless citizenry. When Hugo Chávez was deposed by a U.S.- engineered coup d'état the Venezuelan people intervened to reinstate him as president. In Venezuela, Chávez invokes not just, or even primarily, the historical legacy of European socialism. He invokes Simon Bolivar, Fidel Castro and José Marti. There is an awareness of the need to build a social movement rooted in the history and culture of Latin America rather than slavishly following the European model.

Albo, Gindin and Panitch (2010: 126) write that "Looking for alternatives in a return to the good-old pre-neoliberal days misunderstands the connection between then and now, and ignores the extent to which the working classes have been integrated into financial markets." They argue that "[a]lternatives must begin with people's immediate material needs, but must at the same time be oriented to strengthen popular capacities to act independently of the logic of capitalism" (127).

Workman suggests that the Left must quit politics. He notes that "The rehabilitation of the Left in Canada must occur off the mainstream political grid—this," he notes, "is the only chance" (2010a: 135). This means that the Left must set its own agenda, forge a new vision, a new expectation rooted in addressing the needs of humanity and acceding to the limitations of nature. All too often even those Left analysts who recognize and write about the crisis nature of capitalism and the endemic propensity for capitalism to create great wealth for the few and grinding misery for the many can only posit some vague notion of socialism as an alternative. Left academics and Left activists simply must do better. After the historical experience of the Soviet Union, China, the British Labour Party and the New Democratic Party in Canada (which for most people, courtesy of the mass media, has come to define socialism), to posit such government as an alternative, without deconstructing much of what has become its defining essence, does not hold much credibility.

Michael Lebowitz (2010) writes that we must "challenge and defeat the logic of capital." He adds: "[t]he struggle for an alternative vision will not result from twentieth century attempts to build socialism," and argues that "we must 'reinvent socialism."

Progressives on the Left who aspire to a different kind of society must deconstruct and reinvent socialism, wrest it from its twentieth-century sordid past and breathe new life into it. We can no longer rest on some imagined laurels of socialism. The reality of the identified socialist states has been a series of "fearsome dictatorships" (Lynd and Grubacic 2008: 12), no matter how much their lingering supporters try to sugarcoat them.

Marxism, as interpreted though the experience of these states, has little credibility for most people. Marx provides the deepest analysis of capitalism (for a recent Marxist analysis of the current crisis, sees Smith), yet the so-called communist/socialist states that claim to be Marxist have disgraced the name of Marx and seriously marginalized Marxism as a viable tool for analysis. The Left must resurrect Marxism as an analytical tool but shun the vision of Marxism that has been manifest in dictatorial states like the Soviet Union and its satellites. Let us not forget that in spite of his many contributions to socialist thought it was Lenin and the early Bolsheviks who dismantled the workers' councils known as soviets. It was Stalin who betrayed the workers' councils in Spain, an action that led directly to the fascist rule of Francisco Franco.

Socialism in the twenty-first century must learn from the negatives of its past as well as the positives. However, it must also look to traditions beyond the traditions of Europe. It must look beyond a Eurocentric view, a view which posits that all human progress will flow out of Europe and the clones, such as the United States, Canada and Australia, of its empire.

There is much to learn from the traditions, history and experiences of people in non-European societies, particularly societies in the South and indigenous people from both North and South who offer different paradigms from which to build. In 2008 I saw a large sign on the outside of a UCIRI (union of indigenous communities in the isthmus region) facility in Lachivizo in Mexico's Oaxaca State, which stated: "Don't let Individualism Destroy You." This echoed for me an alternative to the culture of capitalism. It echoed a society where people worked together in a communal relationship where individuals are respected and honoured for their contribution to the whole society. This is part of the vision that must inform twenty-first-century socialism.

Another European tradition that has been vilified by much of the Left, anarchism, needs to be given another look. One thing that has become clear to me is that twenty-first-century socialism cannot be built with or on the mechanisms of the capitalist state. The centralized power that characterized twentieth-century socialism did not and cannot bring a new socialist humanist society.

In speaking about how change can happen David McNally argues that "[t]he difference between those committed to socialist transformation of society and those who confine themselves to piecemeal reform [according to Luxemburg] is not that the latter support reform and the former do not. Both groups," she insisted, "including those dedicated to revolutionary change, are utterly committed to reforms." After all, McNally continues, "everything that improves the well-being of the poor, the oppressed, and the exploited is to be welcomed." But more significant, he adds, "the *struggle* for reforms is the rich and indispensable soil without which no genuinely mass democratic movement for change can grow."

It is in and through such struggles, McNally argues, "that people challenge authority, overcome deference, discover new capacities in themselves, build new solidarities, acquire a hitherto unknown self-confidence, and begin to believe that ordinary workers can run society." Consequently, as Luxemburg insisted, "the issue is not reform *or* revolution, but reform *and* revolution. The 'struggle for reform' is its means; the social revolution its goal" (McNally 2011: 175–77).

In his book McNally provides a cogent argument for the process of social change. However, if the seeds planted in the soil do not reach beyond the capitalist vision of the good society (i.e., a society of never-ending materialist growth and expansion), all the struggles in the world will not lead to a new twenty-first-century socialist society. The new seed must present a new vision, must articulate a culture that instills a new ethos, one that meets human needs and respects the limits of the environment. It must create a new vision of what it means to be human built on a communal collectivity, a socialist humanism, where all share in the resources available to us.

If this break with capitalist culture is not made, then any struggle will be meaningless, presenting only false hope and in the long run allowing capitalism to continue to successfully redefine itself as it has done more than once in the twentieth century. We must ask what kind of society, what societal organization (and notice I didn't say "economy," because economies of the future must be embedded in society and serve the goals of society) will provide the justice and equality that we all strive for. Left academics and Left activists must break the bonds of our past and the bonds of our capitalist oppressor and forge our own directions, our own agenda and build our own world.

Finally, let me say that as a publisher who has earned my living publishing progressive books that have come out of academe, I do not exclude myself from this challenge. I have often rationalized what I do by saying that it is important to keep a body of critical literature alive. I still think that this position is valid, but I want to see that critical thought transformed into critical action. I have made my living out of publishing books written about the oppressed. I want to find a way to give something back, find a way of building bridges, make connections and facilitate social action for radical social change. In the end the role of those of us who come from positions of privilege may well be that of facilitators rather than doers, using our connections and our outreach to both engage with and engage the oppressed.

4

The Marginalization of Marx in an Anti-Metaphysical Age

Thom Workman

The general drift of critique over the last century is incompatible with Marxist scientific inquiry. This critical intellectual current was inspired by Nietzsche's historic revolt against philosophy and metaphysics. The Nietzschean consignment gave way to Heidegger, Quine and Wittgenstein, which in turn gave way to several high-profile critics including Adorno, Gadamer, Derrida, Foucault and Rorty. Each novel critical spin had Marx and much of the Marxist tradition firmly in its sights. Whether it was Adorno's notion of "negative dialectics," Derrida's idea of "philosophy without a centre," Taylor's "philosophical anthropology," Gadamer's "philosophical herme-neutics" or Foucault's "geneology," each critique sought to "improve" upon Marx by implicitly or explicitly repudiating his original scientific assumptions. A legion of more recent postmodernist and poststructuralist critics, always purporting to be sensitive to repression and suffering, and forever suspicious of the ideological spin coming out of mainstream culture, energized these new critical paradigms with the hope of surpassing Marxism and its sup-posed failings (Lamont 1987).

Among other things this has encouraged *bona fide* cult followings through-out the academy that sometimes seem to be a parody of the very idea of the out-of-touch critic (Lamont 1987: 613). In some quarters it created inter-minable debates about the nature of non-Marxist critical social science and small-c critical theory (Fay 1987; Hoy and McCarthy 1994). The tension between Marxism and most critical intellectual trends always seems to be in play. As Barbara Epstein writes: "In any discussion of theories of or for social change Marxism is necessarily a reference point; those who see post-structuralism as the theory of radical politics are implicitly if not explicitly arguing that poststructuralism has replaced Marxism" (Epstein 1995: 87). The general confrontation between critical intellectual trends and Marxism has elicited several responses from socialist commentators (Geras 1990). As we survey "what went wrong," Marxist scholars must observe that liberal hostility and indifference has only been part of the challenge; the hegemonic critical intellectual tradition of the twentieth century, a tradition immersed in Nietzschean skepticism, repudiates the very core of Marx's critical science.

To elaborate on this confrontation two related arguments are advanced. The *first* draws out a philosophical critique of the Nietzschean turn in social thought and offers a straightforward philosophical critique of its more recent "postmodern" or "poststructuralist" variants. This critique of the philosophical foundations of Nietzschean-inspired social thought is designed to help us see that the widespread adoption of the Nietzschean outlook, despite its problematic philosophical foundations, is ideological, with a considerable anti-Marxist dividend. The *second* argument focuses on the fundamental incompatibility between a Nietzschean-inspired social critique and Marx's critique of capitalism (Dempsey and Rowe 2004). The chapter concludes by admonishing those Marxist currents that have embraced elements of the Nietzschean turn by championing intellectuals like Foucault, Derrida, Rorty and Kuhn.

It the broadest sense the chapter falls under the rubric of critical cultural diagnostics. Cultural diagnostics have been a prominent part of Western social and political thought, but few cut into issues in the spirit of Marx. The basic character of these writings attempts to explore the supposed ills of modernity with a view to modifying or adjusting its trajectory. Rousseau's critique of European scientific culture and its purported role in the demise of simple virtues, Nietzsche's harangues against the life-disaffirming effects of philosophy and Christianity, Cassirer's critique of irrationalism and modern political mythology, and Freud's identification of the smothering effects of culture upon the instincts are exemplary works within this tradition. They are equally limited insofar as they regard Western culture as undifferentiated at the level of social relations of power.

Such studies accordingly fail to expose many elements of Western culture in terms of their ideological relationship to dominant groups and classes. Some critiques overcome such limitations. For example, Gramsci's notion of hegemony as the multifaceted cultural expression of the world views of the capitalist class, de Beauvoir's critique of the logic of gender in patriarchal culture, Chomsky's critique of cultural "illusions" and Marcuse's claim that capitalist culture suppresses the negating instinct peculiar to all contradictory social formations provide varying examples of cultural criticism that are sensitive to the ideological nature of cultural forms of capitalist development Other such critiques, such as those by David Harvey (1991) and Frederic Jameson (1992), explore the rise of postmodern culture as emanations of capitalist social formations at specific conjunctures. And with more direct attention to the implications for Marxist thought, Alex Callinicos' (1994) exploration of postmodernism and the marginalization of Marxism represents a thought-provoking contribution to the ongoing efforts to explore the relationship between prevailing intellectual currents and Marxism, particularly as regards the nature of capitalism.[1]

Building upon the insights of Callinicos and others we can observe that our struggles against the dominant intellectual currents is hardly new. Indeed, in *The German Ideology* Marx also explored the relationship between cultural and ideological forms on the one side and the deterioration of critique along with the perpetuation of oppressive social relations on the other. In this stimulating study he argued that German intellectuals errantly distilled the movement of history from fermented Hegelian categories, and accordingly failed to grasp the impact of the social relations of production on both history itself and on those theoretical efforts to grasp history. This line of commentary echoed Marx's direct critique of Hegel in the *Contribution to the Critique of Hegel's Philosophy of Law* where he contended that the philosopher had accounted for historical development merely in terms of logically deduced categories of philosophy. Marx was fond of Hegel's efforts to account for history in a sweeping and developmental fashion, but his emerging materialist conception of history led him to lament that Hegel regarded history as a "matter of logic" rather than the "logic of matter." Marx famously countered that the leading categories of social thought and philosophy are best understood as conditions of class struggle and productive life. Over time these categories become ossified and to unsuspecting commentators are taken as true. "Whilst in ordinary life every shopkeeper is very well able to distinguish between what somebody professes to be and what he really is," Marx derisively wrote, "our historiography has not yet won this trivial insight. It takes every epoch at its word and believes that everything it says and imagines about itself to be true" (Marx 1976: 70–71). Elsewhere in *The German Ideology* he claimed that the theories receiving widespread acceptance in any age will be those that accord with the prevailing social relations of power: "in an age and in a country where royal power, aristocracy and bourgeoisie are contending for domination and where, therefore, domination is shared, the doctrine of the separation of power proves to be the dominant idea and is expressed as an 'eternal law."

In the critical spirit of *The German Ideology*, this chapter contends that the dominant intellectual tendencies of the last 150 years, tendencies that have been widely interiorized by scholars and social critics around the world, have played a role in the marginalization of Marxist discourse in a fundamentally idealist critique of all forms of structuralist thought and the rejection of any meta-theories of transformative social change and ideologies derived from it (Veltmeyer 2002). This prevailing intellectual idiom is Nietzschean insofar as it furthers Nietzsche's two central ideas: *perspectivism* (the repudiation of a transcendent knowledge) and *nihilism* (the repudiation of a transcendent ethics). The leading appellations of this intellectual discourse invoke a lexicon of rupture captured in terms such as "post-philosophical" and "postmodern." Although the latter has been subjected to well-deserved criticism (see Brass 1991; Veltmeyer 2002), the terminological and conceptual obfuscations of postmodern thought persist, perhaps precisely because they allow one to elude uncomfortable truths. The leading contributors to this intellectual idiom have embraced the so-called "linguistic turn" in social theory and the associated shift from structuralism (analysis of the real world) to discourse analysis.[2] This manner of thinking also rejects the grounding of ethical and epistemological discourse in anything beyond human culture. Insofar as traditional metaphysics relies on categories such as being, truth, beauty and essence that ontologically fix things beyond the realm of human language it is rejected.

Seen through the prism of the categorical tension between transcendent and immanent modes of thought and being, the anti-metaphysical turn in social and political thought can be regarded as immanent; ethics and all knowledge claims lead back to humanity. There is nothing beyond or above "us" that provides the final measure of thought, just as there is no universal rationality, and no ultimate ground of knowledge that creates the possibility of a conclusion to philosophical or scientific endeavours. At best, philosophical reflection and science are open-ended, ever-changing efforts to come to terms with the world around us—and nothing more.

Contemporary Intellectual Quiet

Given its contradictory richness I am not addressing the entire corpus of recent Western thought. But I refer to those powerful elements of Western thought that embrace both elements of the Nietzschean revolt, namely *perspectivism*[3] and *nihilism*. Although modern skepticism made its debut with writers such as Thomas Hobbes and David Hume the most direct and aggressive challenge to philosophy and metaphysics began with Nietzsche and his revolt against metaphysics. The Nietzschean revolt has elicited some of the most tantalizing themes including the "death of God" or transcendental measure, the "end of man" in the sense of a free-floating rational figure, the demise of philosophy as the privileged or final discourse of natural and human affairs, the rejection of a ground of "critique" in the sense of authentic human beingness and the proper order of things, an attack on the oppressive notion of capital-R-reason or the idea that there can be an authoritative rational rubric for all scientific and social commentary, the celebration of intellectual deconstructionism and its accompanying notion that ideas can be exhaustively surveyed in terms of their historically contingent horizons, the repudiation of scientific "method" and the general ascendancy of the discourses of personal and poetic edification

With the publication, in 1979, of *Philosophy and the Mirror of Nature*

Richard Rorty secured his position as one of the strongest defenders of the Nietzschean way. Over the ensuing years he published a wide-ranging complement of essays that set down the basic elements of his skepticism. His progressive credentials stood out in the North American academy. In a neoliberal world where most American intellectuals had gravitated towards the more conservative side of the political spectrum, Rorty, whose parents were part of a bevy of American Trotskyists targeted by both the U.S. state and Stalin, publicly criticized the generalized assault on the working class that slowly gathered force after the Taft-Hartley Act, saw the revival of the American labour movement as the key to the restoration of strong social programs, and assailed the neo-con Right in the United States for its jingoism and its unrelenting greed. His American intellectual roots along with his Whitmanesque celebration of American ideals are discussed openly in several essays. On the positive socio-political side of things he heartily embraced the spirit of civics engagement, and on the philosophical side of things he often claimed that his work, especially his idea of pragmatism, was indebted to the American philosopher John Dewey more than any other thinker.

In Rorty's writings the first pillar of Nietzschean thought—perspectivism—evolves into the claim that absolutely *all* knowledge, including the achievements of the natural sciences, is an expression of nothing more than human-made conventions. If Nietzsche had gravitated towards a negation of philosophical discourse as a response to both the smothering intellectual atmosphere of the nineteenth century and the European-wide radicalization of social discourse, Rorty could be seen as having transformed the Nietzschean critique into a thorough rejection of the Western philosophical tradition, beginning, as he repeatedly emphasizes, with the rejection of the Platonic distinction between "truth" and "appearance" (Rorty 1999: 23–71). As he elaborated in *Philosophy and the Mirror of Nature* there is no intrinsic reality to be discovered, and no privileged discourse that will settle questions once and for all. All knowledge claims rest on social or intellectual conventions. We cannot arrive at the "absolute" truth of all things that exist. Indeed, there is no ordered reality to be "discovered" via philosophical reflection on the essence of visible phenomena or a scientific analysis of observable social relations, explaining them in terms of laws that govern the hidden structure of social relations. Hence, there will be no final discourse marking the acquisition of "true" knowledge. Such notions are dismissed as outmoded Platonic fantasies (Rorty 1989: 3–22). Knowledge is linguistic rather than ontological, which is to say that it arises from within a theoretical or ideological discourse and does not express any relation of "truth" to the real world. Meaning is discourse bound and does not point towards a relation of truth between the knower and the known.

His basic view can be expressed syllogistically:

> All knowledge is expressed linguistically.
> All language emanates entirely within culturally contingent human conventions.
> Therefore, all knowledge is cultural.

What this means is that there are no extra-linguistic knowledge claims. No language, especially scientific or philosophical language, transcends our culturally formed horizons. Our culturally bound language yields categories that we then impose on the external world.[4] Knowledge claims can only be cultural fabrications. The criteria for knowledge can only be *our* culture, emerge out of *our* history, mesh with *our* codes of understanding, and ultimately be indebted to *our* distinctive, meandering and wide-ranging intellectual evolution.

The second pillar of Nietzschean philosophy that Rorty embraces is nihilism, or the contention that standards of human conduct and behaviour have no transcendent ground. It must be stressed that despite the iconoclastic European nihilism of the nineteenth century, nihilism to Nietzsche specifically meant the denial of an extra-historical or extra-human grounding of reality. Rorty shares the contention that humanity's codes of conduct will reflect the conventions of humanity itself, and that any justifications can only established through dialogue and discussion. In his writing *nihilism* becomes the adamantine claim that absolutely no codes of cultural conduct ever get closer to the would-be standards of imaginary gods. He called openly for the "ontological primacy of the social" over attaching importance to questions like "Does God exist?" (2007: 3–26).

The measure of ethics for Rorty is whatever works well for humanity, "working well" to be determined through cultural intercourse and a sort of historical proof. "We should not look for skyhooks," he wrote, "but only for toeholds" (1991: 14). To this culturally determined process of "the good" Rorty applies the appellation "pragmatism." Pragmatism can be reduced to the formula that "what is good is what works." In questions of ethics there is no "God's eye view," or to utilize a somewhat more provocative term that Rorty sometimes employs, "no spooks." He explicitly contrasts this notion of "ethics without principles" with what he calls the Kantian "tribunal of pure practical reason," i.e., he sets it in contrast to any notion that ethics can be grounded in a final or privileged realm of understanding. With respect to knowledge claims we must not ask whether they are "true" in that they correspond to the intrinsic nature of an external world; rather we must ask if the knowledge claims makes our lives better or worse. This pragmatist view holds that humanity has no inevitable terminus or end-game: "The end of human activity is not rest, but rather richer and better human activity" (1991: 39).

This summary gets to the gist of Rorty's philosophical outlook, which epitomizes the Nietzschean turn in social thought—a fundamental skepticism in regard to the possibility of social science as theoretical discourse on reality. He stands as a leading figure within a rather formidable community of twentieth-century intellectuals who embraced the twin pillars of Nietzschean revolt, and in this embrace not only turned away from Marxism but from all forms of structuralism and associated metatheories.

Before proceeding further with an exploration of the incompatibility between Rorty's skepticism and Marxism it will be helpful to review the main objections that have been made against the Nietzschean turn in social thought. First, much of the discourse after Nietzsche is replete with questionable inferences drawn from the critical thrust of incisive twentieth-century works. Two of the most celebrated sources of skepticism can be found in Thomas Kuhn's *The Structure of Scientific Revolutions* and in Paul Feyerabend's *Against Method*. Both works are compelling cautionary tales about the journey of science and the nature of the scientific method. They are humbling works with a sobering feel for the challenges associated with the natural and social sciences. However, these cautionary tales are all too often turned into a full-blown attack on science as the search for "knowledge" about the "external world." And they have provided fodder for diverse permutations in the idealist attack against materialism and structuralism, i.e., science. Postmodernism represents but the latest foray in a protracted ideological struggle to obfuscate reality and thus cloud class consciousness and inhibit the construction of scientific knowledge and theoretically informed political action.

Let us briefly consider the case of Kuhn and his skepticism vis-à-vis scientific knowledge and the capacity to capture in thought a fundamental logic in the sequence of events and the process of historical development. In his sweeping study of scientific evolution Kuhn emphasized the fact that Darwin's controversial contribution was not evolutionary theory per se but rather the idea that human evolution was an open-ended affair without a *telos*, without design or some kind of evolutionary beacon. "For many men," Kuhn wrote, "the abolition of that teleological kind of evolution was the most significant and least palatable of Darwin's suggestions. *The Origin of Species* recognized no goal set either by God or nature" (Kuhn 1962: 171).

Kuhn argued that the evolution of science as a whole can be analogically compared with this radical element of Darwin's theory. The paradigmatic upheavals of science can adequately be accounted for *without* the idea that each successive paradigm "draws constantly near to some goal set by nature in advance" (1962: 170). That is, we need not believe in the idea of a scientific terminus "set by nature" itself to account for the paradigmatic shifts in science. Such an end-game would be characterized by the acquisition of a limited, knowable set of laws governing the orderly natural world. Writers in the anti-metaphysical tradition have seized on Kuhn's speculations. In

Rorty's writings, Kuhn is identified as one of his "idols" who advanced the notion that scientific knowledge is a thoroughly human affair governed only by the contingency of linguistic conventions. But as has been pointed out by other commentators, Kuhn's inferences are invalid and seem to be driven by the elementary epistemological failure to distinguish between "truth claims" and "truth."[5] To put this criticism in other words, it is one thing to know that we can get things wrong, and even to embrace our fallibility, but quite another thing to draw the epistemological conclusion that we will never get things correct. And the leap from recognizing our fallibility to the ontological conclusion that there is no antecedent natural or social reality is even more fantastic.

A second criticism concerns the undialectical one-sidedness that characterizes the Nietzschean critical turn. This is the kind of criticism that one either makes very briefly with all of the associated pitfalls of brevity, or details in the form of a treatise. To be as pithy as possible, past dialectical knowledge never held the categories of reflection—transcendent/immanent, subject/object, fixity/flux etc.—apart so steadfastly. We have many compelling examples in the history of philosophy advising us against the overly aggressive separation of categories. In Plato's Parmenides, for example, an emphasis is placed on the dialectical notion that being admits of contradictory predication. Inspired by this dialogue Hegel pressed the distinction between the Understanding and Reason and associated the latter faculty with the capacity to recognize that non-identical categories routinely "veer" into their polar opposite. He stressed that the "speculative" moment of Reason sublated such conceptual identities and contradictions into new phases of categorical tensions. In this system the rigid holding apart of apparently contradictory categories in a hard and fast manner was the sign of undialectical thinking.

Hegel, an important theorist of dialectical thinking, stressed that dialectical interpenetration of opposing tendencies pervaded the world around us: "The perception of Dialectic in the province of individual Ethics is seen in the well-known adages: pride comes before the fall; too much wit outwits itself. Even feeling, bodily as well as mental, has its Dialectic. Everyone knows how the extremes of pain and pleasure pass into each other: the heart overflowing with joy seeks relief in tears, and the deepest melancholy will at times betray its presence by a smile" (Hegel 1975: 118).

Such dialectical thinking has characterized a number of celebrated thinkers and critics from the past, not to mention Marx. For example, in writing of intellectual radicalism Paulo Freire once wrote that "the radical is never a subjectivist. For him the subjective aspect exists only in relation to the objective aspect (the concrete reality which is the object of his analysis). Subjectivity and objectivity thus join in a dialectical unity producing knowledge in solidarity with action, and vice versa" (1970: 22).

A dialectical sensibility cautions us against holding categories rigidly apart and running with "one-sided" accounts of the world. The anti-metaphysical position rests on such an undialectical move. Its repudiation of any transcending aspects of thought and being, for example, of the notion that there might be anything "above" or "beyond" human discourse, anything that involuntarily frames our contemplative efforts, anything that necessarily bears down on us as we set about to make sense of the world that confronts us, is really a resolution of outstanding philosophical questions in favour of the immanence of thought and being.

In this manner of thinking, categories with imputed transcendent properties are out; all intellectual claims, including truth claims and assertions about the goodness of anything, are reduced to human sociocultural evolution. In the wake of such one-sidedness science and philosophy are no longer regarded as a matter of navigating our way creatively between the immanent and transcendent poles, of human understanding literally "coming to terms" with a dialectically rich external world, of accounts of life being brought into accordance with the perplexing character of life itself. The anti-metaphysical move makes the austere claim that human discursive conventions impose order upon the external world for the sake of coping with it—that is all! Science is coping; philosophy is coping, as are poetry and all other modes of discourse.

Marx after Nietzschean Skepticism

Nuances aside, the "linguistic turn" in modern philosophy, along with its more recent postmodern variants, rehearses the basic themes of Nietzschean skepticism. I am not suggesting that the *gravitas* of any one of the above observations sinks Nietzschean skepticism. However, each one by itself strongly suggests that the "revolt" against metaphysics is not something to be embraced but rather something to be considered in an intellectually rigorous manner. As an assemblage of monitory observations they render the ascendency of the anti-metaphysical standpoint a bit peculiar, and certainly in need of an accounting. "Why has the anti-metaphysical discourse had such an easy go of things in the last century?" It is supposed here that the dominant Nietzschean current has ascended for less noble reasons. To use Foucault's words, the hegemonic anti-metaphysical current has become part of the sweeping power/knowledge complex of Western thought, especially as this paradigm might work to contain elements of the Marxist critique.

The argument here advanced is that the hegemonic intellectual milieu in the wake of Nietzsche, more than anything else, helps to contain the Marxist critique by undermining the possibility of a sustained engagement with Marx's original works. The focus is not so much on the casual dismissal of Marx for crass careerist or political reasons. The aggressive marginalization of capitalism's fiercest critic by an order composed dominantly of men accustomed to commodious living should scarcely surprise anyone. Rather, the concern is with those intellectual efforts that may incline to a more serious engagement with Marx's writings and some of its central theses. The prevailing metaphysical intellectual orientation after Nietzsche sits awkwardly against the general character of Marx's writing and renders any interpretive efforts all the more difficult. Marx's mature analytical works are bound to seem strange and peculiar in a world bathed in Nietzschean assumptions precisely because his "materialism" is permeated with rich ontological and metaphysical presuppositions. Although it is certainly the case that Marx does not "philosophize" in the sense of alighting too long on the character of the ideational dilemmas that rear up as we reflect on the world around us, his work is replete with those more enduring philosophical categories, ideas and notions that stubbornly transcend the immediacies of political and ideological struggle.

It could be said that Marx more or less brackets those irreducible metaphysical and ontological questions that tend to implicitly permeate all writing. Marx's *corpus*, for example, is threaded by an ontological commitment to the notion that the principal dialectic that governs history is the iteration between humanity and the natural world (it is this assumption that energizes his youthful attack on nineteenth-century Hegelianism).

His critique also embraces a notion of human beingness as a tension between rational and appetitive faculties, a notion that would have been familiar to the ancients. He often commits himself to corresponding ideas about authentic life. Perhaps most importantly, his more mature work coheres around the idea that proper scientific explanation must distinguish between the *essential* and *phenomenal* spheres of social life. These notions blossom into open-ended metaphysical commitments irrespective of the fact that Marx did not take his writing off in such a direction (and we should mercifully be thankful for this since it netted us so much!). Readers of Marx are left to fill in the gaps regarding the relationship between his "materialist" outlook on the one hand and the presence of enduring philosophical questions on the other hand, although his dialectical sensitivities, combined with the fact that he leans heavily on such notions throughout this work, should caution us against believing that he would casually regard *absolutely* all philosophical matters—pun intended—as traceable secretions of the material world.

Insofar as the thrust of Marx's argument hinges on such categories as essential, phenomenal, critique, crisis, alienation and so forth, categories that open up into difficult "metaphysical" questions while retaining a robust sociological and historical residue, the *corpus* runs up against the hostile anti-metaphysical currents of the age—indeed, it is prone to being misunderstood entirely. The categorical architecture of Marx is out of step with the effete intellectual atmosphere of our times, and any engagement with Marx's works is made that much more difficult.

Although the aspects of this tension between the hegemonic intellectual orientation after Nietzsche and Marx's corpus are numerous, and although a full survey of these confrontations is well beyond the scope of one paper, the confrontation can be illustrated by returning to a dominant theme in the writings of Richard Rorty, namely, his *anti-essentialism*. Rorty's philosophy attacks the notion of essences at its supposed origin, that is, the Platonic distinction between *reality* and *appearance*. According to Rorty, abandoning this distinction means giving up on the idea that there are some kinds of things beyond the human mind that are "fixed" or "stable." This fixed or stable feature of something is its "intrinsic" or "non-relational reality" or its "essence." From an ontological standpoint Rorty's view can be dubbed "anti-essentialism." Insofar as his outlook attacks the foundational assumptions and commitments of the Western metaphysical tradition it means giving up on this tradition entirely. This anti-essentialist line of thought is pressed relentlessly by Rorty throughout his *corpus*.

From an epistemological standpoint Rorty labels his anti-essentialism as "anti-representationalism." In the course of gaining knowledge we do not "discover" reality but rather, as Nietzsche once wrote, weave "fresh metaphors." Science and philosophy are elaborate creative intellectual exercises not altogether different from art and literature. This outlook amounts to a sophisticated rejection of the "correspondence theory of truth," that is, of the idea that the social or natural world has an antecedent reality that can be represented linguistically and symbolically.

Anti-essentialism and anti-representationalism find very little traction in Marxism. Marx's thinking was infused with the notion of an antecedent social reality and its corollary that "truth" is the isomorphic representation of that reality. In his analysis of capitalist production Marx distinguishes between the *essential* and the *phenomenal*, i.e., the inner workings of the system, visible only in its objective effects, and the social relations that bear these effects. Science, in this connection, accounts for phenomenal forms of life in terms of the essence or inner truth of capitalist social relations. The essential sphere of capitalist social relations, as Marx understood it, centres around the exchange of commodities in accordance with the "socially average quantity of necessary labour time" embodied therein, a proposition presented as the "labour theory of value." This essential sphere of capitalist production can be grasped in thought in a process of scientific analysis or abstraction in which visible "phenomena," such as chronic unemployment and precipitous economic declines, are explained in terms of systemic tendencies or "laws" of capitalist development—*inter alia* the General Law of Accumulation and the Law of the Falling Rate of Profit. In other words, as the exchange of fungible value plays out in a competitive environment it results in a series of social and economic crises that destabilize capitalist society, and to which capitalists and policy planners must respond in order to avert a full-scale economic collapse. In this regard, Marx's sternest lesson is bound up with the discovery that when capitalism works it necessarily fails working people. Capitalism *qua* capitalism, Marx "discovered," and as Vasapollo, Petras and Veltmeyer argue in this volume, entails and can be understood in terms of a fundamental systemic propensity towards crisis. That is, the tendency toward crisis is the essence of capitalist development, just as exploitation is the essence, or the hidden meaning, of the wage relation.

As an aside, the repudiation of essences elides into anti-totalizing themes. One way to understand this tendency is to resort to Liebniz's distinction between a "dynamic singular" and an "aggregate." The former refers to something with an *essence* and a *dynamic logos*. This accords well with Marx's notion of capitalist society and his corresponding sense that the task of science is to uncover the essence of something. An aggregate, on the other hand, refers to something with functionally related parts and nothing more. A teapot is an aggregate (to use Wittgenstein's famous example) with a handle, a lid, and a spout, but it lacks an essence and a governing logos. Anti-essentialism militates against any tendency to see capitalist society in terms of its inner dynamics, its connections, its driving forces or its inner and outer forms. If it encourages analysts to regard society in terms of its connections at all, they will only be seen as *contingent* or *accidental* relationships. Theorizing society as a series of necessary connections related to an essence amounts to a totalizing narrative that violates the epistemic virtues of the age as ratified by Rorty and so many others. At times the proscription against "totalizing analysis" is expressed dramatically: "I want to stress the danger of the type of *totalizing* critique," Richard Berstein wrote, "that seduces us into thinking that the forces at work in contemporary society are so powerful and devious that there is no possibility of achieving a communal life based on undistorted communication, dialogue, communal judgement, and rational persuasion."

In what might be one of the most unrestrained moments in Western social commentary Jean-François Lyotard connected totalizing narratives with much of the political repression of the twentieth century: we have paid a high enough price for the nostalgia of the whole and the one, for the reconciliation of the concept and the sensible, of the transparent and the communicable experience. Under the general demand for slackening and for appeasement, we can hear the mutterings of the desire for a return of terror, for the realization of the fantasy to seize reality. The answer is: *let us wage a war on totality*; let us be witnesses to the un-presentable; let us activate the differences and save the honor of the name (1984: 81–82). The Marxist analytical tendency to overcome the liberal orthodoxy of the age and connect things, to connect, for example, public policy to underlying exigencies of capitalist economies, always feels like the unmentioned target of such extravagances. Irrespective of this, however, anti-totalizing sentiments are hostile to the spirit of Marx's critique.

A closely related element of Rorty's anti-essentialism is the repudiation of any essentializing elements regarding the conception of human being. Just as there is no "intrinsic" nature to the non-human world so there is no "intrinsic" nature to human beings. An individual, on Rorty's account, is nothing more than a "blind impress" of experiences that accumulate over one's lifetime. There is no authentic self-hood or essential human being outside the tissue of experiences "that make up each 'I'." Every life is a "tissue of contingent relations" that can never get completed before one's death. "It cannot get completed," he wrote, "because there is nothing to complete, there is only a web of relations to be rewoven, a web which time lengthens every day" (1989: 42).

This line of thinking is also fundamentally opposed to Marx's ideas about human beingness. The ontological sensibility that guides Marx's writings from his earliest critiques of Idealist philosophy through to his mature critiques of political economy is the dialectic between humanity and the natural world. The thinking, reflective human being confronts the natural world and the resulting iteration marks the essence of human beingness. The authentic human being, for Marx, emerges as the thoughtful manipulator of the natural world. It is what separates humanity from other species that also manipulate the natural world in a more unthinking, instinctive or habitual manner. This rather "essentialist" understanding then informs his notion of alienation as the interruption of authentic life, that is, as the interruption of the human life as the thoughtful manipulation of nature. Inauthentic life, or estranged labour, deepens as the thoughtful or reflective manipulation of nature recedes in rough proportion to the technological advancement of capitalist production.

Rorty's anti-essentialism also extends to history. Just as a person is a bundle of contingent experiences and nothing more, so human history is an open-ended, meandering, indeterminate passage through time. There is no *logos* to history, no predetermined or necessary trajectory, nor, of course, could there be any end point or *telos*. Such notions require us to believe that history has a *logos* or *essential dynamic*, and, Rorty contends, such convictions are little more than metaphysics by other means, efforts to burrow towards the "truth" of history lurking somewhere behind the mere "appearances" of the triumphs and horrors that unfold. "We should stop using 'History'," he wrote, "as the name of an object around which to weave our fantasies of diminished misery" (Rorty 1989: 229). History should be written as a "collection of cautionary tales" rather than as a "coherent dramatic narrative."

Ultimately, he suggests that all "essentialist" notions of history, citing often the ones offered by Hegel and Marx, are substitutes for transcendental illusions about God's plan and vague ideas about divine measure.

As we might expect, there is a more temporal aspect to Rorty's criticism. In the aftermath of the dismantling of the Soviet Union, Rorty's critique of a deified capital-H History was often equated with the notion of capitalism itself. Capitalism should not be an essence-defined thing to be overcome. If we admit this we will be willing to settle for social democracy—the only viable alternative to rapacious capitalism. He warmly embraces Ernesto Laclau's thesis that "the transformation of thought—from Nietzsche to Heidegger, from pragmatism to Wittgenstein—has decisively undermined philosophical essentialism and that this transformation enables us to reformulate the materialist position in a much more radical way than was possible for Marx" (Rorty 1998: 229). Rorty immediately added: "Fukuyama suggested, and I agree, that no more romantic prospect stretches for the Left than an attempt to create bourgeois democratic welfare states and to equalize life chances among the citizens of those states by redistributing the surplus produced by market economies" (1999: 30).

Rorty himself surmised that his notion that all history is contingent history ran up against Marx's understanding. In speaking of John Dewey's reading of Marx he approvingly wrote: "Dewey concluded that Marx has been taken in by the bad, Greek side of Hegel—the side which insisted on necessary laws of history" (1999: 30). Historical necessity is very much a part of Marx's work. Marx's pre-*Capital* notions of history and its governing class *logos* are perhaps his most widely touted observations. History has its necessary historical trajectories; there is an inevitable end that awaits capitalism. His later work can be regarded as a detailing of the mechanisms through which capitalism might wobble and finally collapse. The immanent tendencies of capitalism lead to crises. The resilience of the capitalists in responding to the occurrence of crisis suggests that the propensity toward crisis does not mean an immediate collapse. Indeed, Marx himself pointed to all sorts of counteracting measures at the disposal of capital. Nevertheless, it is safe to assume that sooner or later the capitalist system will exhaust its capacity to offset the tendency towards crisis, creating the objective and subjective conditions of revolutionary transformation. A developmental sense that capitalism is doomed pervades Marx's writings. Dewey's uncharitable remarks were correct in at least this respect.

The political implications of the Nietzschean turn is now thrown into full relief. The repudiation of philosophy is followed by the repudiation of the basic political idea of socialism, namely, the conviction that capitalism must be swept aside. The notion that capitalist social relations are necessarily unbearable and destabilizing for humanity finds no succor in the Nietzschean train of twentieth-century critique. The labyrinthine connections are not easy to follow, but the outcome seems clear enough a century later. With the absorption of *nihilism* and *perspectivism* into the mainstream critical vision of the twentieth century an unsuspecting attitude towards capitalism became commonplace. Critic after so-called critic has lined up to announce that the capitalist world that stands before us is not wrong. Rather, it merely needs a bit of tweaking. And so we come upon one of the greatest ironies of our age: as human misery mounts, as Euro-military aggression expands, as ecological degradation deepens and as the planet is plunged into one crisis after another, the suspicion that capitalism might be at the casual root of things has waned. Marxism is the enduring custodian of a fundamental critique of capitalism; it alone links our dispiriting capitalist past with the bleakness of the capitalist present; it alone informs the socialist promise of a postcapitalist future. But if we have had anything reaffirmed in the last century it is that the ideological aegis of capitalism extends from the vulgar lows of the cable news networks all the way up to the grandest predilections of intellectual life.

Conclusion

Given the dominant intellectual currents of today, the angular nature of Marx's writings is striking. His work contradicts and opposes Nietzschean theoretical principles. It rests on a notion of science as the fixing of essences at a time when the very notion of essences has been thoroughly repudiated. In this sense Marx's writings have been discredited at the level of philosophy. It could even be suggested somewhat provocatively that Nietzschean thought is the loftier counterpart to the more vulgar anti-Communism of the Western world. Marx has been attacked through the floor. That is, irrespective of its intellectual sophistication, the anti-metaphysical shift seems to foreclose the possibility of a serious engagement with Marx's work. At times, moreover, various cannibalistic currents of Marxism have embraced the hegemonic Nietzschean paradigm with the surefire effect of forcing an outright rejection of Marx's starting premises. The writings of Ernesto Laclau and Chantal Mouffe in *Hegemony and Socialist Strategy* come to mind. Similarly, the editorial line of *Rethinking Marxism*, a line reiterated in 2007, embraces a similar position:

> We reject the notion that class is the sole object of Marxist analysis and the related idea that class is the primary determinant of social activity and human behaviour. In line with our *rejection of such determinism*, we reject the claim that class functions as an essence in Marxist discourse. Nor do we accept the claim, central to some parts of the Marxist tradition, that class is the determinant in the first,

last, or any instance of all other aspects of social life. In our day, *the dominant tendencies in philosophy, including the persistence of both rationalist and empiricist epistemologies, have been increasingly challenged by philosophers of science and language.* From the work of Thomas Kuhn and Richard Rorty in the United States to the work of Michel Foucault and Jacques Derrida in France, the underlying epistemological positions of the human and natural sciences have been thoroughly criticized. (emphasis added)

We must keep asking why this philosophical outlook has arisen at this point in history. It is perfectly reasonable to suggest that Marxists engage the last century of philosophical and social commentary, and quite another thing to suggest that we unproblematically accept it with an eye to extirpating Marx's most rudimentary intellectual framework. As for those outside of the Marxist tradition it is unfortunate that the intellectual horizons in the aftermath of Nietzschean skepticism make it much more difficult to engage the classical corpus. Marx's original works are bound to appear peculiar, perhaps even quaint or vulgar or naive, and such impressions reveal much about the contemporary intellectual milieu and precious little about the intellectual or scientific integrity of the original texts.

Notes

1. On the role of postmodernism in the ideological struggle against Marxism and the "corruption of the academic intelligentsia" (the production of "modern political myths"), see Sanbonmatsu (2006: 227) and more generally Brass (1991).
2. On the difference and implications, both theoretical and political, between structural and discourse analysis, see Veltmeyer (2002).
3. Nietzsche's "perspectivism," reflected in his notion that "there are no facts; only interpretations," is reproduced in the sociological notion that reality is socially "constructed" and that there is no reality apart from or beyond the shared interpretations of reality.
4. Rorty's epistemology is akin to Nietzsche's perspectivist view of human knowledge—the notion that we "delicate" and "suffering" souls construe the chaos of the external word in accordance with our needs and desires.
5. This failure in writers like Kuhn and Feyerabend is stressed by Alan Sokal in *Beyond the Hoax: Science, Philosophy and Culture* (2008: 171–227).

5

The Role of the Political Instrument

Marta Harnecker[1]

The recent popular uprisings at the turn of the twenty-first century that have rocked numerous countries such as Argentina and Bolivia—and, more generally, the history of the multiple social explosions that have occurred in Latin America and the rest of the world—have undoubtedly demonstrated that the initiative of the masses, in and of itself, is not enough to defeat ruling regimes. Impoverished urban and rural masses, lacking a well-defined plan, have risen up, seized highways, towns and neighbourhoods, ransacked stores and stormed parliaments, but despite achieving the mobilization of hundreds of thousands of people, neither their size nor their combativeness have been enough to develop from popular insurrection into revolution. They have overthrown presidents, but they have not been able to conquer power and initiate a process of deep social transformations.

On the other hand, the history of triumphant revolutions clearly demonstrates what can be achieved when there is a political instrument capable of raising an alternative national program that unifies the struggles of diverse social actors behind a common goal; that helps to cohere them and elaborate a path forward for these actors based on an analysis of the existent balance of forces. Only in this manner can actions be carried out at the right place and right time, always seeking out the weakest link in the enemy's chain.

This political instrument is like a steam engine that compresses a piston at the decisive moment and—without wasting any energy—converts it into a powerful force. In order for political action to be effective, so that protests, resistance and struggles are really able to change things, to convert insurrections into revolutions, a political instrument capable of overcoming the dispersion and fragmentation of the exploited and the oppressed is required. An instrument that can create spaces to bring together those who, in spite of their differences, have a common enemy; that is able to strengthen existing struggles and promote others by orientating their actions according to a thorough analysis of the political situation; that can act as an instrument for uniting the many expressions of resistance and struggle.

We are aware that there are a number of apprehensions toward such ideas. There are many who are not even willing to discuss them. Such positions are adopted because they associate this idea with the anti-democratic, authoritarian, bureaucratic and manipulating political practices that have characterized many Left parties.

I believe it is fundamental that we overcome this subjective barrier and understand that when we refer to a political instrument, we are not thinking of just any political instrument, we are dealing with a political instrument adjusted to the new times, an instrument that we must build together. However, in order to create or remodel this new political instrument, the Left has to change its political culture and its vision of politics. This cannot be reduced to institutional political disputes for control over parliament or local governments; to approving laws or winning elections. In this conception of politics, the popular sectors and their struggles are completely ignored. Neither can politics be limited to the art of what is possible.

For the Left, politics must be the art of making possible the impossible. I am not talking about a voluntarist declaration. I am talking about understanding politics as the art of constructing a social and political force capable of changing the balance of forces in favour of the popular movement, so as to make possible in the future that which today appears impossible.

We have to think of politics as the art of constructing forces. We have to overcome the old and deeply-rooted mistake of trying to build a political force without building a social force. Unfortunately, there is still a lot of revolutionary phrase-mongering among our militants; too much radicalism in their statements. I am convinced that the only way to radicalize a given situation is through the construction of forces. Those whose words are filled with demands for radicalization must answer the following question: what are you doing to construct the political and social forces necessary to push the process forward?

But this construction of forces cannot occur spontaneously, only popular uprisings happen spontaneously. It needs a protagonist. And I envisage this political instrument as an organization capable of raising a national project that can unify and act as a compass for all those sectors that oppose neoliberalism. As a space that directs itself toward the rest of society, that respects the autonomy of the social movements instead of manipulating them, and whose militants and leaders are true popular pedagogues, capable of stimulating the knowledge that exists within the people—derived from their cultural traditions, as well as acquired in their daily struggles for survival—through the fusion of this knowledge with the most all-encompassing knowledge that the political organization can offer. An instrument that orients and unites—at the service of the social movements.

Convince, Not Impose

Popular movements and, more generally, the different social protagonists who today are engaged in the struggle against neoliberal globalization both at the international and national levels reject, with good reason, attitudes that aim to impose hegemony or control over movements. They do not accept the steamroller policy that some political and social organizations tended to use that, taking advantage of their position of strength and monopolizing political positions, attempt to manipulate the movement. They do not accept the authoritarian imposition of leadership from above; they don't accept attempts made to lead movements by simply giving orders, no matter how correct they are.

Such attitudes, instead of bringing forces together, have the opposite effect. On the one hand, they create discontent in the other organizations; their members feel manipulated and obligated to accept decisions in which they have had no participation; and on the other hand, it reduces the number of potential allies, given that an organization that assumes such positions is incapable of representing the real interests of all sectors of the population and often provokes mistrust and skepticism.

But to fight against positions that seek to impose hegemony does not mean renouncing the fight to win hegemony, which is nothing else but attempting to win over, to persuade others of the correctness of our criteria and the validity of our proposals.

To win hegemony does not require having many people in the beginning: a few is enough. The hegemony reached by the July 26 Movement led by Fidel Castro in Cuba, seems to me to be a sufficiently convincing example of this.

More important than creating a powerful party with a large number of militants is to raise a political project that reflects the population's most deeply felt aspirations, and thus win their minds and hearts. What is important is that its politics succeed in procuring the support of the masses and consensus in the majority of society.

Some parties boast about the large numbers of militants they have, but in fact they only lead their members. The key is not whether the party is large or small; what matters is that the people feel they identify with its proposals.

Instead of imposing and manipulating, what is necessary is convincing and uniting all those who feel attracted to the project to be implemented. And you can only unite people if the others are respected, if you are willing to share responsibilities with other forces.

Today, important sectors of the Left have come to understand that their hegemony will be greater when they succeed in bringing more people behind their proposals, even if they may not do so under their banner. We have to abandon the old-fashioned and mistaken practice of demanding intellectual property rights over organizations that dare to hoist their own banner.

If an important number of grassroots leaders are won over to these ideas, then it is assured that these ideas will more effectively reach the different popular movements. It is also important to win over distinguished national personalities to the project, because they are public opinion makers and will be effective for promoting the proposals and winning over new supporters.

I believe that a good way to measure hegemony obtained by an organization is to examine the number of natural leaders and personalities who have taken up its ideas and, in general, the number of people who identify with them.

The level of hegemony obtained by a political organization cannot be measured by the number of political positions that have been won. What is fundamental is that those who occupy leading positions in diverse movements and organizations take up as their own and implement the proposals elaborated by the organization, despite not belonging to it.

A test for any political organization that declares itself as not wanting to impose hegemony or control is still being capable of proposing the best people for different positions, whether they are members of that very party, are independent or are members of other parties. The credibility among the people of a project will depend a great deal on the figures that the Left raises. Of course, this is easier said than done. Frequently, when an organization is strong, it tends to underestimate the contribution that other organizations may have to offer and tends to impose its ideas. It is easier to do that than to take the risk of rising to the challenge to winning people over. While more political positions are obtained, the more careful we have to be of not falling into the desire to impose hegemony or control.

Moreover, the concept of hegemony is a dynamic one, since hegemony is not established once and for all. To maintain it requires a process of permanently re-winning it. Life follows its course, new problems arise, and with them new challenges.

To Be at the Service of the
Popular Movements, Not to Displace Them

I have stated that politics is the art of constructing a social and political force capable of changing the balance of forces in order to make possible tomorrow what today appears impossible. But to be able to construct a social force it is necessary for political organizations to demonstrate a great respect for grassroots movements; to contribute to their autonomous development, leaving behind all attempts at manipulation. They must take as their starting point that they aren't the only ones with ideas and proposals and, on the contrary, grassroots movements have much to offer us because through their daily struggles they have also learned things, discovered new paths, found solutions and invented methods which can be of great value.

Political organizations have to get rid of the idea that they are the only ones capable of generating creative, new, revolutionary and transformative ideas. And that therefore their role is not only to echo the demands of the social movements, but also to be willing to gather ideas and concepts from these movements to enrich its own conceptual arsenal.

Political and social leaders should leave behind the method of pre-established schemas. We have to struggle to eliminate all verticalism that stifles the initiative of the people. The role of a leader must be one of contributing with ideas and experiences in order to help grow and strengthen the movement, and not displace the masses.

Their role is to push the mass movement forward, or perhaps more than push, facilitate the conditions necessary so that the movement can unleash its capacity to confront those who exploit and oppress them. But helping to push forward is only possible if we fight shoulder to shoulder in local, regional, national and international struggles.

The relationship of political organizations with grassroots movements should therefore be a two-way circuit: from the political organization to the social movement and from the social movement to the political organization. Unfortunately, the tendency continues to be that the relationship only functions in the first direction.

It is important to learn to listen and to engage in dialogue with the people; it is necessary to listen carefully to the solutions proposed by the people themselves to defend their conquests or struggle for their demands and, with all the information collected, we must be capable of correctly diagnosing their mood and synthesize that which could unite them and generate political action, and at the same time tackle pessimistic and defeatist ideas they may hold.

Wherever possible, we must involve the grassroots in the process of decisionmaking, that is to say, we have to open up new spaces for people's participation, but people's participation is not something that can be decreed from above. Only by taking as our starting point the true motivations of the people, only if one helps them to discover the necessity of carrying out certain task for themselves, and only by winning over their hearts and minds, will they be willing to fully commit themselves to the actions proposed. This is the only way to ensure that efforts made to help orient the movement are not felt as orders coming from outside the movement and to help create an organizational process capable of involving, if not all, then at least an important part of the people into the struggle and, little by little, win over the more backward and pessimistic sectors. When these latter sectors understand that, as Che Guevara said, the aims we are fighting for are not only necessary but possible, they too will choose to join the struggle. When the people realize that their own ideas and initiatives are being put into practice, they will see themselves as the protagonists of change and their capacity to struggle will increase enormously.

Taking all that has been said above into consideration, it becomes clear that the type of activists we need cannot be drillmasters—today, it is not about leading an army, which is not to say that at some critical junctures this may and should be the case, or about a demagogic populist—because it is not about leading a flock of sheep; political cadres should fundamentally be teachers, capable of fostering the ideas and initiatives that emerge from within the grassroots movements.

Unfortunately, many current leaders have been educated in the school of leading the people by issuing orders, and that is not something that can be changed overnight. Thus, I do not want to create an impression of excessive optimism here. Achieving a correct relationship with the social movements is still a long way off.

Should We Reject Bureaucratic Centralism and Simply Use Consensus?

For a long time, Left-wing parties operated along authoritarian lines. The usual practice was that of bureaucratic centralism, influenced by the experiences of Soviet socialism. All decisions regarding criteria, tasks, initiatives, and the course of political action to take were restricted to the party elite, without the participation or debate of the membership, who were limited to following orders that they never got to discuss and in many cases did not understand. For most people, such practices are increasingly intolerable. But in challenging bureaucratic centralization, it is important to avoid falling into the excesses of ultra-democracy, which results in more time being used for discussion than action, since everything, even the most minor point, is the subject of rigorous debates that frequently impede any concrete action.

In criticizing bureaucratic centralization, the recent tendency has been to reject all forms of centralized leadership. There is a lot of talk about organizing groups at all levels of society, and that these groups must apply a strict internal democracy, ideas that I obviously share. What I do not agree with is the idea that no effort needs to be put in the direction of giving these ideas a common organic link. In defending democracy, flexibility and the desire to fight on many different fronts, what is rejected are efforts to determine strategic priorities and attempt to unify actions.

For some, the one and only acceptable method is consensus. They argue that by utilizing consensus they are aiming not to impose decisions but instead to interpret the will of all. But the consensus method, which seeks the agreement of all and appears to be a more democratic method, can in practice be something profoundly anti-democratic because it grants the power of veto to a minority, to such an extreme that a single person can block implementation of an agreement that may be supported by an overwhelming majority. Moreover, the complexity of problems, the size of organizations and political timing that compels us to make quick decisions at specific junctures make it almost impossible to use the consensus model on many occasions, even if we leave aside the manipulating uses of the consensus model.

I believe that there cannot be political efficacy without a unified leadership that determines the course of action to follow at different moments in the struggle and to achieve this goal it is vital that a broad ranging discussion occurs, where everyone can express their opinions and where, in the end, positions are adopted and everyone respects them.

For the sake of a unified course of action, lower levels of the organization should respect the decisions made by the higher bodies, and those who have ended up in the minority should accept whatever course of action emerges triumphant, carrying out the task together with all the other members.

A political movement that seriously aspires to transform society cannot afford the luxury of allowing undisciplined members to disrupt its unity, without which it is impossible to succeed. This combination of single centralized leadership and democratic debate at different levels of the organization is called democratic centralism. It is a dialectic combination: in complicated political periods, of revolutionary fervour or war, there is no other alternative than to lean toward centralization; in periods of calm, when the rhythm of events is slower, the democratic character should be emphasized.

Personally, I do not see how one can conceive of successful political action if unified action is not achieved, and for that reason I do not think that another method exists other than democratic centralism, if consensus has not been reached. A correct combination of centralism and democracy motivates the leaders and, above all, the members. Only creative action at every level of the political or social organization will ensure the triumph of our struggle. An insufficient democratic life impedes the unleashing of the creative initiative of all the militants, with its subsequent negative impact on their participation. In practice, this motivation manifests itself in the sense of responsibility, dedication to work, courage and aptitude for problem-solving, as well as in the capacity to express opinions, to criticize defects and exercise control over the higher-up bodies in the organizations.

Only a correct combination of centralism and democracy can ensure that agreements are efficient, because having engaged in the discussion and the decisionmaking process, one feels more committed to carry out the decisions. When applying democratic centralism we must avoid attempts to use narrow majorities to try and crush the minority. The more mature social and political movements believe that it is pointless imposing a decision adopted by a narrow majority. They believe that if the large majority of militants are not convinced of the course of action to take, it is better to hold off until the militants are won over politically and become convinced themselves that such action is correct. This will help us avoid the disastrous internal divisions that have plagued movements and Left parties, and avoid the possibility of making big mistakes.

Minorities Can Be Right

Democratic centralism implies not only the subordination of the minority to the majority, but also the respect of the majority toward the minority. Minorities should not be crushed or marginalized; they should be respected. Nor should the minority be required to completely subordinate itself to the majority. The minority must carry out the tasks proposed by the majority at each concrete political junction, but they should not have to renounce their political, theoretical and ideological convictions. On the contrary, it is the minority's duty to continue fighting to defend their ideas until the others are convinced or they themselves become convinced of the ideas of others.

Why should the minority continue defending its positions and not submit to the position of the majority? Because the minority may be right; their analysis of reality might be more accurate if they have been capable of discovering the true motivations of specific social forces. That is why those who hold minority positions at a determined moment should not only have the right, but the duty, to hold their positions and fight to convince the maximum amount of other militants of their positions through internal debate.

Moreover, if the majority is convinced that their propositions are correct, then they have nothing to fear in debating ideas. On the contrary, they should encourage debate and try to convince the minority group. If the majority fears a confrontation of positions it is probably a sign of political weakness. Is this not the case if we look at some of the Left parties and social movements in Latin America? How many splits could have been avoided if the minority view had been respected? Instead, on many occasions the entire weight of the bureaucratic apparatus has been used to crush them, leaving them with no choice but to split. Sometimes minorities are accused of being divisive for the simple reason that they want their ideas to be respected and be given space to debate them. Could it be that the true splitters are those who provoke the division by leaving the minority with no other option than to split if they hope to continue their struggle against positions they believe to be wrong?

The topic of majorities and minorities also has to do with the disjunction or non-correspondence between representatives and the represented. This phenomenon may occur for different reasons, including: the organic incapacity of those who represent the real majority to achieve better representation in the mass organizations; the bureaucratic manoeuvers of a formal majority to keep itself in positions of power; the rapid change in political consciousness of those who elected these representatives due to developments in the revolutionary process itself. Those who only days before truly represented the majority may today simply represent a formal majority because the revolutionary situation has demonstrated to the masses that the position of the minority was correct.

The new culture of the Left should also be reflected in a different approach toward the composition of leadership bodies in political organizations. For a long time it was believed that if a certain tendency or sector of the party won the internal elections by a majority, all leadership positions would be filled by cadres from that tendency. In a certain sense, the prevailing idea was that the more homogenous the leadership, the easier it would be to lead the organization. Today different criteria tend to prevail: a leadership that better reflects the internal balance of forces seems to work better, as it helps to get all party members, and not only those of the current majority, feel more involved in the implementation of tasks proposed by the leadership. But a plural leadership, along the lines that I am proposing, can only be effective if the organization has a truly democratic culture, because if that is not the case, then such an approach will produce a wave of unrest and render the organization ungovernable. Moreover, a real democratization of the political organization demands more effective participation by party members in the election of their leaders: they should be elected according to their ideological and political positions rather than personality. That is why it is important that the different positions be well known among the party membership via internal publications. It's also very important to ensure a more democratic formulation of candidates and to safeguard the secret vote.

Finally, it is essential to remember that the internal democratic culture of a political organization is the public face it offers to the social movements with which it wants to work. If it demonstrates, on the one hand, that its internal decisionmaking process occurs according to a democratic procedure based on tolerance and, on the other hand, that it carries out its work in a unitary manner, it can offer the social movements a model for successful action.

Need to Unite the Party Left and the Social Left

Rejection by a majority of people of the globalization model imposed on our continent intensifies each day given its inability to solve the most pressing problems of our people. Neoliberal policies implemented by large transnational financial capital, which is backed by a large military and media power, and whose hegemonic headquarters can be found in the United States, have not only been unable to resolve these problems but, on the contrary, have dramatically increased misery and social exclusion, while concentrating wealth in increasingly fewer hands.

Among those who have suffered most as a result of the economic consequences of neoliberalism are the traditional sectors of the urban and rural working classes. But its disastrous effects have also affected many other social sectors, such as the poor and marginalized, impoverished middle-class sectors, the constellation of small and medium-sized businesses, the informal sector, medium and small-scale rural producers, the majority of professionals, the legions of unemployed, workers in co-operatives, pensioners, the police and the subordinate cadres of the army (junior officers). Moreover, we should not only keep in mind those who are affected economically, but also all those who are discriminated against and oppressed by the system: women, youth, children, the elderly, indigenous peoples, blacks, certain religious creeds, homosexuals.

Neoliberalism impoverishes the great majority of the population of our countries, those impoverished in the socioeconomic sense and also in the subjective sense. Some of these sectors have transformed themselves into powerful movements. Among those are women's, indigenous and consumer rights movements, and movements that fight for human rights and in defence of the environment.

These movements differ in many ways from the classical labour movement. Their platforms have a strong thematic accent and reach across classes and generations. Their forms of organizing are less hierarchical and rely more on networks than those of the past, while their concrete forms of actions vary quite a lot.

New social actors have also appeared. What is surprising, for example, is the capacity to mobilize that has manifested itself among youth, fundamentally organized through electronic means, with the object of rejecting actually existing globalization; resisting the application of neoliberal measures, promoting very powerful mobilizations against war and against military occupation, and spreading experiences of revolutionary struggle, breaking up the information blockade that had been imposed on left and progressive ideas.

This growing rejection is being expressed through diverse and alternative practices of resistance and struggle. The consolidation of Left parties, fronts or political processes in opposition to neoliberalism is undeniable in various countries: Venezuela, Brazil, Colombia, Uruguay, El Salvador, Bolivia. In some, such as Brazil, Argentina, Bolivia, Ecuador and Mexico, powerful social movements have arisen, which have transformed themselves into major political actors, becoming important opposition forces that occupy the front lines of the fight against neoliberal globalization. However, despite the depth of the crisis that this model has provoked, the breadth and variety of affected sectors that embrace the majority of the population, the multiplicity of demands that have emerged from society and which continue to remain unmet—all of which have produced a highly favourable situation for the creation of a very broad anti-neoliberal social bloc with enormous social force—the majority of these growing expressions of resistance and struggle are still far from truly representing a real threat to the system.

I believe that one reason that helps explain this situation is that parallel to these objective conditions which are favourable for the construction of a broad alternative social bloc against neoliberalism, there are very complicated subjective conditions which have to do with a profound problem: the dispersion of the Left. And that is why I believe that for an effective struggle against neoliberalism, it is of strategic importance to articulate the different Left sectors, understanding the Left to mean all those forces that stand up against the capitalist system and its profit-driven logic, and who fight for an alternative society based on humanism and solidarity, built upon the interests of the working classes.

Therefore, the Left cannot simply be reduced to those that belong to Left parties or political organizations; it also includes social actors and movements. Very often these are more dynamic and combative than the former, but do not belong to or reject belonging to any political party or organization. Among the former are those who prefer to accumulate forces by using institutions to aid transformation, while others opt for revolutionary guerrilla warfare; among the latter, some attempt to create autonomous social movements and different types of networks. To simplify, I have decided to refer to the first group as the political Left and the second group as the social Left, even though I recognize that this conceptual separation is not always so in practice. In fact, the more developed social movements tend to acquire socio-political dimensions.

To sum up, I believe that only by uniting the militant efforts of the most diverse expressions of the Left will we be able to fully carry out the task of building the broad anti-neoliberal social bloc that we need. The strategic task therefore is to articulate the party and social Left so that, from this starting point, we can unite into a single colossal column, the growing and diverse social opposition.

Reasons for Popular Skepticism
Concerning Politics and Politicians

Elsewhere I have stated that in order to wage an effective struggle against neoliberalism, it is necessary to unite all those suffering its consequences, and to achieve this objective we must start with the Left itself, which in our countries tends to be very dispersed. But there are many obstacles that impede this task. The first step to overcoming them is to be aware of them and be prepared to face them.

One obstacle is growing popular skepticism regarding politics and politicians. This has to do, among other things, with the great constraints that exist today in our democratic systems, which are very different from those that existed prior to the military dictatorships. These low-intensity, controlled, restricted, limited or monitored democratic regimes drastically limit the effective capacity of democratically elected authorities. The most important decisions are made by unelected institutions of a permanent character, and which therefore are not subject to changes produced by electoral results; such is the case with national security councils, central banks, institutions for economic advice, supreme courts, ombudsmen, constitutional tribunals.

Groups of professionals, and not politicians, are responsible for making decisions, or at minimum have a decisive influence over the decisions made. The apparent neutrality and depoliticization of these entities conceals the new way in which the dominant class does politics. Their decisions are adopted outside the framework of parties. We are dealing with controlled democracies, where the controllers themselves are not subject to any democratic mechanism. Moreover, instruments for manufacturing consensus—monopolized by the ruling classes—have been dramatically improved, conditioning to a great extent the way in which people perceive reality. This explains why the most conservative parties, which defend the interests of a tiny minority of the population, have been able to quantitatively transform themselves into mass parties, and why the social bases that support their candidates, at least in Latin America, are the poorest social sectors of the urban peripheries and countryside.

Other elements that explain this growing popular skepticism include, on the one hand, the unscrupulous appropriation by the Right of the language and discourse of the Left—words such as "reforms," "structural changes," "concern for poverty," "transition"—today form part of its everyday discourse; and, on the other hand, the quite frequent adoption of political practices by some parties on the Left that hardly differ from the habitual practices of traditional parties.

We must bear in mind that, increasingly, people are rejecting clientelist, non-transparent and corrupt party practices carried out by those who reach out to the people only at election time; that waste energy in internecine fighting between factions and petty ambitions; where decisions are made at the top by party elites without genuine consultation with the ranks; and where personal leadership outranks the collective. People are increasingly rejecting messages that remain as mere words and are never translated into action.

Ordinary people are fed up with the traditional political system and want renewal, they want positive change, they want new approaches to doing politics, they want clean politics, they want transparency and participation and they want to regain confidence. This distrust of politics and politicians— which also permeates the social Left—which is growing daily, is not a serious issue for the Right, but it is for the Left. The Right can operate perfectly well without political parties, as it demonstrated during periods of dictatorship, but the Left cannot do without a political instrument, be it a party, a political front or some other formula.

Another obstacle to the unity of the Left—following the defeat of Soviet socialism, and the crisis of the welfare state promoted by European social democracies and Latin American populist developmentalism—is that it has had great difficulty in elaborating a rigorous and credible alternative to capitalism—socialist or whatever you want to call it—that takes into account the new world reality.

Capitalism has revealed its great capacity to reinvent itself and utilize the technological revolution toward its own ends: fragmenting the working class and limiting its negotiating power, creating panic over unemployment. Meanwhile, on many occasions, the Left has remained anchored in the past. There is an excess of diagnosis and an absence of remedy. We tend to navigate without a political compass.

Most of the obstacles outlined above come about due to realities imposed on us from outside, but there also exist obstacles that disrupt attempts to unite all the Left that come from within. Moreover, during the last decades, the party Left has had many difficulties in working with social movements and winning over new social forces. On the other hand, there has been a tendency in the social Left to dismiss parties and magnify their own roles in the struggle against neoliberal globalization, an attitude which has not helped in overcoming the divisions within the Left.

The Left Must Strive to Set the Agenda for Struggle

I stated above that a large section of the party Left has found it very difficult to work with social movements and develop ties with the new social forces in recent decades. This has been due to several factors. While the Right has demonstrated great political initiative, the Left tends to be on the defensive. While the former uses its control of the institutions of the state and the mass media, as well as its economic influence, to impose its new model, subservient to financial capital and monopolies, that has precipitated privatizations, labour deregulation and all the other aspects of the neoliberal economic program to increase social fragmentation and foment anti-partyism, the party Left, on the other hand, has almost exclusively limited its political work to the use of current institutionality, subordinating itself to the rules of the game imposed by the enemy, and hardly ever taking them by surprise. The level of absurdity is such that the calendar of struggle of the Left is set by the Right.

How often have we heard the Left complain about the adverse conditions it had to face during election campaigns, after discovering that its electoral results were not what it was expecting? Yet the very same Left seldom denounced the rules of the game imposed on it, nor proposed electoral reforms, during its electoral campaigns. On the contrary, what tends to occur is that in seeking votes—instead of carrying out an educational, pedagogical campaign that serves to increase the organization and awareness of the people—the Left uses the same techniques to sell its candidates that the ruling classes use.

On the other hand, the current rules of the game imposed by the dominant classes hinder the unity of the Left and foment personality-based politics. In some countries, the Left is forced to work to support its own party instead of for a broader front because if it doesn't the party tends to disappear from the political sphere. This means that, when electoral defeats occur, the frustration, wearing down and debts incurred during the campaign are compounded by the fact that the electoral effort does not translate into political growth, leaving a bitter sense of having wasted time. The situation would be very different if campaigns were conceived from a pedagogical point of view, where election campaigns were used to deepen awareness and popular organization. Then, even if the electoral results were not the most favourable, the time and effort invested in the campaign would not be wasted.

It is not surprising that some argue that the cult of the institution has been the Trojan horse that the ruling system has been able to introduce into the fortress of the revolutionary Left, thus attacking the Left from inside. The work of the ranks is progressively delegated to people who hold public and administrative positions. Most of the effort stops being directed toward collective action and is redirected toward parliamentary action or building a media presence.

Militant action has tended to be reduced to activities on election day, putting up posters and other such trivial public acts. And, even worse, party financing is increasingly reliant on the participation of party cadres in state institutions: parliament, local government, election boards, with all that that entails, in terms of dependency and undue pressure.

The political activity of the Left cannot be reduced to the conquest of institutions; it must be directed toward changing those institutions in order to be able to transform reality. A new balance of forces must be created so that the necessary changes can be implemented. We have to understand that we cannot build a political force without building a social force. At the same time, we must also avoid "party-izing" all initiatives and the social move-ments we relate to; on the contrary, effort must be made to bring together their practices into a single political project. Additionally, the party Left has had a hard time adjusting to the new realities. On many occasions it has remained firmly locked into rigid conceptual frameworks that prevent it from appreciating the potential of the new social subjects, exclusively focusing efforts on forces that have traditionally mobilized, such as trade unions, that today are much weaker due to a variety of factors.

Finally, one of the greatest difficulties for the party Left regarding work with the social Left has been the viewpoint that sees social movements as conveyor belts for the party. The leadership of the movement, positions in leadership bodies, the platform of struggle, that is everything, is decided by party leaders and only afterwards is the line of march taken to the social movement members in question, without allowing them to participate in the process of deciding the matters that affect them directly.

Summing up, in order for the party Left to develop strong bonds with the social Left, the party Left must renew itself ideologically, change its political culture and work methods and incorporate into its arsenal the innovative forms of struggle and resistance utilized by the social Left.

Respect Differences and Be Flexible Regarding Activism

Among the Left, there continues to be difficulty in working together while respecting differences. In the past, the tendency of political organizations, especially parties that self-declare as "parties of the working class," was always toward homogenizing the social base within which they carried out political work. If this attitude was once justified due to the past identity and homogeneity of the working class, today it is anachronistic when confronted with a working class that is quite differentiated, and with the emergence of a diversity of new social actors. Today, we increasingly have to deal with a unity based on diversity, on respect for ethnic and cultural differences, for gender and for the sense of belonging of specific collectives.

It is necessary to try to channel commitments to activism by starting with the actual potential of each sector, and even of each person, that is willing to commit to the struggle, without seeking to homogenize these actors. It is important to have a special sensibility toward finding all those points of agreement that can allow for the emergence of a common platform of struggle.

This respect for differences should also reflect itself in our discourse. We must break with the old style of attempting to take a uniform message to people with very different interests. We cannot think of them as an amorphous mass; what exists are individuals, men and women who live in different places, who do different things and who are under different ideological influences; the message has to adopt flexible forms in order to be able to reach these real men and women.

When all our speeches and messages are cut from the same cloth and are transmitted in the same manner and with the same words, pronounced in the same tone and through the same megaphone, and when the years go by and the posters and slogans don't change, our words lose their value. They can no longer win the imagination of anyone.

We have to individualize the message, but without losing sight of the common objectives. I believe that the issue of respect for differences can help shed light on the issue of the crisis of activism. Furthermore, everyone knows that over the last few years, a fairly generalized crisis of activism has occurred, not only among Left parties but also in the social movements and grassroots communities influenced by liberation theology, something that is not removed from the changes that the world has suffered. Nevertheless, in many of our countries, together with this crisis of activism, we have witnessed a parallel increase in the influence of the Left in society, and an increase of progressive sentiments among popular sectors.

This leads to the conclusion that one factor present in the origins of this crisis is the type of demands placed upon people in order for them to be able to involve themselves in organized political activity. We have to examine whether the Left has been able to open up avenues for activism and help nurture that growing progressive sentiment in society, because not all people have the same activist vocation nor do they all feel inclined to be active on a permanent level. This fluctuates a lot depending on the political climate at the time. To ignore this fluctuation and demand a uniform level of activism is self-limiting and weakens the political organization. For example, there are those who are willing to be active over a specific issue: health, education, culture and not within a local branch in their workplace or community. There are others who only feel the need to be active at certain junctures (such as elections) but are not willing to do so all year round, even though during key moments of the political struggle you can always count on them to be there, and in their daily lives they are promoting the project and values of the Left.

To try to pigeonhole people who are willing to be active into a single norm, based on a twenty-four-hours-a-day/seven-days-a-week level of activism, which is the same for everyone, means excluding all these potential militants. We have to create a type of organization that can house the widest range of militants, allowing for diverse levels of membership. Organic structures have to abandon their rigidity and become more flexible in order to make the most of the different levels of activist commitment, without establishing a hierarchy between these different levels. In order to facilitate the different levels of activism, it is necessary to adapt the structures and grassroots units of the organization in order to suit the character of the surroundings in which their political activism is carried out.

A Strategy for Building Unity

I have referred to the necessity of building unity among all Left forces and actors in order to be able to group a broad anti-neoliberal bloc around them. Nevertheless, I do not think that this objective can be achieved in a voluntarist manner, creating coordinating bodies from above that end up as simple sums of acronyms. I believe that this unity can emerge through concrete struggles for common objectives. And that is why I think that we can help create better conditions for this unity if we put into practice a new strategy of anti-capitalist struggle.

I am talking about a strategy that takes into consideration the important social, political, economic and cultural transformations that have occurred across the world in the twentieth century. A strategy that understands that the new forms of capitalist domination go far beyond the economic and state sphere and have infiltrated all the nooks and crannies of society, fundamentally through the mass media, which has indiscriminately invaded the homes of all social sectors and in doing so changed the conditions of struggle.

Today more than ever we have to confront not only the dominant classes' apparatuses of political coercion but also the mechanisms and institutions present in civil society that generate a popular acceptance of the capitalist social order. These tend to achieve a significant hegemony over important popular sectors, a cultural leadership over society; they have the capacity to ideologically subordinate the dominated classes. As already \noted, propaganda is to bourgeois democracy what the truncheon is to the totalitarian state. Our challenge therefore is to elaborate a revolutionary strategy within the conditions of a bourgeois democracy that enjoys a level of acceptance by an important part of the popular sector that allows it to maintain itself without having to recur to repression; what is more, we have to take as our starting point the recognition that large parts of the popular sector accept as good coin the capitalist leadership of the process.

For this reason, simple propaganda about an alternative society is not enough. The greater complexity that domination has assumed, the presence of important extra-state factors that produce and reproduce the current popular fragmentation and that attempt to delegitimize the thought and project of the Left in the eyes of the public, means that we must practise what we preach. To do so, we must develop a process of popular construction opposed to capitalism in the territories and spaces won by the Left, that seeks to break with the profit logic and the relations this imposes, and tries to instill solidarity-based humanist logic.

We must promote struggles that are not reduced to simple economic demands—although they must necessarily be included—but that advance in the development of a more global, social project that encourages authentic levels of power from the grassroots. What we are dealing with is the construction of experiences in popular democracy that are tangibly superior to bourgeois democracy. For example, the elaboration of a project for a humanist and solidarity-based city in a local government, promoting diverse spaces for participation that allow local residents to transform themselves into active members of their community. Or the construction of a pole of rural settlements where peasants can establish diverse forms of collaboration among themselves, not only in agricultural production, but also in industrialization and commercialization of their products, in the education of their children and the formation of their cadre according to a model that foreshadows the new society. Or the building of a student federation that defends the democratic participation of students in the running of a university committed to society. Or the construction of a trade union confederation that puts an end to bureaucratic leadership separated from the grassroots, that defends a sociopolitical unionism, that overcomes simple economism, and that proposes as its objective an active insertion in the struggle for social transformation.

A strategy of this type can enormously facilitate the cohering of all sectors of the Left, both those that are members of parties as well as social movement activists, because it involves a different type of call to action. In order to be active, one does not necessarily have to become a member of a party, a mass organization, a movement; one can be active simply by participating in putting into practice the project of an alternative model.

More than just a propagandized utopia that is sterilely introduced into the minds of men and women in a passive manner, as enlightened education without any practice in concrete construction, we are dealing with the construction of popular democratic reference points which, given that they reflect different practices, tend to attract new sectors. Moreover, it is only through these practices that many people begin to understand why it is that in order to expand their humanist and solidarity-based projects it is necessary to put an end to the capitalist system that, with its logic of profit, raises enormous hurdles to any type of alternative model.

It is therefore an urgent priority to put an end to the "tactics" of shortcuts, of focusing only on the conjuncture, and thread together a practice centred on the promotion of democratic struggles from the grassroots; in the local construction of forms of power and popular democracy; that allow us to define the meaning and timing of electoral struggle, and other forms of struggle. Otherwise, these practices will not overcome the long string of "short-termism" that we have encountered in recent years. But it is also urgent that we overcome grassrootism, localism, apoliticism and corporatism, which limit the struggle of the popular sectors to trade union horizons or economic struggles.

Popular Consultations: Spaces that Allow
for the Convergence of Different Forces

I have previously argued the case for the need to create a large social bloc against neoliberalism that can unite all those affected by the system. To achieve this, it is fundamental that we create spaces that allow for the convergence of specific anti-neoliberal struggles where, safeguarding the specific characteristics of each political or social actor, common tasks can be taken up that aid in strengthening the struggle.

In this respect, I think that popular consultations or assemblies are very interesting spaces. These can allow us to mobilize behind a single concrete task of convincing—undertaking door-to-door popular education—a large number of people and youth who are beginning to awaken to politics, who want to contribute to a better world, who very often don't know how to do it and who are not willing to be active in the traditional way because many of them reject politics and politicians.

Moreover, this concrete door-to-door work leads toward having to directly relate to poor popular sectors and their arduous living conditions. Many can be radicalized by coming into contact with so much poverty. A recent example was the referendum held in Uruguay on December 8, 2003 to decide whether to repeal or ratify a law supporting the partnership of the state oil company ANCAP—that has held a monopoly over oil since its foundation in 1931—with foreign private capital. The new company was to be managed and run by the foreign partner.

The vote to reject privatization of the state oil company won by a wide margin (62.02 percent of the vote), and by a bigger percentage than was foreseen in the polls leading up to the vote (50.2 percent). The law had been approved in 2002. Having proven that irregularities were committed by the new managers of ANCAP, the left-wing political coalition, Frente Amplio FA (Broad Front), and allied social and union organizations decided to promote a campaign to collect signatures in support of a referendum against the law. Around 700,000 signatures were required.

In the midst of the petition campaign, the financial crisis of mid-2002 occurred, the value of the currency collapsed within days, some people lost their life savings, many bank accounts were frozen, there were massive company closures and unemployment surpassed the historic high of 13 percent, rising to 20 percent, something unbearable for a country like Uruguay. Social discontent increased. The possibility of turning the popular consultation into a symbolic act of rejection of the government's policies allowed the campaign to grow, gain strength and motivate people.

Even though the mass media was totally hostile and tried to ignore the existence of the initiative, the house-to-house campaign across the country to collect signatures was more powerful than the media blockade. The strong point of the campaign, once again, was the work done in the grassroots, talking with people in their homes and using local radio stations that supported the cause.

The initial weight of the campaign was shouldered more by the social organizations than the political instrument (party), which was somewhat hampered by its initial hesitations. But when Frente Amplio joined the campaign, it once again demonstrated its clarity in the debates and the great potential of neighbourhood, unionist and propagandistic activism. The initiative was supported by all the tendencies in the union confederation, PIT-CNT, the FUCVAM, the Federación Unitaria de Cooperativas de Ayuda Mutua (Unitary Federation of Mutual Aid Co-operatives), which carried out an important mass mobilization across the whole country, and the student movement (FEUU) also joined the campaign, although with little force.

The Right took the initiative to start with, even covering the walls of Montevideo with slogans attacking Tabaré Vasquez, then FA presidential candidate, and supporting the law. Within weeks, thousands of walls were recovered and the Right disappeared off the streets. From that moment on (August–September 2003) fractures began to appear in the traditional parties: the Partido Nacional mayor from Paysandú (a large city on the border with Argentina, a former industrial centre, today in ruins) declared himself in support of abolishing the law. The same occurred with many local leaders from outside the capital and some mid-level national leaders. Although the Right found it hard to accept, an electoral triumph of this sort and by such a wide margin was a sign, perhaps limited but an eloquent one, of what was to come in the Uruguayan presidential elections set for the end of 2004 (when Tabaré Vasquez won).

Another example, if we focus on recent ones, is the consultation over the Free Trade Area of the Americas (FTAA) held in Argentina in November 2003, where more than 2 million votes were cast. It was organized by the Autoconvocatoria No al ALCA (Convention Against FTAA), a diverse and large space that brought together a growing number of trade unions and movements such as professionals, women, farmers, environmentalists, religious, human rights, political, neighbourhood, co-operative and business organizations.

Even when these consultations lack legal backing, they can have important political effects. Proof of this was the declaration made by Argentina's then head of cabinet, Alberto Fernández, who stated that the result of the consultation should be taken into consideration by the government at the time of making decisions concerning the FTAA. On the other hand, this experience allowed thousands of activists from different backgrounds to work together in carrying out the popular consultation. Participation within this large and diverse space is what enabled the proposal to reach out to different popular sectors that are usually separated among themselves, both geographically and socially.

Conclusion: Don't Confuse Desires with Reality

Unfortunately, there tends to be a lot of subjectivism in our analysis of the political situation. What tends to occur is that leaders, driven by their revolutionary passion, confuse desires with reality. An objective evaluation of the situation is not carried out, the enemy is underestimated and, on the other hand, one's own potential is overestimated. Moreover, leaders tend to confuse the mood of the most radical activists with the mood of the grassroots popular sectors. More than a few political leaderships make generalizations about the mood of the masses simply based on their own personal experiences, whether it is in the region they are in or the social sector they are active in, or their guerrilla front, or, in the most general sense, based on the perception of those around them, who are always the most radicalized sectors.

Those who work with the most radicalized sectors will have a different vision of the country compared to those who carry out their political activities among the least political sectors. Revolutionary cadres who work in a militant popular neighbourhood will not have the same vision of the country as those who are active in middle-class sectors. The same thing occurs in countries where both war zones and political spaces exist. Guerrillas who have real confrontations with the enemy, and who have won control of certain zones thanks to their military victories, tend to believe that the revolutionary process is more advanced than militants who work in legal political spaces in the large urban centres, where the ideological power and military control of the regime are still very large.

The only guarantee for not committing these errors is ensuring that leaders are capable of evaluating the situation not on the basis of their mood, but rather taking as their starting point the mood of the bulk of the people, the mood of the enemy and the international reality. Once this evaluation is carried out, it is necessary to come up with proposals that allow us to take advantage of the situation as a whole.

It would seem to be a truism to say that it is important for the top leaders to learn to listen. I believe that this is fundamental. Nevertheless, what occurs is that some leaders are so impregnated by preconceived ideas regarding the current state of affairs, of how things are, of what can be done and what can't be done, that in their contact with intermediary leaders and the grassroots, they tend more toward transmitting their vision of things than informing themselves about the actual mood of the people.

What therefore can occur is that, when one has to make an analysis of the situation, errors occur, not so much due to the lack of information, but because, despite information having been transmitted correctly and in a timely manner by the ranks, it has not been assimilated by the leadership. But it is also important that the ranks and middle layers of leaders be objective in providing information. Sometimes they can misinform rather than inform by providing, for example, inflated numbers for certain mobilizations or actions.

The tendency to delude oneself, to falsify data regarding mobilizations, meetings, strikes, the weight of each organization, is quite common in politics—for instance, saying that thousands were mobilized when it was really only hundreds. This triumphalist focus is the product of the mistaken idea that we are always right, that we are always the best, that everything we do ends up in a positive result for us.

It is not only in regard to numbers where self-delusion has existed, but also in the evaluation of actions that have been proposed. If the objective was to achieve a certain representation in parliament but this was not achieved, recognition is not given to the fact that the number of votes received was below the expectation that had been created; instead, there is always an attempt to seek a way to present the event as a triumph, such as by stating that the number of votes increased compared to the previous election. If a national strike is proposed, but only a partial strike is achieved, this is not recognized as a defeat; rather the success of the strike is talked up because more workers did not go to work compared to previous actions of this type.

If leaders do not know how to listen—something that requires a large dose of revolutionary modesty—and, at the same time, they receive falsified information, then proposals are made which—taking false premises as their starting point—are not adjusted to the real possibilities of the forces on the ground; battles that are planned can lead to significant defeats because they are not based on the real balance of forces.

Note

1.   Translated by Federico Fuentes.

6

Organizing for Socialism: The Communist Network of Italy

Mauro Casadio and Luciano Vasapollo[1]

After two decades of experience with an ideology that views and presented capitalist democracy as the pinnacle of human achievement and the endpoint of "history," the system was stretched to the limits of its normal functioning in a crisis that resurrected fears that capitalism could only survive if it managed its way out of the crisis. But the "global financial crisis," which hit the system at its centre rather than on the periphery as in earlier outbreaks, not only signifies a fundamental disorder in the normal functioning of the economic system, but also has generated forces that threaten the stability of the political system and its capacity to govern—governability. Indeed we are entering a political cycle marked by growing political conflict and conditions of warfare at the level of international relations and the governing regimes that make up the imperial world order and its system of nation states. Unlike the economic crisis, which primarily affects the capitalist democracies at the centre, the political disorder is predominantly a matter of peripheral capitalism, as the governing regimes in the global south search to manage the forces unleashed by the efforts of the global ruling class to advance its economic and geopolitical interests, and impose order among the major blocs of capital locked in a competitive struggle to command the resources of the system.

There is rarely a day in which some research centre somewhere fails to report on the growing developmental divide between the rich and the poor, the critical state of the world's environment and the deterioration of social conditions for one group or the other, a problem that in different national contexts impacts even the class and groups in the middle strata of the social structure, and that in some places and some parts is also reaching crisis proportions. In the political and ideological apparatus of global governance and class rule there is a growing awareness that the forces and conditions of systemic crisis are spreading, even as order is restored in the financial system.

A reading of the research and analysis of colleagues and comrades both in Italy and elsewhere in the world over recent months leads us to conclude that there is a virtual consensus among Marxists as to the fundamental dynamics of these developments and the situation brought about by them. But there have also emerged theoretical and political differences that need to be assessed and dealt with in the interest of forging an international socialist movement and, in the arena of our own class struggle, a counter-hegemonic bloc in Italy. At issue here is construction of a research-and-action plan that raises and addresses the relevant questions as to where we are going and what needs to be done.

To focus on the diverse dimensions of the systemic crisis of capitalism puts us in a position of understanding better or best how to organize and construct a political strategy to advance and mobilize the forces of resistance against capitalism and imperialism in its contemporary form of neoliberal globalization and to direct these forces in a socialist direction. But to begin we refer to two questions that have dominated our attention in recent years, namely the evolution of imperialism as a form and condition of capitalist development, and the composition of the class structure and the correlation of class forces generated by it.

Dynamics of Colonialism and Neoimperialism

The evolution of imperialism in its various forms can be traced to post-World War II in a context that saw the transformation of an empire dominated by Europe and led by Great Britain to one dominated by the United States. This context included the construction of an imperial world order and a system of international organizations, institutions, rules and agreements designed to provide the necessary conditions of security and development, to bring about the economic reconstruction of Europe and the hegemony of the United States over the system and also to ensure that the economically backward countries on the periphery of the system and undergoing a process of decolonization would not succumb to the siren and temptations of communism, and instead tread a capitalist path towards national development (Petras and Veltmeyer 2009, 2011).

In 1953 there were only four independent countries in the African continent, but by 1960 the number had grown to more than twenty. India had broken away from a British Empire in tatters, the revolutionary forces of socialist transformation had triumphed in China and forces for revolutionary change and national liberation were building across Asia and Latin America. However, under conditions of "international co-operation," and despite several experiments with socialism on the African continent, most of the countries in the diverse outposts of European colonialism responded to the pressures and overtures of the capitalist democracies at the centre of the system to pursue a capitalist path towards their development. In Latin America only Cuba managed to break out of the trap of capitalist peripheral development set by the international organizations of the U.S.-led imperialist system. In other countries in the region, a combination of the state's iron fist, wielded at the behest of the imperial masters in Washington, and the soft velvet glove of development broke the back of both the labour movement and the struggle of the peasants for land. By the early 1980s, with the installation of the new world order, labour had been defeated, the associated social and political movements disarmed, its forces disarticulated and the rural movements for land decapitated or brought to ground with the instruments of repression and armed force.

The development process during this period unfolded under the aegis of the state, which in the global south not only assumed responsibility for the "function of capital" (investment, entrepreneurship, management, and marketing) but also the functions of social welfare, human capital formation and economic development. However, the engine of economic growth and social development began to stall in the late 1960s, ending the "golden age of capitalism" and ushering in a prolonged period of crisis and restructuring, and with it a global class war launched by capital against labour in the 1970s as a strategic response to the crisis and a concerted effort to reactivate the accumulation process. Other strategic and structural responses[2] to the economic crisis of overproduction included the relocation of labour-intensive industrial operations closer to sources of cheap exploitable labour, technological restructuring of global production in the form of computer-generated information (advances in information technology) and the regulation of labour (flexibilization, Fordism), structural reform in macroeconomic policy (structural adjustment to the requirements of the new world order), and above all, a fundamental change in the capital-labour relation, increasing the share of capital in national income and concomitantly reducing the share of labour.[3]

Forces of Change and the Social Structure

The forces released in the process of capitalist development and imperial rule had a profound impact on the social structure and the capital-labour relation at the base of this structure. The forces of change—industrialization, modernization, proletarianization—were conceptualized by development theorists in terms of a process of "structural" transformation of a traditional and precapitalist agrarian society and economy into a modern industrial capitalist system (Petras and Veltmeyer 2011: Ch. 3). In the process, according to the economists and sociologists at the World Bank (World Bank 2008), with the capitalist development and modernization of agriculture, and the consequent shift of the population from the countryside to the towns and cities, the rural peasantry of small landholders was transformed into an urban proletariat of wage-workers as well as those who worked "on their own account" in the streets in the so-called "informal sector" of the urban economy (Davis 2006). World Bank economists (2008) conceptualized this process of "primitive accumulation by dispossession" (to use David Harvey's apt phrase) as "pathways out of poverty," namely labour and migration. Under conditions of neoliberal globalization and capitalist development in the 1980s the industrialization process, and the capitalist labour market, in a number of contexts in the global south (Latin America in particular) was truncated, resulting in a profound change in the nature of the working class. One of these changes was the relative decline of the industrial proletariat formed in an earlier phase of capitalist development and imperialism, and with it the weakening of the movement of unionized labour in both the private and public sectors.

With the informal sector of the non-capitalist urban economy accounting for up to 80 percent of jobs generated in the 1980s and since, more than half the working class in the major cities no longer exchange their labour power against capital, but work on their own account under precarious forms of employment and deteriorating social conditions, which are documented and analyzed so eloquently by Mike Davis in his study of "planetary slums" (2006). What Davis does not analyze, however, is the continuing decline in the organizational capacity and class power of labour, or the difficulties faced by the Left in organizing workers in this new context and mobilizing the forces of resistance against the neoliberal agenda of the governments, both those (on the Pacific coast from Mexico to Chile, with the exception of Correa in Ecuador), which are essentially lackeys of U.S. imperialism, and the more pragmatic and social liberal or centre-left regimes formed in Brazil, Argentina, Bolivia, Ecuador and elsewhere in the region (Petras and Veltmeyer 2009). Although in Argentina the unemployed workers and the "new urban poor" did in fact (in 2001) rise up against this agenda and confront the forces of neoliberal globalization in the form of the state (see Petras and Veltmeyer 2009), the organization and mobilization of the new working class in peripheral capitalist social formations remains a major challenge for the Left in building twenty-first-century socialism (21cs).

In countries closer to the "centre" of the system the social structure formed in the era of neoliberal globalization assumed a different form than that which defined the global south. For one thing, the social structure of these societies is more clearly based on the capital-labour relation. Notwithstanding the declining power of the labour movement in Europe and elsewhere in the global north—labour having lost many of the battles in the class war launched by capital against labour in the 1970s (Davis 1984; Crouch and Pizzaro 1978)—the working class remains a bastion of organized resistance to the neoliberal capitalist world order, the major social base for any possible rebuilding of a socialist movement in the twenty-first century.

But any strategy for mobilizing the forces of resistance in a socialist direction has to take account of the structural and political features of this working class and the fundamental change brought about in recent years in the social conditions of the social strata located in the middle of the social structure. The relation of this class to both capital and labour is less direct or more ambiguous. First, as in the global south on the periphery of the system, the industrial proletariat and public sector unions have borne the brunt of the economic restructuring process and the massive multifaceted assault on labour over the past three decades. As a result, their organizational capacity and political power have been undermined and is seriously diminished.

Second, as discussed by James Petras and Henry Veltmeyer in this volume, the class and policy dynamics of neoliberal globalization over the past three decades (and the appropriation by the capitalist class and its upper middle class "service providers" of the lion's share of the wealth generated) has resulted in the polarization of "society" between the rich and poor, and the spread of poverty. This is particularly the case in the U.S., where this process is very advanced, but current attacks on the welfare state in Europe threaten to bring about similar developments in Europe. Only a concerted response of the Left to this reform agenda will stave off this development, setting a possible stage for revival of the socialist movement.

Third, capitalist development of the forces of production under conditions of neoliberal globalization, and with it the increased polarization of society—what the Economic Commission for Latin America and the Caribbean (ECLAC 2010) conceptualizes as a "structure of inequality"—is resulting in a hollowing out of the middle class, putting the savings and property and even the jobs of class members at risk and threatening their middle-class lifestyle and "life chances," pushing the lower strata of this class into poverty. Although most members of this class tend to retain middle-class (i.e., false) consciousness, they constitute a major potential base for socialist development.

Fourth, in the political economy of globalization there has emerged a growing south-north labour migration trend. As a result, migrants from the global south make up an increasing part of the working class and a potential contribution to the labour movement, if the Left can succeed in organizing this sector of workers and work to counteract the exclusion of migrants from the hard-won benefits won by labour in previous cycles of class struggle, embracing migrant workers as a critical factor in the labour movement. This is another major challenge for the Left, which to date has failed in its ability to appeal to and organize this growing sector of the working class.

Fifth, political developments in Greece in 2010 prefigure likely developments elsewhere in Europe, as governments under the sway of capital are forced to accede to the demands for "reform," which include a further dismantling of hard-won concessions and benefits, and that constitute a major assault on the social condition of the European working class. In this connection, it is imperative that the Left rise to the challenge, which is to work to increase the class consciousness of workers—their awareness of the forces at play and the need for a concerted, organized political response to the latest assault on labour. One contribution to this class-consciousness among both workers and the socialist government in the case of Greece is to draw possible lessons from class struggles elsewhere. For example, the government could learn a lot from the experience of Argentina in 2001, when the government of the day, under pressure from a mobilized if unorganized (and dis-employed) working class as well as an angry middle class, held the IMF at bay in refusing to accede to its demands for reformist austerity measures and financial "discipline." As it turned out, in standing firm against the IMF and the U.S. state, the Kirchner regime managed to pull the country out of a deep recession and successfully manage an economic recovery program that led to the highest rate of economic growth in the region in recent years (Petras and Veltmeyer 2009). The government's firm stance against the demands for "reform, under pressure from an actively mobilised population, was the key to this effective response to a crisis that bears resemblance to the crisis now threatening the working classes of Europe."

Crisis of Capitalism

It is evident that the question of the essential characteristics of the economic and financial crisis is the nub and central focus of our work at the level of analysis and theory. This is not only because of an evident propensity of capitalism towards crisis. It is also because the dynamics of capitalist development, and strategic and political responses to it, tend to generate both the objective and subjective conditions of socialist transformation. This is one of the "eternal verities" of capitalism established by Marx and evidenced by a century of capitalist development (Veltmeyer 2010). It is also why our organization in recent years has focused on the dynamics of the crisis as a major object of theoretical and political analysis. Our organization, via the RdeC and CESTES/Proteo, has undertaken and produced a solid body of theoretical and empirical analysis of the dynamics of the systemic crisis and the objective conditions that this crisis, together with the tragic responses of the state to it. In both the academic world and the business press and policy-making circles, the most recent manifestation of the tendency towards crisis is interpreted as a global phenomenon—although the evidence and several studies suggest that the crisis is far from global, hitting primarily the economies at the centre of the system. The crisis is also widely interpreted as primarily if not exclusively financial, affecting mainly the institutional functioning of the financial system. But a number of studies suggest and our interpretation is that the crisis is both multidimensional in scope and systemic, reaching down into the very foundations of the system, threatening the pillars of production as well as the functioning of the financial system.

If, as we suggest, it is true that the crisis is systemic, and not merely financial in nature, it allows us to theoretically grasp the potential of future developments, and construct alternative scenarios of these developments. But it also points to the direction of theoretical and political debate, and the form that our class intervention might or should take. What is needed is a research strategy and a plan of action that takes into account the systemic tendencies of the system and the range of potential and possible developments.

However, if an analysis of the most immediate effects of the crisis is the most practical, taking into account the recent debate among Marxists about the manifest form of the crisis, it is also necessary to take the more complicated step of theorizing the medium-term effects and potential developments of the crisis, and the Marxist debate on these issues is highly relevant here. In this case the appropriate method of analysis is to theoretically construct the possible and likely alternative scenarios. At issue in this analysis is to determine whether we have on the horizon a possible continuation (or even the reinforcement) of U.S. hegemony, or whether we are at the threshold of a new phase of stagnant capitalist development, the internal contradictions of which will have political effects that can be anticipated and grasped in theory.

In tracing alternative scenarios it is evident that we need to take account of and consider diverse contingent factors as well as systemic tendencies. One of these is technological innovation and associated developments. At issue here is the question of a paradigmatic shift in the productive system—in the method employed to increase the productivity of labour and capital. Another critical factor in the capitalist development of the forces of production is geopolitics. In this connection the contemporary phase of development in what might be understood as the postneoliberal era is characterized by a shift in the geopolitical and economic centre of the system towards Asia, and China in particular. But this is by no means the only geopolitical trend that can be discerned. Russia, India and Latin America (especially Brazil), as well as Eurasia are also critical variables in the process of what *The Economist* visualizes and understands in a somewhat (if not highly) simplified tripartite division of the world economy into three poles and sets of alliances—North America, Europe and the "emerging markets," with two major powers, the U.S. and China, the one in decline and the other ascendant.

A third factor to consider in the possible alignment of international and national relations and forces is the class conflict generated by these developments and associated struggles. At issue here are the forces of resistance against neoliberalism, globalization, capitalism and, in some contexts, imperialism; and also, and in particular, the strategic responses "from below" to conditions that in some contexts are reaching crisis proportions. Thus we should interpret recent political developments in Latin America, which, according to some analysts have "transformed a continent" (Zibechi 2011). In this connection, Zibechi argues that "[i]n many ways, the first decade of the new millennium was the flip side of the last decade of the twentieth century in South America. There have been numerous and significant changes. We still don't know," he adds, "if it's a glitch in time or a new beginning." In any case "the region will never be the same." Carlos Menem, Alberto Fujimori, Carlos Andrés Pérez, Fernando Henrique Cardoso, Julio María Sanguinetti, Gonzalo Sánchez de Losada, Hugo Bánzer—the names of the figures who dominated the 1990s say it all: "it was an era of privatization and deregulation, of the unprecedented shrinking of the state, an intense concentration of wealth and a dramatic increase in the presence of transnational corporations." Calculations made by Brazil, where whole sectors of the economy were privatized, estimate that 30 percent of the GNP changed hands in these years. "A veritable earthquake," writes the Brazilian sociologist Francisco de Oliveira (2009) in this regard.

The Washington Consensus "left no stone unturned" (Zibechi 2011). In some cases, as in Argentina, the neoliberal model threatened the entire future of the country for several generations. The transformations were even more threatening because the privatizing hurricane came immediately after the dark years of the dictatorships or, as some would say, formed an integral part of the work of the dictators. But, Zibechi notes, and Petras echoes in his opening chapter in this volume, "those terrible years were also the years of the awakening of societies, the activation of old and new social movements, the continental coordination of the Left in the Forum of Sao Paulo and global coordination in the World Social Forum." As Petras documents in this volume and Zibechi argues, "a wave of social activism, such as the region—and the world—had not seen since the 1970s spread the carpet for the grand exit of neoliberal governments and the gradual but persistent appearance of a new generation of governments that presented themselves as Left or progressive." Petras and Veltmeyer (2009, 2011) dispute this point, arguing that these regimes are not nearly as radical as they appear or present themselves. But even so, these regimes did and still do oppose the Washington Consensus as well as the neoliberal policy agenda, and they do take issue with U.S. imperialism, if not capitalism.

The Communist Option [Italy] within the Crisis

It is a truism for Marxists that the working class in each country has to come to terms with (that is, oppose) its own bourgeoisie and the capitalist system as it manifests itself in their own experience. Thus the importance of discussing and deciding as to the "communist option" within the current crisis—how best to advance the interests of the working classes in this context. In the medium to long term, and certainly on the horizon of thought and action, this means the overthrow of the capitalist system and the construction of socialism. This is not on the immediate agenda, however, requiring Marxists to adjust their thinking and action to "what is possible" in the immediate context, and "what is to be done" in this context. The issue here is to identify the points of weakness in, or vulnerability of, the system—to reflect on the "window of opportunity" provided by a particular conjuncture of objective and subjective conditions. In this connection, it is important to understand that any crisis situation weakens the institutional structure of the system, exposing both the inevitable underlying fissures and releasing forces of change. As emphasized by Petras and Veltmeyer in their concluding chapter in this volume, the opportunity and the need to take action apply as much to those on the Right as to those on the Left; and the forces of change released in the process can be mobilized in either direction. The point is that we as a network of Italian communists on the basis of theoretical reflection and debate might understand what is necessary (what needs to be done), but we also need to correctly diagnose what is possible in the current conjuncture—and not miss the "moment"—the opportunity to act when conditions are right.

On the other hand, the evident transformation of the Italian Left in recent years has to be contextualized with reference to political developments both inside the country and abroad. These developments include a tendency towards fragmentation of the Left, retreat from the class struggle, lack of militancy, and a generalized disorientation and lack of organization all too evident in the so-called "anti-globalization movement," including its most militant youth sector. These developments raise serious questions about the lack of militancy, political education and effective organization on the Left that can no longer be avoided.

At issue in this situation, shared (it would seem) with the Left all over the world, is the failure to connect a concrete analysis of the specific situation in which working people find themselves to both the workings of the system, i.e., to a theoretical analysis of the dynamics of capitalist development in specific contexts, and the current conjuncture of neoliberal globalization and the actions and policies of the state in the service of the capitalist class. In this connection, what our organization needs is to gather the relevant data and to conduct both a qualitative and quantitative analysis of these data regarding the condition of the working class in diverse sectors of the economy, both public and private—data on work conditions and forms of employment, both precarious and regular; inflation and the cost of living; and the gender and age dimensions of these conditions. We also need collective discussion of the results of this analysis, to communicate them to our membership and translate them into effective political practice, i.e., figure out how to use them as a weapon in the class struggle.

Class Struggle from Below

The alternative scenarios constructed by our organization as the basis for political action refer to and point towards contradictions of capitalist development that can be managed or resolved by the system's agents and guardians on the condition that the dominated or subordinate class does not acquire the political subjectivity, i.e., class consciousness, with which to construct an adequate political practice from below and within. In this connection, political developments in Latin America, particularly those related to diverse efforts to construct an alternative socialist path towards national development (see the contributions of Petras and Webber, and the reflections of Harnecker and Lebowitz in this volume) are revealing and useful. Not only do these developments, and the vicissitudes of diverse efforts in the region to construct the "socialism of the twenty-first century" illuminate the opportunities and pitfalls of socialist political practice in conditions of crisis, but they also provide useful tools for analysis, organization and action. However, it is too soon to conceive of a politically irreversible counteroffensive to the latest offensive of capital in the long and ongoing global class war.

If we are all too aware of the difficulties that the Left faces in the project of constructing an alternative socialist form of society we should not lose sight of the opportunities provided by a system in crisis. The anti-imperialist movement that is taking form in the global arena of the class war, and that in Latin America has found its moment of greatest clarity at the level of political strategy, makes clear that although we cannot yet speak or write about an imminent socialist revolution, history has not come to an end with capitalism. Socialism remains very much on the agenda both as a necessity and a possibility. The problem is how to build it in the current conjuncture of capitalist development, and what form might or will it take—questions of scientific analysis, both concrete and theoretical, and political organization and strategy.

The theoretical and political space between the objective and the subjective, between the opportunities provided by the contradictions of a system in crisis and the capacity for effective intervention in the development process continues to be the keystone of debate on the "Left" within the social movements and among us communists. The urgency of this debate reflects the evident fact that the correlation of forces in the current crisis favours the "Right." Forces on the reactionary Right appear to be better equipped than the Left to respond to the economic, social and moral crisis that afflicts Italy. This we cannot let stand and must change.

The political intervention of the Left in conditions of a growing contradiction is a matter of great urgency. At issue is the need for organization—to create an anti-capitalist consciousness and a communist subjectivity among workers and the general population that is adequate to the needs of the moment and the current situation. But the political culture that has sustained at least two generations of our comrades no longer exists, making it difficult to come up with an adequate response to the current situation, a situation also characterized by a siege mentality regarding the forces of reaction on the "Right" of the political spectrum.

A vigorous debate vis-à-vis an alternative political project (the socialism of the twenty-first century), and the construction of a counter-hegemonic bloc (see the chapter by William Carroll), are both possible and necessary today, and rendered more feasible than utopian by the development of reality itself. But the issue for us is how best to organize in this context (in this phase and under the conditions of the current situation), taking into account matters of theory and political contingency. In other words, the question is whether and how, if correctly and well organized, the network of communists can contribute to the construction and growth of an antagonistic class movement.

The debate as to how to construct a communist organization in twenty-first-century Italy (with the determination and consciousness needed to build a party) is concretized in the formation and broadening of a Leftist political collectivity and a leadership capable of meeting the challenge and confronting the complexities of political organization in the current conjuncture of the class struggle. In our opinion, to fully engage the project of reconstructing an organization that is both aware and able to embrace responsibility for and the strategic and political role required of it necessitates a break with the existing political culture. It is evident to us that the model of organization used by the political parties derived from dissolution of the Italian Communist Party (PCI), hierarchical in structure, is inadequate for the task. For one thing, in this organization the political line of the organization and militant action, and also the militant, is subordinated to the hierarchy and institutional structure, with a consequent negative impact on cadre formation and communist practice. Our experience with this form of organization has revealed the problems caused by limiting militant communist practice to simply participating in propaganda, elections and organizing parties and other events. In this connection the Communist Network (RdeC) that we have constructed has introduced the democratic practice of collective leadership and experimented with various ways of enhancing the level and diverse forms of active participation of its members. Organizing in a spirit of experimentation has resulted in creation of a more flexible structure for collective political action, with a notable positive impact on the level and forms of cadre formation and active militant participation in the political struggle.

As for the subjective or political dimension of the organization and the broader communist movement, theoretical debate is crucial, as is the need to adjust theory to changing conditions, to confront our ideas about what must and can be done with the real world, taking into account and reflecting on these conditions. This is what used to be called "concrete analysis of concrete situations," which is theoretically informed but not based on a commitment to preconceived ideas, i.e., that can adjust to changing conditions in the real world.

The aim of our theoretical practice is to capture in thought those tendencies and structural forces the working of which can be substantiated through empirical analysis and that can serve to either validate or invalidate our ideas and action on them. The aim is to understand which elements of thought and practice should be retained and which can be discarded. Naturally, or importantly, we need to avoid the evident tendency, in our experience and prior political practice, to decontextualize ideas and use them formulaically in situations in which the underlying conditions are different, so that the ideas do not apply. That is, our reflections on the real world and our own political practice should not tempt us to search for and "discover" formulaic answers to substantive questions—to think mechanically rather than dialectically, which requires us to adjust our ideas to the real world rather than adjust reality to our ideas. For one thing, as noted above, consciously directed action on different ideas, and the agency of different organizations in the pursuit of diverse strategies, have both intended and unintended consequences, leading to developments that cannot be preconceived or theoretically determined. These developments in turn will undoubtedly create new material conditions for the working class and a new configuration of class forces in response to these conditions. And, as Marx established in his conception of historical materialism, these conditions and forces should be theorized and analyzed scientifically, i.e., on their own terms rather than with speculation or preconceived ideas.

Contradictions of Capital:
Crisis, Restructuring and Resistance

The propensity of capitalism towards crisis arises out of a fundamental contradiction. In the drive to accumulate capital, capitalists are prone to overproduce and saturate markets, limiting their capacity to realize surplus value, thus leading to a reduction in capital available for productive investment and a cutback in production and a layoff of workers, which reduces consumption and thus the market, further restricting the capacity to extract surplus value on the basis of expanded production and the exploitation of labour. Marx theorized this developmental tendency in terms of a law that average profits will tend to fall over time. The theory of this law (in mathematical form: s/c+v) assumes that (a) the organic composition of capital (i.e., c/v, or the ratio of constant over variable capital), under conditions of competition and a resulting drive for technological innovation and advantage, tends to rise over time; and (b) the rate of surplus value, i.e., s/v, or the rate of surplus value production (s) over the total value of labour power (v), under conditions of a class struggle, tends to remain constant. The contradiction consists in the fact that on the one hand capitalism is based on exploitation of labour and generation of a profit on invested capital under conditions of expanded production; on the other hand, it is geared to a tendency for the rate of average profits to fall. Under these conditions Marx theorized that the capacity of capitalism to expand production would be pushed towards its limits, generating both the objective and subjective conditions of a revolutionary transformation of the conditions and form of production, namely socialism. In abstract terms, as a principle of historical materialism, Marx saw in this propensity towards overproduction and crisis a cycle of downward production and falling profits, as a fundamental conflict between the forces of production and the corresponding social relations of production. Under these conditions, the existing system of production relation, or the legal relation of property in the means of production, tends to become a fetter on the capacity of the system to expand production, bringing into conflict one class intent to accumulate capital and another, the working class—that class whose conditions of existence are defined by lack of access to production (the proletariat is the class that owns nothing except its labour power, which it is thereby forced to exchange for a living wage). The inevitable result, Marx concludes, is that the system has a built-in tendency towards crisis, pushing the system to its limits and thereby creating the objective conditions of revolutionary transformation (the incapacity of the system to expand production) and its subjective condition, a class that is conscious or theoretically aware of being exploited and thus disposed to confront to resist the class power of capital. To be precise, or make clear Marx's thinking in regard to the unfolding of this contradiction and the resulting class conflict, he did not anticipate that the system would collapse under the weight of this contradiction, or that the regime would inevitably be overthrown. As he saw it, socialist transformation hinged on the conversion of a class "in itself" (in a position to be objectively exploited) into a class "for itself" (conscious, and thus disposed to resist the efforts of capital to profit at its expense).

But, as Marx theorized, the system also has at its disposal the capacity to offset the tendency for profits to fall and thus extend its capacity to expand production by restructuring the system, releasing thereby forces of change that can be mobilized in support of or against the system. One method (way of offsetting the tendency towards crisis) is to raise the level of exploitation by increasing the workday under the same wage rate, or, alternatively, to reduce wages. Another is to increase the rate of surplus value or exploitation through technological advance or conversion of the production apparatus—the "revolutionary" way of advancing the forces of production. A third method is to internationalize production in the search for new markets or sources of cheap labour, in the process—according to later generations of Marxist or neo-Marxist theorists—creating conditions of uneven capitalist development on a global scale.

However (although it was left to later generations of Marxist scholars to theorize), the propensity towards crisis will reassert itself, pushing capitalism once again towards its limits to expand production, and reproduce the conditions of socialist transformation, including the contradiction between the forces and relations of production (and a resulting pattern of crisis, economic restructuring and political resistance). But this time these conditions are generated, and the process unfolds, in a system of global production—in the global arena of the class struggle, which is to say, as a global class war.

An understanding of these dynamics of capitalist development does nor necessarily signify discontinuity with past political practice—to promote change and systemic transformation via the institutional mechanisms of liberal democracy (such as party politics and elections) or the building of a socialist movement. But it does mean better theoretically informed practice (including an understanding of the dynamics of imperialism and class rule), and thus a way out of the crisis that more likely works in the interest of labour rather than capital.

One dynamic of capitalist development on a global scale, the outcome of what Marx theorized as the "general law of capital accumulation," is a twofold tendency towards the concentration of capital, thus leading to the emergence of finance capital and monopolies, and what David Harvey (2005) has theorized as "accumulation by dispossession," leading (in Marx's formulation of this theory) to the "multiplication of the proletariat." Another dynamic—apart but not disconnected from a fundamental propensity towards crisis—of capitalist development on a global scale is associated with the battle for the global market among diverse national forms of capital, namely, inter- and intra-imperialist rivalry.

The inter-capitalist struggle for competitive advantage,[4] and a resulting inter-imperialist rivalry (with the state intervening on behalf of capital), plays an important role in the global dynamics of uneven capitalist development and installation of a "new world order" (neoliberal globalization) that has facilitated the free movement of capital, and the restructuring of macroeconomic policy. This restructuring, as it turns out, has been one way that capitalists were able at least temporarily to offset the crisis tendency but, as noted at the outset, the tendency reasserted itself in different contexts and points of time in the 1990s and the new millennium, most notably in the so-called recent "global financial crisis." It is particularly important to the Left, in its diverse expressions in Italy and elsewhere, to study, research and analyze the dynamics of this development, and, in order to mobilize them in some way, to gauge the strength of the forces of resistance to this development. For the network of Communists (RdeC) this means not only drawing lessons from the class struggle elsewhere (especially, in the current context, in Latin America) but coming to terms and settling accounts with capitalism and the bourgeoisie in our own country—to analyze the policy and political dynamics of this development, and to connect these dynamics to the changing, and deteriorating, social condition of the Italian working class; to make a concrete (albeit theoretically informed) analysis of the situation in which workers find themselves.

A clear understanding of the contradictions of capitalist development in this specific context, and the weight of these contradictions on the working class, will allow us to construct an appropriate and effective political practice, thereby determining or shaping the process of political organization, the object of an ongoing debate within the organization. This debate has to do not so much with the evolution of events, and the changing conditions of social existence and everyday life, as with systemic tendencies and the way that the objective conditions of these tendencies are expressed in government policy and Italian politics.

Spontaneity Versus Organization

Another critical factor in the debate on how best to organize for socialist transformation is a matter of political subjectivity—whether engagement in the class struggle should be organized or whether it is a spontaneous response of workers to the objectivity of their social condition. On this issue our position is that no "spontaneity" can respond adequately to the demands of the class struggle. Our past experience leads us to assert this position without equivocation. However, how best to organize and what form such organization should take are matters of continuing debate. But on one point we are clear. It is critical that no militant be excluded and that all are invited, if not expected, to participate actively in the formulation and execution of strategy, and that collective decisionmaking requires a horizontal, rather than vertical, form of organization. Hence our preference to organize in the form of a democratic network rather than a party along traditional Marxist-Leninist lines. It is our experience that organization in the form of a network not only ensures a higher level and better form of active participation but also is less likely to lead to the sectarianism that was so destructive in diverse efforts to unify the forces of resistance.

The political demands of the class struggle—i.e., an organized and effective political response to the machinations of capital against labour—not only organized political leadership but construction of an organization that encompasses and brings together as broad a representation of the working class as possible, and that inhibits or minimizes the formation of antagonistic relations within the working class and among its leadership cadre.

For us these and other issues of organization, strategy and militant action are complicated by the many elements that obscure or obfuscate the possibility of creating a different form of society, another world as it were—socialism to be precise. The historic defeat of the working class—labour lost many battles in the long class war launched by capital in the 1970s—is one of these elements. Others include changes in the structure and composition of the working class, as well as the bureaucratization of unions and the labour movement, and the formation of a labour "aristocracy." These and other such changes in the popular sector created all sorts of divisions that worked against class-consciousness and militant action. In addition, political parties or social movements on the Left failed to respond to the demands of the situation, first, because of institutionalism, and second, due to ideological and organizational issues. Both the parties and the movements essentially, if not totally, separated themselves from the profound agitations in the popular sector of Italy. We are still paying the price for this separation today in the political impotence, sectarianism and internal divisions of the Left.

In the wake of such problems, and with reference to the deteriorating condition of the working class in its diverse and multitudinous forms, it is incumbent upon us to more effectively engage the class struggle against the economic model of neoliberal globalization and the hegemony of capital on the ideological level, at the major points of production, in different workplaces and on the streets. What is needed in a context of deepening crisis is hard political work to expose the contradictions of the system and take political advantage of existing opportunities for substantive change, to mobilize and direct the forces of change in a socialist direction. This does not mean that socialist transformation is at hand; we are all too aware that we are in no position to make the revolution. But we need to place socialism on the agenda and undertake the diverse complex tasks of building a new socialist movement. This requires a commitment to socialism, an ideological struggle in the construction of a counter-hegemonic bloc, political education and effective organization, a clear understanding of the issues that confront and concern people as well as the forces at play in the class struggle and non-sectarian but militant and collectively organized action.

Our analysis of different phases of capitalist development of the forces of production has shown that each advance and change brings about the need for, and produces, a corresponding change in the form of class organization. In this context the mass party, as we came to know it, exhausted its political limits, the result not so much of the particular characteristics of the leadership cadre as the political process in which political practice at the time was embedded. In any case, the form of organization and action characteristic of a Marxist-Leninist mass party, with a vertical organizational structure and sectarian politics (a politically divisive party line) is no longer functional for building a socialist movement in the objective and subjective conditions of capitalist development today.

"What needs to be done" remains the critical issue, but we need to be more self-critical and flexible in our form of organization and political practice. We need to take account of both the subjectivity and objectivity of conditions experienced by people today in the current phase of worldwide capitalist development, to make connections and to extend our reach as wide and far as we can into the working class, working collectively to mobilize, and if and where possible to unify, the many and diverse forces of resistance against capitalism, neoliberal globalization and imperialism. In this context, we must be well aware of the fact that the working class today is not the working class of the past, and that the capitalism and imperialism of today assume forms that are in some respects different from the past, creating conditions that must be understood, and responded to, in their specificity as well as in their more general systemic dynamics.

An effective political response to the requirements of the situation in which we find ourselves, a clear understanding of "what is to be done," must be based not only on a scientific theory of systemic dynamics and concrete analysis of concrete situations, but also guided by a clear idea as to what is both necessary and possible—the form that socialism could take and how to move towards and build it. It is in this connection that a comparative analysis of, and reflections on, other relevant experiences are particularly useful. At the present time, some of the most significant examples of how to deal with capitalism (and imperialism) can be found in Latin America—in Cuba (how it managed to defy all odds in building socialism in conditions of neoliberal globalization and crisis; the construction of a revolutionary social-ist consciousness; its socialist internationalism), in Bolivia (how to achieve power by means of a social movement, combining electoral politics with active mobilization of the forces of resistance), in Venezuela (in the ongoing project to construct and experiment with 21cs) and in ALBA (constructing international trade relations on the basis of socialist principles).

Conclusion

In conclusion, as a network of communists we need to take more seriously the need for a profound analysis of the social condition and concrete situation of the working class in an incipient and deepening crisis—to expose the contradictions and developmental tendencies of the system and the possibilities for change. This requires a clear theoretical—and political—

understanding of systemic tendencies and a correct reading of the forces at play, the objectivity and subjectivity of conditions confronted by people in the current system.

We need to be self-critical and upgrade our toolbox of ideas and method of actions, to adjust them to the demands of the moment—critical events, the concrete situation and changing conditions. Also useful is the study of and serious reflection on the class struggle. For example, some aspects of the Cultural Revolution in China, the reflections of Che Guevara and the debate on the Soviet model and the Cuban economy, current and recent developments in Latin America, and, in particular, efforts to construct the "socialism of the twenty-first century"—these and other such struggles and developments (anti-imperialist struggles and the active mobilizations of the oppressed and the exploited) all provide grist for our mill of theoretical reflection and political debate. They constitute experiences from which we can learn and that can be used to adjust our critical thinking and political practice, to inform action and the modalities of how we confront the demands of the class struggle in the current conjuncture of capitalist and socialist development. In conducting a theoretical analysis of systemic tendencies and a concrete analysis of concrete situations, we need to reflect on these experiences and debate the possible lessons to be derived from them—the way they connect to the diverse but similar situations of people today.

By means of CESTES and Proteo, the RdeC has demonstrated the critical importance of theoretical debate on the dynamics of capitalist development on a global scale, and the machinations of imperial power, in diverse contexts. Study of these dynamics, and open debate about their consequences and meaning for political action, have provided critical inputs into our political education programs, and are reflected in advances made in expanding our network of communists and connecting to the Italian working class. Our reflections and experience lead us to conclude that extension of this debate, political organization and an internationalist orientation are important building blocks in the construction, or reconstruction, of a socialist movement towards socialism in the twenty-first century.

Notes

1. Translated from Spanish by the editor.
2. In terms of theory, the difference between "strategic" and "structural" is that the former refers to the intended consequences of actions taken in the direction of change, while the latter specifies the unintended consequences of these actions.
3. For a theoretical exposition of these dynamics of crisis and restructuring from a Marxist perspective, see Vasapollo 2011.
4. In fact, economists at UNCTAD have determined that close to half of all international trade transactions take the form of intra-firm transfers, i.e., they do not enter the market. An estimated another 50 percent of the remaining international trade

operations is subject to monopoly, and thus does not involve competition. But there remaining 25 percent of the global market operates under conditions of inter-capitalist competition, thus releasing the forces of capitalist development theorized by Marx (on these dynamics see Vasapollo 2011).

7

Socialist Strategy, Yesterday and Today: Notes on Classical Marxism and the Contemporary Radical Left

Murray E.G. Smith and Joshua D. Dumont

A century has now passed since capitalism exhausted whatever historically progressive role it once played. In the twentieth century, the stubborn persistence of capitalism's competitive and exploitative social relations resulted in two horrific and massively destructive world wars (not to mention countless localized conflicts), in severely restricted and distorted patterns of economic development in regions of the world subject to imperialist pillage and in untold misery for masses of human beings condemned to unemployment/ underemployment, grinding poverty, malnourishment and disease. It is with bitter contempt that socialists observe that hundreds of millions of people who might have contributed to the betterment of our species have suffered wretchedly and had their lives cut tragically short because capitalism refused to shuffle off its mortal coil.

As we enter the second decade of the twenty-first century, the capitalist system can inspire little confidence that it has purchased a new and progressive lease on life. The current economic crisis, the worst since the Great Depression of the 1930s, has definitively ended the period of capitalist triumphalism inaugurated by the fall of the Soviet Union—that boon for "market democracies" which the more impressionistic of bourgeois ideologues had thought heralded the final triumph of liberal-democratic capitalism and even "the end of history." Certainly, in spite of rapidly worsening conditions for the working population, there is no likelihood of a return to the sort of expansionary "welfare state" that arose in the advanced capitalist countries following World War II. Attempting to repair the damage associated with the global economic slump that began in 2008, capital and capitalist states have instead ushered in a period of savage attacks on the living standards and security of working people throughout the world. The gradual erosion of the hard-won gains of the working class in the capitalist core which began after the onset of the profitability crisis of the 1970s, and which facilitated a partial recovery from that crisis, is now being eclipsed by concerted efforts to transfer unprecedented amounts of wealth directly into the hands of the super-rich, allegedly with a view to "stabilizing" the system.

Capital's new class strategy, in response to its latest crisis, might aptly be described as *neoliberalism with a vengeance*.[1] The failure of the labour movement to take the offensive politically in the face of this onslaught—a failure attributable above all to a refusal to adopt a resolutely class struggle perspective—has emboldened the capitalist class almost everywhere to close ranks behind the neoliberal nostrums that have prevailed globally since the 1980s. Our point of departure in this chapter is the proposition that *this class strategy of capital can only be met with an effective counter-offensive through a major revival and reassertion of the fundamental programmatic tenets of Marxist socialism.*

As a body of ideas and as a movement toward a society beyond capitalism, Marxist socialism stands for the dissolution of capitalist private property, collective ownership of the means of production and distribution, a democratically planned economy and the replacement of antagonistic social relations of exploitation, competition and domination with relations of equality, co-operation and solidarity: a classless, communist society. From the Marxist perspective, socialism is not merely an ethical ideal: it is the only fully rational response to the intensifying contradictions of the capitalist world order. Socialism aims at eliminating the deeply entrenched material inequalities—between classes, "races," nations and genders—that have been fostered and perpetuated by all class-antagonistic modes of production, inequalities that have reached truly monstrous proportions in the world capitalist system. Its goal is not the "formal equality" sanctified by liberalism—a merely juridical and legal equality, which effaces and ignores the persistent differences that distinguish human beings in their concrete circumstances. Rather, its goal is to achieve a global society in which, in the words of *The Communist Manifesto*, "the free development of each is the condition for the free development of all."

The fundamental contradictions of capitalism, as identified and analyzed by Marx, may be subsumed under four overarching themes that remain every bit as germane today as they were in the past: (1) the contradiction between the growing power, sophistication and labour-displacing bias of productive technology and the social imperative of the capitalist mode of production to subordinate wealth creation (the satisfaction of human needs) to profit-making (the creation of surplus-value via the exploitation of living labour); (2) the contradiction between the increasing "objective socialization" of production and the private appropriation of wealth; (3) the contradiction between the internationalization (and "globalization") of production and human intercourse and the persistence of the capitalist nation state as the pre-eminent political unit for promoting and safeguarding the interests of nationally-based "social capitals" and managing the recurrent crisis tendencies of capitalism; and (4) the contradiction between the imperative of the capitalist law of value to measure wealth in terms of "abstract social labour" (as manifested in money) and the humanistic-ecological requirement to define and measure wealth in terms of the joint contributions of nature and human labour, that is, in a way that takes full account of the metabolic exchanges between nature and society as mediated by human labour.[2] These contradictions, and the systemic irrationality and crises to which they give rise, can be positively transcended only through a global socialist transformation carried out by the international working class.

On the face of it, the conditions for a renaissance of socialist theory and practice, and the widespread promulgation of the Marxist theses enunciated above, should be highly favourable. And yet at no time since the fall of the Paris Commune of 1871 has the socialist project been worse off. Proponents of socialism are relatively isolated and few in number—a faint echo of a time when tens and even hundreds of millions of people eagerly anticipated and struggled to bring about a world without capitalism. What's more, many self-styled socialists seem wilfully ignorant of the crucial strategic questions and debates of the past—not to mention the close resemblance of their own political positions to ideological trends within the international labour movement that proved to be dead-ends in the past. Vladimir Lenin's aphorism that there can be no revolutionary movement without revolutionary theory is taken seriously by few; and yet the need for the conscious activity of the working-class movement to be guided by Marxist theory is greater than ever.

In the remainder of this chapter we pursue two basic aims. First, we review some of the more important theoretical features and strategic dimensions of "classical Marxism" as a distinct body of thought originally formulated by Karl Marx and Friedrich Engels and subsequently developed by several major figures of the revolutionary socialist movement. Second, we critically survey some of the main strategic themes and theoretical propositions typical of many academics and activists identified with what we will call "the contemporary radical Left."

Classical Marxism

Marx's most important contribution to socialist theory was his insight that the working class is the sole historical actor with the consistent objective interest, structural location and social power to replace capitalism with socialism, and that this class must organize itself as an *independent political force* to achieve that goal. Already in 1843 Marx had concluded that the modern wage-earning working class is the central and indispensable agent of human emancipation.

The proletariat, for Marx, is a class with "radical chains"—a class that is:

> the dissolution of all classes, a sphere which has a universal character because of its universal suffering and which lays claim to no *particular right* because the wrong it suffers is not a *particular wrong* but *wrong in general*; a sphere of society which can no longer lay claim to a *historical* title, but merely to a *human* one…; and finally a sphere which cannot emancipate itself without emancipating itself from—and thereby emancipating—all the other spheres of society, which is, in a word, the *total loss* of humanity and which can therefore redeem itself only through the *total redemption of humanity*…. When the proletariat demands the *negation of private property*, it is only elevating to a *principle for society* what society has already made a principle *for the proletariat*. (1975: 256, emphasis added)

Marx argued that the proletariat, as the class upon whose labour and oppression the entire social edifice rested, could only liberate itself by abolishing private property as a social institution and creating a classless society. The mechanism by which the working class, in the course of its labouring activity under capitalism, is perpetuated as a property-less class was first grasped by Marx in his *Estranged Labour* manuscript of 1844, where he observes that "[l]abour not only produces commodities; it also produces itself and the workers as a *commodity* and it does so in the same proportion in which it produces commodities in general" (1975: 324). This insight into the *alienation* of labour was deepened with the formulation of Marx's theories of labour-value and surplus value, and it was extended in his magnum opus, *Capital*, where he echoes his earlier discovery: "The capitalist process of production, therefore, seen as a total, connected process, i.e. a process of reproduction, produces not only commodities, not only surplus-value, but it also produces and reproduces the capital-relation itself; on the one hand the capitalist, on the other the wage-labourer" (1977: 724).

The proletariat is not only "negatively" predisposed to reject private property; it is "positively" inclined toward the socialization of productive property inasmuch as it operates the means of production *co-operatively* (albeit under the domination and discipline of capital). Indeed, the capitalist division of labour encompasses an ever-increasing degree of co-operation, which is paradoxically constrained by an ever-increasing concentration of capital into fewer and fewer hands. In the course of its struggle, the working class is pushed toward resolving this contradiction through the establishment of a democratic, producer-run and collectivized economy. From this perspective, the emergence—in different times and places, and as moments in the real history of the class struggle—of strikes, picket lines, workplace occupations, factory councils, forms of workers' control and, at the highest level of struggle, soviet-type bodies as the institutional foundation of workers' power, is neither an accident nor the mere result of "communist agitation." Rather it is *socially determined* by the structure and contradictions of capitalist production itself.

Recognizing the (largely unconscious) striving for communism that is implicit even in the most "economistic" of labour strikes is key to a specifically Marxist understanding of class struggle. As Marx noted in a letter to Joseph Weydemeyer in 1852:

> As to myself, no credit is due to me for discovering either the existence of classes in modern society or the struggle between them. Long before me bourgeois historians had described the historical development of this class struggle and bourgeois economists the economic anatomy of the classes. What I did that was new was to demonstrate: 1) that the *existence of classes* is merely linked to *particular historical phases in the development of production*, 2) that class struggle necessarily leads to the *dictatorship of the proletariat*, 3) that this dictatorship itself only constitutes the transition to the *abolition of all classes* and to a *classless society*. (Marx and Engels 1975: 64, emphasis added)

The capstone to Marx's insistence upon the centrality of the proletariat to the struggle for socialism is the principle that the working class (even in situations where it is expedient for it to temporarily ally itself with other forces) must jealously guard its organizational and political *independence*—as incarnated, ultimately, in a revolutionary workers' party. The enduring programmatic thread of such a party, Marx believed, had to be a commitment to guiding the working-class struggle at every step toward a transcendence of "bourgeois Right." Addressing the Communist League in March 1850, Marx and Engels advanced this fundamental principle in the following terms:

> [I]t is our interest and our task to make the revolution permanent until all the more or less propertied classes have been driven from their ruling positions, until the proletariat has conquered state power and until the association of the proletarians has progressed sufficiently far—not only in one country but in all the leading countries of the world—that competition between the proletarians of these countries ceases and at least the decisive forces of production are concentrated in the hands of the workers. Our concern cannot simply be to modify private property, but to abolish it, not to hush up class antagonisms but to abolish classes, not to improve the existing society but to found a new one. (1973: 323–24)

In the twentieth century, several revolutionary socialists made critically important extensions and refinements to this Marxist program of working-class self-emancipation. As it is clearly impossible to summarize in a short essay all of these contributions, we will concentrate on some of the central ideas of three outstanding Marxists—Rosa Luxemburg, V.I. Lenin and Leon Trotsky—with a view to identifying what is *distinctive* about revolutionary Marxism in relation to other nominally socialist approaches.

In her pivotal 1900 polemic *Social Reform or Revolution*, Rosa Luxemburg elaborated an uncompromising critique of the "revisionist" current that had emerged in the Second International in the 1890s. Revisionism had drawn upon pre-existing tensions and tendencies within Social Democracy to formulate for the first time an explicitly reformist strategy, summed up in Eduard Bernstein's famous formula: "The final goal, whatever it may be, is nothing to me; the movement is everything." Bernstein's strategic conception boiled down essentially to the proposition that the Social Democratic party should not be fighting for socialist revolution but should instead advance the struggle for socialism by building up the strength of the working class through incremental social reforms wrested from capital and the state. An evolutionary, and not a revolutionary, road to socialism was thereby proposed.

In a vigorous defence of the revolutionary socialist perspective, Luxemburg maintained that reformist socialism is, in fact, not a genuine socialism at all:

> He who pronounces himself in favor of the method of legal reforms *in place of and as opposed to* the conquest of political power and social revolution does not really choose a more tranquil, surer and slower road to the *same* goal. He chooses a *different* goal. Instead of taking a stand for the establishment of a new social order, he takes a stand for surface modifications of the old order. (1971: 115–16)

At the heart of revisionist theory, Luxemburg argued, is a corruption of Marxism. Marx's understanding of the class struggle, for instance, is formally acknowledged, as is the need for socialism. But whereas Marxism sees the dictatorship of the proletariat as the mighty oak contained within the acorn of class struggle and works to cultivate it, revisionism seeks to mitigate class antagonisms and to "*attenuate* the capitalist contradictions" (89) through social reform: "As soon as immediate practical results become the principal aim, the clear-cut, irreconcilable class standpoint, which has meaning only in so far as it proposes to take power, will be found more and more an obstacle" (87). In opposition to the revisionist view, Luxemburg insisted that the existing state is a "class state"—the political-repressive organization of the ruling class—and that "the natural limits of social reforms lie with the interest of capital" (76).

Rather than limiting themselves to a fight for reforms, Marxists had to orient the struggle toward the destruction of the capitalist state: "Only the hammer blow of revolution, that is, *the conquest of political power by the proletariat*, can break down [the 'wall between capitalist and socialist society']" (84--85). Here Luxemburg echoes Marx's famous declaration that "the working class cannot simply lay hold of the ready-made state machinery, and wield it for its own purposes" (Marx 1974: 206) and anticipates Lenin's insistence in *The State and Revolution* (1917) that the proletariat must establish its own unique organs of class rule and "smash" the capitalist state.

Luxemburg's position was undeniably revolutionary, but it must be placed in its proper historical context. As a socialist leader writing at the turn of the twentieth century, her framework remained that of classical Social Democracy, which had traditionally bifurcated the party's program into immediate "minimum" demands for social reform and the distant "maximum" goal of socialism (codified most clearly in the Erfurt Program of 1891). Luxemburg charged the revisionists with *counterposing* the minimum and maximum programs, whereas, in her view, the "struggle for reform is [the party's] *means*; the social revolution, its *goal*" (1971: 52). Her pamphlet seethes with revolutionary vigour, but the critique is constrained by the limits imposed by the historical period in which she was writing.

Two key developments would soon pose the need for significant changes and extensions to the programmatic and strategic corpus of classical Marxism: the consolidation (and crisis) of an imperialist stage of capitalist development (expressed most sharply by World War I) and the Russian Revolution of 1917. Lenin and Trotsky, the two principal leaders of that revolution—the *only* successful working-class revolution in history—are also the two most important theoreticians of twentieth-century revolutionary Marxism.

Lenin's most important theoretical contribution was to draw out and systematize the politico-organizational lessons of the experience of the Second International in the wake of the support the national leaderships of most Social Democratic parties gave to their own governments at the start of World War I. In two central texts ("The Collapse of the Second International" [1915a] and "Socialism and War" [1915b]), Lenin argued that the political basis for "social imperialism" or "social chauvinism" was the *opportunist* trend in the Second International, which found definite, albeit varying, expressions in most Social Democratic parties before the war. Ultimately, the social basis for opportunism is the petty bourgeoisie and, most importantly, a relatively privileged and conservative layer of the working class—"a petty-bourgeois upper stratum or aristocracy (and bureaucracy) of the working class" (1915a: 243)—supported by the surpluses associated with imperialist plunder. Lenin observed: "An entire social stratum, consisting of parliamentarians, journalists, labour officials, privileged office personnel, and certain strata of the proletariat, has sprung up and has become *amalgamated* with its own national bourgeoisie, which has proved fully capable of appreciating and 'adapting' it" (1915a: 250).

Before the war, the opportunist trend was seen as ultimately harmless, marginalized insofar as the proletarian character of the party remained predominant. Yet the "all-encompassing" breadth of the Social Democracy (formulated by Karl Kautsky as "a party of the whole class") involved a problematic "unity" between revolutionaries and reformists and led, in reality, to the growing influence of the latter at the expense of the former, at least in the mass parties of western and central Europe.

On the eve of World War I, with disputes in the Russian Social Democracy uppermost in his mind, Lenin was already insisting that: "Unity is a great thing and a great slogan. But what the workers' cause needs is the unity of Marxists, not unity between Marxists, and opponents and distorters of Marxism" (1914: 231). A year later, he was arguing that Kautsky's conception of "*unity* with the opportunists *actually* means subordinating the working class to their 'own' national bourgeoisie" (1915b: 311). This marked the beginning of Lenin's transformation from a revolutionary Social Democrat into the founder of a new, revolutionary-communist International.

By 1915, Lenin had concluded that the need for "a *new* form of organisation and struggle," as definitively demonstrated by the betrayal of the Social Democracy, flowed from the demands of a new historical epoch:

> The crisis created by the great war has torn away all coverings, swept away conventions, exposed an abscess that has long come to a head, and revealed opportunism in its true role of ally of the bourgeoisie. The complete organisational severance of this element from the workers' parties has become imperative. The epoch of imperialism cannot permit the existence, in a single party, of the revolutionary proletariat's vanguard and the semi-petty-bourgeois aristocracy of the working class. (1915a: 254, 257)

On this basis, Lenin re-evaluated the experience of the Russian Social Democratic Labour Party, which had been split de facto into two separate parties for several years: the Mensheviks and the Bolsheviks. Using the Bolshevik Party as a model, Lenin (1915b: 329) proposed to construct a new international socialist organization that would regroup the revolutionary *vanguard* of the working class as a Third International. The Hungarian philosopher Georg Lukács, an early convert to Lenin's project, observed that this "vanguard party" perspective involved a basic reassertion of the role of the "subjective factor" in history:

> Lenin's concept of organization therefore means a *double break with mechanical fatalism*; both with the concept of proletarian class-con-

sciousness as a mechanical product of its class situation, and with the idea that the revolution itself was only the mechanical working out of fatalistically explosive economic forces which—given the sufficient "maturity" of objective revolutionary conditions—would somehow 'automatically' lead the proletariat to victory. (1972: 31)

It is Lenin's clarification of the role of the working-class vanguard as the key subjective agent in revolutionary transformation that accounts for his dogged insistence on *programmatic clarity*. Differences over principled and strategic questions are not secondary matters to be set aside in the name of "unity"; rather, revolutionaries must place "program first."

If Lenin's concept of the vanguard party provided a solution to the problems created by a broad socialist party of "the whole class"—a solution predicated on the imperative for revolutionaries to organize themselves separately from the bureaucrats, revisionists and opportunists who seek an armistice with the bourgeoisie in the class war—it was Trotsky's contribution to raise revolutionary Marxist strategy decisively out of the morass of the "minimum-maximum" programmatic dichotomy. In 1938, Trotsky, distilling and clarifying the methods and experiences of the Russian Bolshevik Party and the early Communist International, codified the idea of a "transitional program" in the founding manifesto of his fledgling Fourth International:

> The Fourth International does not discard the program of the old "minimal" demands to the degree to which these have preserved at least part of their vital forcefulness. Indefatigably, it defends the democratic rights and social conquests of the workers. But it carries on this day-to-day work within the framework of the correct actual, that is, revolutionary perspective. Insofar as the old, partial "minimal" demands of the masses clash with the destructive and degrading tendencies of decadent capitalism—and this occurs at each step—the Fourth International advances a system of *transitional demands*, the essence of which is contained in the fact that ever more openly and decisively they will be directed against the very bases of the bourgeois regime. The old "minimal program" is superseded by the *transitional program*, the task of which lies in systematic mobilization of the masses for the proletarian revolution. (1998: 36–37)

Among the demands included in Trotsky's transitional program were the call for a sliding scale of wages and hours, workers' control of industry, opening the books of the employers, militant picket lines, workers' self-defence guards and labour-based militias, factory councils, soviets, the expropriation (without compensation) of industry and the banks, and, as a crowning demand toward which all other transitional demands point, a workers' government. Trotsky proposed that the selection and presentation of demands by the revolutionary vanguard would have to be tailored to the specific needs and level of consciousness of the workers in a given context of struggle. Yet he also insisted that putting forward socialist solutions in terms readily understandable to workers did not mean *adapting* one's program to their consciousness—it meant building a "bridge" between "today's conditions and from today's consciousness of wide layers of the working class and unalterably leading to one final conclusion: the conquest of power by the proletariat" (36). Crucially, Trotsky's conception of a transitional program does *not* project "reforms" that gradually erode the power of the bourgeoisie; rather, it was an attempt to provide a flexible and open-ended basis of struggle around a system of demands that, taken as a whole, cannot be satisfied so long as the capitalist state and the institution of private property in the means of production remain intact. The essential idea is that concrete struggle on *this* basis will be key to educating workers on the need to seize power and build socialism.

A strategy involving a transitional program was not only employed by the Bolshevik Party from April to October 1917 (the slogan of "All Power to the Soviets" constituting its most famous element)—it had been the essential approach of Marx and Engels in *The Communist Manifesto*. Shortly before her death, Luxemburg explicitly rejected the minimum-maximum division and argued that it was necessary "to place our program upon the foundations laid out by Marx and Engels in 1848": "Our program [of the newly-founded Communist Party of Germany] is deliberately opposed to the leading principle of the Erfurt program; it is deliberately opposed to the separation of the immediate and so-called minimal demands formulated for the political and economic struggle, from the socialist goal regarded as the maximal program" (1970b: 408, 413).

Following the Russian Revolution of 1917, the strategic orientation embodied in the transitional programmatic approach was taken up for only a comparatively brief period by the national sections of the early Communist International and the trade union currents allied with them. After the defeat of the German Revolution in 1923, and the consolidation of Stalinist, bureaucratic domination over the Soviet state and the International, the policies of these Communist parties were decisively subordinated to the short-term twists and turns of Soviet foreign policy. The goal of world revolution was replaced by the program of building "socialism in one country" and promoting "peaceful coexistence" between the capitalist world and the U.S.S.R. In its new role, Trotsky argued, the Stalinized Communist International became the "gravedigger" of revolutions. It fell to Trotsky's small band of followers, at first within the International Left Opposition and later the Fourth International, to defend and carry forward the programmatic legacy of revolutionary Marxism.

The Contemporary Radical Left: A Critical Survey

One of the defining political events of our era—and one that has unquestionably weighed heavily on all elements of the contemporary radical Left—was the collapse of Stalinism and the restoration of capitalism in what was once the Soviet Bloc. The identification of Stalinism with revolutionary Marxism (that is to say, Leninism) since the 1920s—an identity assiduously promoted by the Stalinist regimes, the ideological apparatuses of world capitalism, and much of the radical Left—has done incalculable damage to the socialist/communist project. In part, this damage resulted from widespread acceptance of the fundamentally false notion that the crimes of Stalinism (such as famines, frame-up trials, despotic rule, forced labour camps) were the necessary and unavoidable product of a revolutionary transformation from capitalism to socialism, and that therefore socialist revolution exacts too high a price in human suffering. At least equally important, however, was the profoundly conservatizing and sometimes outright counter-revolutionary influence that the Stalinist regimes exerted on the majority of forces that had defined themselves as anti-capitalist and identified with Russia's socialist revolution of 1917.

Stalinism is not fundamentally an ideology, still less the "logical" continuation of Marxism or of Lenin's Bolshevism. Rather it is the social phenomenon of bureaucratic rule on the basis of proletarian-socialist property forms. It is associated with what Trotsky and his followers defined as "degenerated and deformed workers' states"—postcapitalist regimes that constitute *qualitatively distorted* expressions of the "dictatorship of the proletariat" (Trotsky 1970a, 1970; Smith 1996–97). In each of the bureaucratized workers' states, the working class had either been politically expropriated by a privileged oligarchy (as was the case in the Soviet Union due to the isolation of the young workers' republic and the exceptionally adverse material circumstances it faced) or it had never exercised its direct political rule in the first place, owing to the pre-eminent role of the Soviet military or of non-proletarian popular forces in their establishment (as was the case in eastern Europe, Yugoslavia, China, North Korea, Vietnam and Cuba). While there has been some controversy concerning the nature and extent of bureaucratic rule—particularly in Cuba—it is safe to say that most of those who continue to claim Trotsky's political mantle believe that any significant advance toward socialism in such countries must involve an anti-bureaucratic political revolution and the establishment of a *revolutionary workers' state* committed to socialist democracy and world revolution.

Within the international labour movement, the authority and prestige enjoyed by Stalinist regimes (particularly those headed by Joseph Stalin and his successors, and to a lesser extent that of Mao Zedong) were linked to their historic association with successful anti-capitalist social revolutions.

But there is considerable evidence that this authority was repeatedly used to discourage proletarian-revolutionary policies on the international arena and to transform Communist-led workers' movements in the capitalist world into guardians of the "socialist motherland" and instruments of the foreign policy of the Soviet or Chinese governments. The revolutionary energy of the most advanced and socialist-minded layers of the working class was dissipated as the bureaucratic, national-reformist projects of building "socialism in one country" collided with the imperatives of the international workers' movement to advance along the road of socialist revolution. Eventually, as they asserted their independence from Moscow, many of the larger Communist parties came to resemble mass social-democratic parties—a process that was evident in the "Eurocommunist" turn of the 1970s and accelerated following the collapse of the Soviet Union in 1991. Repeated defeats—often resulting from policies predicated on the false notion that "progressive reform" of capitalism was all that was needed to promote "peaceful coexistence" and to improve the conditions of the working masses in the capitalist-dominated world—led to a fatal weakening of working-class leadership, organization and consciousness on a global scale. The deliberate derailing by the Stalinist and social democratic parties of a succession of potentially revolutionary working-class upsurges helped stabilize world capitalism, and thus indirectly strengthened the forces of capitalist restoration in the "Communist world."

It would have been a miracle if the global regression in class and socialist consciousness that resulted from these many defeats had not taken a heavy toll on those who continue to regard themselves as socialists or communists, that is to say, if it had not produced a significant demoralization and disorientation in the ranks of the putatively socialist Left. No such miracle transpired. The upshot has been the ascendancy on what is euphemistically called 'the Left' of a spectrum of ideas that, notwithstanding their diversity, have tended to converge in opposition to Marxist "scientific socialism" and its proletarian-revolutionary perspective. The entry of the world capitalist economy in 2008 into its most severe crisis since the Great Depression and the "business as usual" (essentially Left-reformist) response of most of the radical Left only underscores the vast distance that separates the thinking of these Leftists from the urgent task of constructing a new, socialist leadership for the international labour movement.

Today's radical Leftists may still cling to an abstract socialist ideal, but they often do so with a diminished capacity to think with clarity and resolve about the elementary requirements of an effective strategy to overcome capitalism and replace it with a socialist order. Debates about the very real, life-and-death issues that have historically divided socialists—debates that were engaged inadequately but with some seriousness by would-be socialists in the 1960s and 1970s—have not been settled so much as swept to the side, replaced by arid calls for unity, tired and simplistic denunciations of sectarianism, theoretical "innovations" that rehearse the ideas of anarchism, utopianism and evolutionary socialism, vague platitudes about the need to build new "capacities" in the struggle against exploitation and oppression, and a political practice far more oriented to the progressive reform of capitalism than to its supersession.

The contemporary radical Left in most advanced capitalist countries is thus both theoretically and politically distant from the core principles of classical revolutionary Marxism.[3] Even many individuals and groups that continue to formally identify in some manner with the latter tradition have rejected its applicability to the present period, thus facilitating varying degrees of rapprochement with avowedly "Left-reformist" socialists. Indeed, the basic ideas of Lenin, Luxemburg and Trotsky are, when encountered today, often characterized as dogmatic and hopelessly sectarian by the contemporary radical Left. Those who continue to espouse them are sometimes described as "dinosaur Marxists" seeking to build "sects" rather than vibrant socialist movements.[4]

Four distinct but also interrelated theoretical/strategic propositions seem to be shared in one form or another by much of the radical Left. First, not only workers but "broad sectors of society" must be drawn into the struggle for socialism, since contemporary capitalism is marked by a diversity of forms of oppression. Second, while a socialist political organization is necessary to resist the depredations of neoliberalism and pose a challenge to the rule of capital, such an organization will have to be of a fundamentally new character and quite unlike any major project of the past (particularly those that identified with Leninism). Third, concern for programmatic clarity and/or "purity" is inherently sectarian and must be set aside if any real progress toward building a mass movement is to be made. Fourth, socialist organizing may be characterized as revolutionary to the extent it achieves tangible progress in developing the "capacities" of those who are oppressed by capitalism to "alter the relationship of forces." These four propositions are accepted either as categorically correct and universally applicable or as conjuncturally necessary and expedient (the latter tending to be the rationale for self-indentified Leninists participating in and building such formations as France's New Anti-Capitalist Party, Portugal's Left Bloc, Britain's Respect coalition and Canada's Socialist Project or Québec Solidaire).

While most contemporary radical Leftists continue to argue that the working class is a vitally important component of any anti-capitalist movement worthy of the name, many other sections of the population (who may or may not also be workers) are considered to be indispensable strategic "allies" in the struggle for socialism. This conception goes well beyond, and indeed negates, the traditional Leninist notion that the revolutionary workers' party must act as a "tribune of the people" (that is, the most ardent opponent of all forms of oppression). Instead it involves the problematic notion that because capitalism is at the root of the oppression of women, indigenous peoples, homosexuals, immigrants, people of colour, youth, the disabled and so on, the struggles of these groups to better their conditions are implicitly anti-capitalist in some general sense and possess an anti-capitalist "logic" or "dynamic." Socialist transformation, from this point of view, will grow out of a multiplicity of struggles, which need to be "linked up" in a project of mutual solidarity. While socialists should help "clarify" the anti-capitalist content of various social struggles, what is *not* proposed is to have a pro-socialist workers' movement *leading* the oppressed.

If the working class is not the sole social agent with both the material interest and capacity to bring about socialism, then proletarian vanguardism in a general sense must be rejected. More specifically, the idea of a vanguard within the working class is rejected in favour of anti-vanguardism or (what amounts to the same thing) multi-vanguardism. On the organizational front, this translates into an argument for a very broad and "inclusive" socialist organization (sometimes, but not always, a party-type formation).

It follows from these propositions that the strategic orientation and pro-grammatic clarity associated with Leninism are anathema to effective socialist organizing. In the view of the contemporary radical Left, differences that once divided activists are now outdated or reduced in significance in light of recent historical developments. In some measure this reflects the opinion of some elements who still identify with revolutionary socialism that perspectives they once considered Left-reformist have taken on an objectively revolutionary significance in the context of the need to "rebuild the Left" in what is viewed as a qualitatively new era. Thus Alex Callinicos, the leading theoretician of the Socialist Workers Party (Britain's largest "far-left" formation and one which formally identifies with Leninism and Trotskyism), has put forward an argument that is, in its essentials, congruent with the contemporary radical Left's rejection of Leninist vanguardism:

> The political experience of the twentieth century shows very clearly that in the advanced capitalist countries it is impossible to build a mass revolutionary party without breaking the hold of social democracy over the organised working class. In the era of the Russian Revolution it was possible for many European communist parties to begin to do this by splitting social democratic parties and winning substantial numbers of previously reformist workers directly to the revolutionary programme of the Communist International. October 1917 exercised an enormous attractive power on everyone around the world who wanted to fight the bosses and imperialism.

Alas, thanks to the experience of Stalinism, the opposite is true today. Social liberalism is repelling many working class people today, but, in the first instance, what they seek is a more genuine version of the reformism that their traditional parties once promised them. Therefore, if the formations of the radical Left are to be habitable to these refugees from social democracy, their programmes must not foreclose the debate between reform and revolution by simply incorporating the distinctive strategic conceptions developed by revolutionary Marxists. (Callinicos 2008)

The concrete approach to practical work associated with Callinicos' perspective is one that is concerned not to "alienate" the broad sectors of society engaged in actually existing struggles against oppression. Rather than fighting for a transitional programmatic approach within social movements dominated by reformist perspectives, the job of socialists, from this point of view, is to deepen and radicalize these movements by drawing out connections and advancing more militant demands. The rationale for this approach is in part informed by the belief that the major obstacle to socialist transformation is not, as Trotsky argued in the *Transitional Program*, a "historical crisis of the leadership of the proletariat" (1998: 33), but rather that the masses no longer possess a generally pro-socialist disposition and revolutionary yearning. The solution for the present stage of history, it follows, is to "build capacities" and develop socialist consciousness by getting people involved in struggles that make real advances within the framework of capitalism—baby steps that will teach them how to walk and one day to run.[5] In the final analysis, this perspective is an *objectivist* one that relies on the "spontaneous" dynamic of "struggle" to change consciousness—precisely the sort of perspective criticized by Lenin in his polemic against "economism" in *What Is to Be Done?*

In the Canadian context, a good exemplar of the contemporary radical Left is the Socialist Project, a loose organization that brings together Leftist academics and pro-socialist activists involved in organized labour and a variety of social movements. In an article entitled "What Should We Do to Help Build a New Left?" appearing in *Relay* (a Socialist Project journal), Greg Albo and Herman Rosenfeld offer a succinct and revealing analysis of what they consider to be the root causes of the recent malaise of socialist organizing:

The defeat of the Left and the workers' movement dates from the end of the post-war boom and the militant attempts through the 1970s to develop alternatives in multiple forms—a radicalized social democracy, reform communism, liberation struggles carrying the banner of socialism, workers' control and participatory democracy movements, and still others. The ascendancy of neoliberalism to revitalize capitalist power as a response to these developments still haunts us. This also has deeper roots in the often ossified ways that Marxism was translated into the political, cultural and economic realities of developed capitalist society. (2009: 4)

It is perhaps highly significant that no mention is made in this account of the perfidious policies of Stalinism and Social Democracy (including their more "Left" variants), nor of the activities of many self-styled revolutionary organizations that failed to present a coherent alternative to these misleaderships. The implication is that the defeat of the workers' movement and "the Left" (that amorphous entity that is repeatedly evoked but seldom defined) must be attributed to two other factors: the "ascendancy of neoliberalism" (in other words, *the success of capital's class strategy*—an explanation that really amounts to a tautology), and the "ossified ways that Marxism was translated" in the context of advanced capitalist societies ("ways" that remain as ill-defined by Albo and Rosenfeld as their conception of what constituted "Marxism" in the 1970s).

Advancing their own perspective on how "a new revolutionary politics" might be developed, Albo and Rosenfeld (2009) cite favourably some passages from veteran Latin American Leftist Marta Harnecker's 2007 book, *Rebuilding the Left*:

> Our efforts should be realistically focused on changing the current balance of power so that what appears to be impossible today becomes possible tomorrow…. [I]n order to respond to the new challenges set by the twenty-first century we need a political organisation which, as it advances a national programme which enables broad sectors of society to rally round the same battle standard, also helps those sectors to transform themselves into the active subjects building the new society for which the battle is being waged.

While not defining what this "new society" will actually look like, Albo and Rosenfeld argue that "we need to push beyond the present disorganization and divisions of the Left to what Harnecker refers to as 'the creation of an alternative social bloc'." What this means exactly remains unclear, but it should be noted that the neo-Gramscian notion of an "alternative social bloc" has often been adduced by radical Leftists who argue for new forms of "popular frontism"—a class-collaborationist strategy (of impeccably Stalinist vintage) for "changing the current balance of power," moving the struggle forward through discrete "stages" and postponing indefinitely the fight for working-class independence and a socialist program.

In his 2008 book *Renewing Socialism*, Leo Panitch rounds out the radical-Left perspective with a critique of what he calls "insurrectionary socialism," by which he means the revolutionary Marxist tradition of Lenin, Luxemburg and Trotsky. While critical of contemporary Social Democracy, Panitch argues that its earlier rejection of Leninism was basically sound: "the premise that underlay the social-democratic position—that an insurrectionary strategy was impossible in the West—must be recognized as having been fundamentally correct" (22). Instead of working toward the overthrow of the bourgeois state, "the first task of a democratic socialism, in remaking the state, no less than movement building, is to actively facilitate the creation of democratic capacities" (8).

It must be said that the leading representatives of classical revolutionary Marxism would have strenuously objected to the notion that they were exponents of an "insurrectionary" *strategy*. Insurrection is in one sense no more a "strategy" than is a general strike or participation in an election (whether for parliament or a soviet-type assembly). Rather, it is essentially a military-technical operation, a tactic of great importance that is appropriate to the penultimate phase of the struggle for power by the working class. As Smith pointed out in a response to Ralph Miliband's (1994) Left-reformist critique of Trotskyism's so-called "insurrectionary position": "Insurrectionary activity can be envisaged only during genuinely revolutionary situations—and these arise only periodically, and under exceptional circumstances" (1994: 57). Moreover, a genuinely revolutionary situation in which the seizure of power by the working class is an immediate possibility is precisely one in which a revolutionary Marxist vanguard is not only present but is capable of vying in a serious way for the leadership of the mass movement. To dismiss the possibility of a successful insurrection in the absence of a mass revolutionary party is entirely sensible; to reject it when such a party is "on the ground" (as was the case in Germany in 1923, for example) would be to effectively side with the counter-revolution ("democratic" or otherwise). Rather than preoccupying themselves with theoretical abstractions violently wrenched from actual historical circumstances, partisans of the radical Left need to think carefully and concretely about the implications of such an "anti-insurrectionary" stance. Above all, they need to decide whether—in the context of events like the October Revolution of 1917, the German Revolution of 1923, the Spanish Revolution of 1936 or the Portuguese Revolution of 1975—they would stand with those "seeking to limit the mass movement to constitutionalist avenues or with those seeking to lead the working class forward to the conquest of state power" (Miliband 1994: 58).

Conclusion

Even the rather cursory comparison that we have offered here reveals the vast gulf that separates the contemporary radical Left from classical Marxism. At the risk of generalization and over-simplification, we would submit that the contemporary radical Left recapitulates many of the themes and ideas of Bernsteinian revisionism and even pre-Marxist, "utopian" socialism: the rejection of working-class centrality and independence; the advocacy of broad, and even cross-class, political formations that are programmatically vague enough to appeal to self-styled socialists looking to "get rich quick" as well as to radical activists involved in more narrowly-focused campaigns (such as immigration law reform, gay and lesbian rights); and, finally, the promotion of a new variant of the "minimum-maximum" approach premised on the view that "the movement" is everything and the socialist program "nothing."

The strategic perspective of the contemporary radical Left falls well short of even the best traditions of classical Social Democracy. When Kautsky codified the minimum-maximum approach in the 1891 Erfurt Program of the German Social Democrats, the latter were still resolutely committed to the political independence of the working class, even as they recognized that, in their epoch, considerable scope for progressive reform remained possible within the framework of capitalism. Moreover, the Erfurtian Social Democrats of the 1890s (and beyond) were serious about building what Kautsky described as a "party of the whole class" on an explicitly socialist programmatic basis and recognized, as both Kautsky and Lenin did, that "socialist consciousness" cannot arise spontaneously within the labour movement (or any other social movement), but that socialist ideas, initially at least, must be brought into the struggles of the oppressed "from the outside"—by those who have assimilated the main theoretical discoveries of Marxism and the principal lessons of working-class history.

In contrast, the "mini-maxi" radicals of today are far more tentative in their advocacy of a *class against class* politics and much more hesitant to speak explicitly about socialism in their day-to-day practice. While quick to denounce "sectarianism" (by which they really mean an active defence of Marxist-socialist principle), they are often just as quick to immerse themselves in projects that are reminiscent of the failed strategies of the past (notwithstanding their pretensions to "new thinking"). The inclination toward *opportunism* is pronounced, finding expression in an increasing focus on electoralism and softness toward class collaboration, while eschewing any serious perspective of building class-struggle oppositions in the trade unions to politically combat the bureaucratic misleaders of the labour movement.[6] Rather than seeking to rediscover the precious programmatic and strategic heritage of Marxism—which, as we have sought to show, involves a synthesis of the theory of working-class self-emancipation, the vanguard party principle and a transitional programmatic approach to the struggle for workers' power—much of the radical Left is retreating, in the name of a false "realism," to strategic conceptions that have much more in common with social-democratic revisionism and even Stalinism.

The idea that one can more "realistically" advance the socialist project by abandoning (or hiding) the revolutionary Marxist tradition is a foolish and opportunist illusion that reflects the pressures of the reactionary ideological climate prevailing today in the West. Key to the revival of Marxism will be the reassertion of a genuine *internationalism*. In fighting for the ideas of Marx, Luxemburg, Lenin and Trotsky, revolutionary socialists must not be concerned merely with building "national" organizations (which will inevitably face widely differing local conditions) but an *international working-class party* that will incorporate its understanding of the uneven development of global class struggle into its strategic perspective. Realistically, the establishment of a revolutionary workers' state in even one country in the world would do incomparably more to transform mass consciousness on a global scale than any amount of opportunist manoeuvering conducted on national and local levels by the contemporary radical Left.

We recognize that our argument will be seen by many as a paean to "sectarianism"—which most radical Leftists mistakenly view as the main current obstacle to building a mass and effective socialist movement. But sectarianism can be understood in different ways, and we consider the label substantially inapplicable to Marxists who uphold the need to work within the mass organizations of the working class (in particular the trade unions), who are prepared to engage in united-front activity with other groups around issues of common concern, who do not refuse "on principle" to use electoral campaigns as a platform for socialist ideas, and who are willing to debate their Leftist opponents in ways that do not preclude mutual understanding and principled collaboration. The conception that the defence of revolutionary Marxist ideas is *inherently* sectarian is a liberal and reactionary notion, one that should not be countenanced by any sincere socialist.

That said, we are in no way oblivious to the genuinely sectarian, cultist and bureaucratic tendencies that have prevailed in many of the groups that have laid claim to revolutionary Marxism. In part these tendencies and deformations can be attributed to the *isolation* of the groups afflicted by them—an isolation imposed by the concrete historical conditions in which they have functioned. But it must be acknowledged that many of these groups have also laboured under their own "crisis of leadership" and that formal adherence to the principles of Lenin's democratic centralism and ostensible fidelity to Trotsky's *Transitional Program* provide no guarantee against the emergence of bureaucratic centralism and sectarian or cultist degeneration. The fight against such tendencies must be consciously incorporated into the program and practices of a revolutionary socialist formation, even as it is recognized that no organizational or strategic formula can provide an iron-clad "guarantee" against either opportunism or sectarianism. The experience of the Bolshevik Party prior to the Russian Revolution remains, in this connection, a tremendous source of inspiration and optimism: for here was a party of *cadres*, of professional revolutionaries, that successfully resisted all such tendencies, and, precisely because it did so, was able to lead a workers' revolution to victory.

The desire of many radical Leftists to break out of isolation and to "make a difference" in a world gone mad is both understandable and healthy. But if they are to make a positive contribution to the building of a real socialist movement, they must abandon the prejudice that the fight for a principled socialist program and a revolutionary, internationalist workers' party is an impediment rather than a vital prerequisite for transforming the actually existing struggles of workers and all the oppressed into an all-out battle to fundamentally change the world.

Notes

1. While the massive increase in public debt and deficit spending associated with the bailouts and "stimulus" packages aimed at propping up the capitalist system in the wake of the 2008 financial meltdown violate the tenets of neoliberal orthodoxy, no alternative ideological or strategic framework for capital has yet emerged. It is to the anti-working class offensive that we refer when we speak of "neoliberalism with a vengeance." This new, more draconian strategy of capital, involving both continuities and discontinuities with pre-2008 neoliberalism, may eventually be designated by an entirely new and widely accepted name. See the contributions to the issue of *Development Dialogue* devoted to "postneoliberalism" (various authors 2009).

2. For an elaboration of the contemporary relevance of Marx's analysis of the capitalist profit system, see Smith 2010.

3. Our focus in this chapter is on the radical Left of the developed capitalist world. Even so, we believe that much of what we will say about it applies with equal force to its counterparts in Asia, Africa and Latin America.

4. In making these claims, many radical Leftists are perfectly aware that they are playing to the prejudices and ignorance of elements newly attracted to socialist ideas. Instead of educating the uninitiated to the profound differences between anarchism and Marxism, Stalinism and Leninism, Maoism and Trotskyism, etc., they often pander to their naïve view that what is needed on "the Left" is greater "unity." But how can a Trotskyist committed to the independence of the working class achieve unity with a Stalinist committed to supporting "lesser-evil" bourgeois politicians? How can a Leninist committed to "smashing" the capitalist state achieve unity with a Social Democrat who seeks to "democratize" it?

5. It should be noted that this general approach is not really "new" to much of the ostensibly revolutionary Left. Even in the 1970s, when socialist consciousness was much more widespread in the working class, many groups claiming to be Leninist and Trotskyist found other reasons to reject a strategy based on a transitional program.

6. The case for building such anti-bureaucratic, class struggle alternatives in the unions is made in complementary ways by Knox (1998) and Butovsky and Smith (2007).

8

The Prospects for Socialism: A Question of Capital and Class

Hugo Radice

Crisis of the Left

The current crisis has starkly revealed the low ebb of socialism in the early twenty-first century: at no point since 2007 has there been any doubt, realistically, that capitalism would survive and recover.[1] Even the revival of the Keynesian ideology of more extensive state regulation and intervention, which was apparent from late 2008 as governments struggled to contain the financial meltdown that threatened after the collapse of Lehman Brothers, has now subsided in the face of the bondholders' assault on the European sovereign debt markets. In short, this has been a crisis *within* neoliberalism, not a crisis *of* neoliberalism.

If socialists are to respond effectively to this situation, we cannot rely upon reminding society of what seem to us to be obvious truths about exploitation and injustice, and about alternative forms of social order within which these issues could be resolved. After thirty years of neoliberalism, the most basic ideas that were associated with the Left have been largely excluded from the "common sense" of society. Before that, it was "natural" to associate the idea of socialism with equality, social justice and the opportunity for all citizens to participate actively in economic and political affairs: these were considered as social rights, as normal objectives to be pursued, and they were generally associated with the political Left over many decades. Today, however, it is instead "natural" to place at the forefront not social, but *individual* rights, centred specifically—as in classical liberalism—on property rights, the freedom to trade, and the strict limitation of the powers of the state. In the common sense of today, socialism is understood not as a set of positive values, but rather as the denial of these liberal ideals, the denial of freedom and choice.

Those who still remain socialists have to take responsibility for this historic reversal by a relentless critical examination of *why* neoliberalism was able to triumph. In this regard, we need to follow the example of Antonio Gramsci, who in his *Prison Notebooks* (Gramsci 1971) sought to understand how it was possible to make the journey from the Turin days of 1919–21, when everything seemed possible for the northern Italian working class, even the overthrow of the bourgeois state, to a fascist prison cell. The British historian E.P. Thompson summarized Marx's own critique thus: "what concerned Marx most closely was not 'economics' nor even… epistemology but *power*" (Thompson 1981: 400, his italics). Yet recognizing the power of the powerful does not absolve from responsibility those who have sought to challenge that power, but have failed; as the old saying has it, "if at first you don't succeed, try, try again."

In this chapter I try to renew Marx's critique in three stages. First, I examine the meaning of socialism and the ways in which the goal of building a socialist society has been pursued through the twentieth century. Then I develop a critique of these efforts with regard to how socialists have understood capitalism, starting with the concept of capital. Finally, I go on to look at the concept of class in relation to political agency. This points to the need to re-examine alternative forms of socialist politics that have been submerged by the dominant forces of social democracy and communism.

Socialism: Idea and Reality

Socialists have been notoriously reluctant to set out just what sort of society they would like to live in. This may simply be because those who call themselves socialists, and are in a position to publish their ideas, are for the most part relatively well-educated and affluent—members of what are commonly termed the "middle classes," a concept that will be examined critically later on. Since they are motivated by a desire to improve the lot of the exploited and oppressed, they face the obvious paradox that it is they themselves, rather than the people who ought to benefit most from socialism, who are best placed to articulate a critical alternative to the existing order. On the one hand, you can deal with this paradox by assuming "leadership in the first instance" (e.g., notably as the "vanguard party," or "the organic intelligentsia of the working class," which amounts to the same thing); on the other hand, you can assert that you will "learn faithfully from the masses," an approach which is rarely more than a figleaf for the worst sort of authoritarianism, as in the Maoist case. The most depressing and disastrous approach is to argue that "this is for the people to decide," and then when "the people" do not support this or that socialist group or initiative, say that they are suffering from "false consciousness"—a concept wholly absent from Marx's own work (McCarney 2005).

Yet discussion of what socialism might look like cannot just be dismissed with a sneer as "utopian," as Marxists are wont to do. When Marx and Engels criticized "utopian socialists," it was not because they thought such discussion was pointless, but because it needed to be based on an understanding of the current disposition of social forces and social interests. Overcoming my own reluctance, I define socialism for present purposes as a society in which inequalities of wealth and power are substantially eliminated, all resources of nature and society are held in common, and all adult members of society have an equal voice in the disposition of those resources. This definition is of course only the starting point, but I hope it provides an agenda for further development. It corresponds roughly to Marx's succinct phrase, "the free association of producers," but breaks this down into its component terms.

Taking equality as a starting point directs attention precisely to the problem of reconciling freedom and democracy, and the conditions under which democracy can fully embody equal rights for all. Equality cannot be reduced to the liberal concept of "equality of opportunity," with its necessary corollary that the poor are always with us (after all, someone has to lose, to fail to convert opportunity into outcome). If citizens are to hold resources in common, and to play an equal part in their disposition, they must be in a common condition of mutual dependency in which the concerns of all are the concerns of each. For this purpose, civil or human rights entail important social requirements, as the U.N. Declaration of Human Rights tried to insist. If socialists really want to transcend the limitations of the present order, basic conditions of social existence such as health, education and subsistence should be set and achieved at a common level. In the field of education, for example, the goal should be not, as at present, to create a hierarchy of educational achievements which is then transformed into a hierarchy of income, wealth and power, but rather to ensure that everyone reaches adulthood with broadly similar levels of attainment, capable of fulfilling the human need for creativity and self-development.

The actual history of socialist theory and practice is the best available guide to the many different ways in which such an ideal can be pursued, differences that centre on the problem of transition—how to get from here to there. As Cees Nooteboom puts it in his remarkable novel *All Souls' Day*, "If you want to find out more, you have to move backward, against the flow of time, while simultaneously moving forward" (Nooteboom 2001: 45). But, overcome by the sheer weight of history, his protagonist goes on: "As a result you never get anywhere" (ibid. 45). If that is really true, then we should stop right now, and go and enjoy the painful pleasures that capitalism has to offer; but I continue to think that actually we *can* get somewhere.

The remarkable thing about the 20th century (by which I mean the "short twentieth century" from 1914 to 1991, as in Hobsbawm 1994) is that at the outset, the idea of socialism sketched above was held in common across a wide spectrum of political thinkers and activists. By the mid-1920s, right across the world, this spectrum had congealed into two broad camps, those of communism and social democracy: other more participatory and radical forms were either absorbed by one or other of the dominant camps, or pushed to the margins.

While both of these camps took a huge variety of forms in different times and places, the essential features of each are clear, and were originally defined in relation not to the eventual goal, but to the means of getting there. Common to both is the view that political power in capitalism had crystallized in the modern nation-state, which presides over a society based on the class rule of the bourgeoisie, the owners of the means of production. Given the state's evident power of legitimate coercion, and what came to be called the "manufacturing of consent" by the intelligentsia through the mass media, the only way of overturning the existing order was to capture the state: but how? In brief, for communists, by revolutionary overthrow; for social democrats, by exploiting those opportunities that existed in the liberal capitalist order for advancing redistributive justice.

The story of how they fared through the century is familiar enough. Communism, in the dire circumstance of Russia in 1917–20, adopted the form of the "dictatorship of the proletariat"—the one-party state, "democratic" centralism, complete state control. Under Stalin this became institutionalized, rationalized, provided with its own justificatory ideology, and with some success exported by force or by emulation over subsequent decades. But precisely in the decade when it reached its greatest geographical extent, 1968–79, it began to reveal the cancer at its core, and after another decade it could only be found in Cuba and North Korea. The greatest indicator of the failure of communism is that in its death throes, its peoples did not just reject communism, but embraced capitalism, albeit in the misguided belief that they were going to get social democracy.

But in the meantime, social democracy, too, had reached its zenith in exactly the same decade, the 1970s. In its northern form of the Keynesian welfare state, this decade saw the advance of social democratic parties (including the Eurocommunists) in much of western Europe and in Britain's white settler enclaves in North America and Australasia; even the U.S. had the legislative measures of Johnson's Great Society. In its southern form of the developmental state, post-colonial solidarity flourished in the calls for a New International Economic Order, while the East Asian tigers began to chart a new challenge to economic free trade imperialism. In both cases, the neoliberal counter-revolution dramatically demolished these reformist pretensions right across the West, before extending its sway through the Soviet bloc and China in the 1990s. Central to the demise of social democracy was the vigorous reassertion of property rights and the rolling back of the state, first theorized by Hayek and Friedman and implemented in Britain and the U.S., and then carried by means of economic and political globalization around the world.

Both the dominant forms of socialism thus collapsed in the face of the neoliberal challenge. What is more, in their trajectories across the twentieth century, they also destroyed other forms of socialism which might have proved more resistant. The common feature of these marginal forms was that they placed less emphasis on the state, and more on the self-activity of working people. From Russia in 1905 to Hungary in 1956, workers' councils emerged spontaneously in conditions of social breakdown, but were crushed by the coercive force of the state, either at the behest of the bosses (e.g., Turin 1919–20) or of communist parties (e.g., Russia 1920–24, Catalonia 1937). The co-operative movement, going back to the 1830s, has offered in many different times and places an alternative vision of the democratic organization of production to meet social needs; but even where, as in Britain, it has developed a formal party-political voice—the Co-operative Party—it has been a junior partner to social democracy. From the trade union movement, syndicalists sought to extend the scope of activity from struggles over pay and working conditions to the wider direction of society, but were rebuffed by conventional social democratic and communist parties except when they proved tactically useful as temporary allies. Other forms which gave rise to specific political movements include guild socialism and council communism. The ease with which radical Left alternatives could be eliminated by state action merely seemed to prove their naivety and political impotence. Perhaps now that both communism and social democracy are dead, it is time for their revival.

But first, the question still remains: why did the dominant forms of socialism fail to sustain the support that they earlier enjoyed, primarily of very large proportions of the working classes (including here the intelligentsia, to which I will return)? In his eleventh thesis on Feuerbach, Marx wrote: "Philosophers have hitherto only interpreted the world in various ways: the point is to change it" (Marx 1845). Usually this is read as a call to turn from analysis to action, but perhaps today, the point is that before we act, we must first understand: at the least, we need to consider whether our failure in practice can partly be explained by a persistent failure of interpretation.

Understanding Capital as a Social Relation

So was there anything wrong with how socialists understood capitalism? I have already noted the common origins of social democracy and communism as political movements in pre-1914 socialism, and it is equally true to say that Marx's critique of political economy informed the understanding of both wings. The economic thinking of social democracy was repeatedly infiltrated by liberal critiques of Marx, but this tended to happen in either the more rarefied realm of abstract economic theory (the law of value, the transformation problem), or the practical but necessarily speculative question of whether central planning was possible or efficient. The reason for this is clear: in the absence of agreement on fundamental (ontological) propositions like Marx's law of value, there was simply no possibility of a joint engagement in the consequent more concrete analysis of the dynamics of production, accumulation and crisis within capitalism.

As a result, at least until the advent (more or less simultaneous) of Keynes and Stalin in the mid-1920s, both social democracy and communism shared a common concrete analysis of capitalism, which they traced back to Marx, or at least to his developers and popularizers from Engels to Bernstein, Bauer, Hilferding, Bukharin, Luxemburg and, of course, Lenin. This common analysis centred on four features of early twentieth-century capitalism in particular: the rise of monopolies; the growing importance of banking and finance; the increasing economic weight of the state; and the extension of economic competition among the major capitalist powers in the form of imperial rivalries.

Of course, very different political implications were drawn from these developments, both individually and taken together. This was most apparent in the split over the 1914–18 war, and the associated general question of whether capitalism had reached "structural" limits beyond which socialism was inevitable: remember that by 1945, this became the considered opinion not only of every revolutionary socialist, but also of Polányi, Schumpeter and even at times Keynes himself. To take a more prosaic example, the problem of monopoly led to the question of whether "natural" monopolies should be subjected to state regulation, or taken into public ownership—a distinction revealed in contemporary neoliberal analysis to be of little practical importance. More significantly, the common remedy for imperialism's subject peoples was political independence and self-determination, whether by means of the bullet or the ballot.

Yet if we consider those four features of early twentieth-century capitalism from the perspective of 2011, perhaps they were not necessarily the inevitable consequence of laws of capitalist development (as both wings of the Left believed). With the benefit of hindsight, it is at least as plausible to see them as contingent developments shaped by historically specific contradictions in the political management of capitalism. At the heart of that political management must surely lie the social relation of capital itself; after all, the reproduction of capitalism as a social order depends in the last analysis on that constitutive relation. If we examine how Marx's critique was interpreted by the early twentieth-century authorities listed above, we certainly find a preoccupation with the functioning of capital, with its circulation, reproduction and accumulation, and above all with its long-term potential. However, this is not capital understood as a social relation, not capital as created by wage-labour, but capital essentially taken as given, as a quantum of produced value (in Marx's imaginative term, dead labour).

I believe that a critical historiography of the work of Marx's successors can be undertaken which opens up a very different approach to socialist politics. My first proposition is that this work has been largely preoccupied with the problems with which Marx grappled in Volumes 2 and 3 of *Capital*. These deal with the conditions of circulation and reproduction of capital, the distribution of surplus value among the different functional segments of capital (productive capital, money capital, merchants' capital), the relation between capital and landed property (rent theory) and the problem of interest-bearing capital. They are about capital "as such." Remember that these volumes were pieced together by Engels after his friend's death, without any but the most sketchy outline from Marx to guide him (Engels 1885: 1–5). Remember too that Marx himself had struggled to put them together effectively from the appearance of Volume 1 in 1867 to his death in 1883.

It is surely not enough just to say that Marx was giving priority to urgent political events, given the importance that he attached to this theoretical work. Supposing instead that Marx simply had not the time and energy, it is instructive to look at the contrast between Volume 1 and Volumes 2 and 3 in terms of structure and continuity. Volume 1 presents a coherence and a unity that is wholly absent from the later works, and stands out in many respects. First, it is about labour as much as about capital, and we are repeatedly reminded that capital is a social relation whose heart is the assertion of property rights over labour's means of subsistence. The conditions of existence of labour as such are presented as codetermined and coterminous with those of capital. Second, at the heart of Volume 1 is the exploration of labour in the production process, where surplus value is created and appropriated; it is only when this has been thoroughly explored that Marx can even begin to analyze accumulation and crises. Third, the state looms large throughout the work, as a fundamental constitutive force in capitalism, suspending the regulatory force of the market whenever it is necessary for the maintenance of the social order. Fourth, this is a deeply historical study, so much so that Marx concludes it with a section that presents the historical roots of capitalism in a way that set the agenda for economic historians until the present day. And finally, this work gives us an exemplary lesson on how to integrate the most abstract concepts and their most concrete materialization in economic and political reality, for example in the account of the struggle over the length of the working day (Marx, 1867: Ch. 10).

And now consider to what extent, if any, these features are replicated in the volumes edited by Engels, and in later Marxist work. The successors have ruminated endlessly on value theory, a topic dealt with by Marx in a few short chapters at the start of Volume 1, but they have paid little attention to the rest of Volume 1 compared to the topics of Volumes 2 and 3. Both labour and the state are at the centre of Volume 1 but are not adequately integrated into the other volumes of *Capital*. Note also that in the later development of Marxist work after the "classics," i.e., after the 1920s at the latest, so little is accomplished beyond an endless recirculation of unresolved analytical problems.

My conclusion is this: we need to reinstate the Marx of *Capital* Volume 1. This is not because we have to have an "authority" to which socialists must refer in order to give their analyses credibility. Rather, it is because, dealing as it does with capital in general and its historical conditions of existence, Volume 1 can be read today and instantly understood in relation to contemporary developments.

The Question of Class

Nowhere is this more clear than in relation to the concept of class. Marx argued that in capitalism there are two classes, the proletariat and the bourgeoisie, founded upon their structural positions in the social relation of capital: the bourgeoisie owns the means of production, and purchases labour-power from the proletariat with the purpose of extracting surplus value from it; the proletariat has been dispossessed of direct access to the means of subsistence through self-activity, and therefore must sell its labour-power in order to subsist. Capitalist production produces and reproduces not only commodities and surplus value, but also the two classes and the relationship between them.

Now Marx is perfectly well aware that within both classes there is enormous differentiation, and that individuals can and do move between classes. But in the course of his exploration of production in Volume 1, he analyzes the processes of differentiation (or as some people put it, decomposition and recomposition) as the consequence of the dynamics of accumulation under capitalist relations of production, or in other words, as the consequence of how those relations develop concretely. These processes are shaped historically by their own contradictory character, and especially by the resistance of workers to their exploitation, in other words by class struggles. They are also shaped by the requirements imposed by nature, through (putting it in abstract terms) the conflict between use value and exchange value.

Class struggles in production were taken up in the 1970s in the new field of labour process studies, initiated by Harry Braverman, André Gorz and Stephen Marglin among others. Although their work has been valiantly sustained within the human resource management field by refugee sociologists mainly working in business schools, in Marxism as a whole the sections in Volume 1 of *Capital* analyzing labour and production have continued to be neglected. This is in part because of a perception that somehow they are "empirical," and merely illustrative; but ironically, the consequence of this is that, when it comes to moving from the abstract to the concrete and from theory to practice—that is, when it comes to strategies of political mobilization in pursuit of socialist goals—the Left has relied upon a crude empiricism. Such a reliance, in a society whose ways of thinking and living are moulded by capitalist values and ideas, is always to risk accepting "the facts" without critical evaluation of their theoretical premises.

Hence, in particular, the lazy conflation of "proletariat" or "working class" with industrial workers. This is in part because the analyst is, as noted earlier, almost invariably from a bourgeois or at least relatively high-status background, and feels the need to defer to, or even romanticize, those who are obliged to spend a lifetime doing manual work to the detriment of their physical and mental health. But mostly it is because bourgeois sociology, drawing on a heritage that starts with Spencer, Durkheim and Weber and has always been counterposed to Marx, has developed an analysis of class that is explicitly designed on the assumption that it is the divisions *within* the working class that are socially significant, and not the division between that class as a whole and capital. In essence, this move is undertaken by denying the existence of the bourgeoisie, and instead postulating the entire social division of labour in occupational terms.

In some respects, this goes back to Adam Smith, or indeed to his mercantilist and physiocratic predecessors, who were interested in the division between agriculture and industry. But for Smith at least, this division was not merely occupational: rather, it was the site of fierce struggle between ascendant capitalists and the *ancien régime* of landed property. This was taken up famously by Ricardo in his critique of Britain's Corn Laws, but it was equally appreciated by Marx in developing his own understanding of the contradictions *within* the new order. Instead, the occupational focus of modern sociology was enabled by the remarkable rise of neoclassical economics from the 1870s, for the neoclassical revolution offered a radically different understanding of capitalism that successfully countered the challenge of Marx's critique.

The neoclassicals argued that everyone, whether worker, capitalist or for that matter landlord, is an economic actor with a predetermined resource endowment and self-determined preferences. These actors interrelate in a universal marketplace, where all prices are determined by the forces of supply and demand. In aggregation, this generates divisions of labour between branches of production (each making a different category of good) and between occupations (with a set of interrelated labour markets). Capital and labour (and also land) are then "factors of production," themselves traded like any other commodity. Yes, insofar as capital is used to purchase labour, there appears to be a conflict of interest over its price; but through the free flow of market forces, these factors of production will both always receive their due and just reward, equal to their marginal productivity.

This radically different ontology has provided the foundations of bourgeois social science ever since. The effect was immediate and direct in the development of economics, where all political and social reference points were removed from the core analysis and treated as *external* to economic life, and ownership was treated as a natural and universal right. But it also powerfully affected the fields of scholarship that became the modern disciplines of sociology and political science, and the ever-longer list of subdisciplines and related areas like management studies. In the pivotal case of sociology, it achieved two effects. First, by adopting the ontological standpoint of neoclassical economics, sociology accepted the latter's "scientific" status and its right to adjudicate on permitted disciplinary boundaries. Second, the dominant Weberian tradition in particular gave effective support to neoclassical economics by privileging the generic concept of status in place of class, with Weber himself developing an economic history in which the Marxian idea of a sequence from feudalism to capitalism is replaced by one from tradition to modernity.

What modern sociology achieves is thus a radical reworking of the classical and Marxian approach to class. Instead of bourgeoisie and proletariat, we are given the upper class (who do not need to work at all), the middle class (who do white-collar, high-skilled or administrative work) and the lower class (who do unskilled work). Of course, no one likes to be lower, so just as you cannot buy a "small" cup of coffee in Starbucks, the lower class is renamed the working class, celebrated in heartwarming movies, and distinguished from the work-shy and the criminal classes (also known as the "undeserving poor").

For socialists this creates a serious problem. In the richest capitalist societies, the working class in the above sense has been steadily shrinking, while the number of supposedly more skilled "middle-class" jobs has risen; this is mostly because of the much faster rise of physical output per worker in manual occupations. This shift is accentuated in statistical measures by capitalist restructuring, one of whose features is the growth in outsourcing of many clerical and ancillary jobs from manufacturing firms. The rapid fall in the workforce size of the average manufacturing plant also makes factory work less salient within surrounding residential communities. At the same time, those defined as middle class have any number of reasons not to regard themselves as working class, unless it is (as, for example, in the U.K.) because they have internalized the idea that this makes them morally superior. With the spread of higher education and home ownership, the social gap between routine administrators and highly-paid entrepreneurs and executives has also diminished, allowing a significant stratum of this middle class to aspire to much higher wealth and therefore status. As for the upper class, they have two alternatives: either they can actively deploy their wealth in occupations such as hedge fund management, investment banking or luxury leisure services, or they can join the ranks of the celebritariat (Young 2008) and consort with footballers, movie stars and drug barons in the marinas of Monaco or Dubai.

But if we return to Marx's concept of class, there are two important consequences for the viability of socialist politics. First, we can re-establish the fundamental existential identity between the much-reduced working class and the ever-growing middle class, for both depend upon the sale of their labour-power to sustain their livelihoods. No matter if they own their own house, or have a pension plan which implies the indirect part-ownership of business enterprises, this dependence remains: indeed, it actually increases their dependence because the consequences of unemployment become in psychological terms much more acute, especially if they are then forced to turn to a welfare state offering only the most threadbare of safety nets.

Second, Marx's concept firmly relates the production of class to the workplace. Within its walls, the rule of capital is not mediated by the market, but is direct and immediate. Try as the boss may to convince you that he is a good chap, and that he is concerned for your well-being and your career development, when the competitive crunch comes, all that remains is that you must pay your way. But, as Marx shows, the reduction of the worker (whatever her or his occupation) to a disposable unit of abstract labour is only an aspiration. A striking feature of the contemporary crisis is the extent to which private enterprises in many of the most severely affected countries have sought to retain their work forces through special measures such as temporary pay cuts or shorter working hours. Capital depends upon labour, not merely in an abstract sense, but concretely in the fact that, especially in the much more competitive environment of globalized capitalism, it is specific workers at all levels who are the repository of knowledge, skills and experience that are necessary for profitable production. And in addition, those workers are increasingly integrated into a *real* collective worker, as Marx argued in *Capital*, Volume 1 Chapter 15 on machinofacture, and in the *Grundrisse*. Why else would modern business have developed its increasingly baroque and universally despised armoury of "human resource management" techniques?

The conclusion is clear: renewing the socialist movement can and should begin in the workplace. And I would only add—for want of time to develop this point—that the home and the local community, and indeed the virtual community on the web, are also workplaces in which vitally important "goods" (in various senses) are produced. For this renewal to be effective, however, we have to offer not only a critique of the existing social order, but also a vision of another way of living. Fortunately, there is that hidden history, of those marginalized alternative varieties of socialist politics discussed briefly earlier, which can inform this work. Perhaps in this way we can finally come to terms with the failings of socialism in the twentieth century, and develop the confidence that we really can do better next time.

Note

1. This chapter was originally prepared as an essay for the conference on "Socialism in Turkey and the World: Problems and Prospects,, Middle East Technical University (ODTÜ), Ankara, December 3–4, 2010. I am grateful to Logie Barrow and Ian Bullock for helpful comments.

9

Crisis, Movements, Counter-Hegemony: In Search of the New

William K. Carroll

Since the global financial meltdown of 2008 and the failure of the 2009 Copenhagen Conference on Climate Change (COP15) to reach a meaningful accord, it has become increasingly clear that a profound economic and ecological crisis is facing humanity. Crisis, as the ancient Chinese proverb says, presents a combination of threat and opportunity. It is a time of danger yet also of new possibilities, as received wisdoms and unreflective practices become open to challenge. The question for activists is how to mitigate the danger while seizing upon the openings. This is a matter both of ends—of articulating an alternative in which human beings and ecosystems might thrive—and of identifying practical means to those ends. Amid the crisis, we hope to find, within the present, elements of a more hopeful future, and to forge alliances that can leverage neoliberal capitalism's failure into a different kind of world based on socialist principles albeit in a new form.

This chapter brings a Gramscian problematic to these efforts and concern for building the socialism of the twenty-first century. It draws upon recent activist and academic insights regarding crisis, movements and counter-hegemony, in order to discern criteria for making choices in current struggles—choices capable of effectively challenging power relations within a capitalist system and bringing about not simply a different, but a better future.

At the outset, a word of clarification is needed. I employ "counter-hegemony" in the neo-Gramscian sense, referring to broad transformative strategies and practices for replacing the rule of capital with a democratic socialist way of life. This project is distinct from two rival approaches on the Left, namely social-democratic electoralism and anarchistic anti-hegemony. Viewed from a Gramscian vantage point, the former relies too heavily on the liberal democratic state as an instrument of change, and underplays the importance of struggles within civil society and vis-à-vis the means of production (Pontusson 1980). The latter (as in Day 2006, 2007) retreats from creative engagement with state-centred politics altogether, substituting a lifestyle politics of "living differently" (Carroll 2006; McKay 2009). The objective here is not to debate these different visions and strategies for the Left, but to demonstrate the value of neo-Gramscian thinking for activists and movements in the early twenty-first century.

In Search of the New

In the most general terms and at the highest level of abstraction, the question of counter-hegemony evokes the dialectic of bringing the new into existence, against the sedimented practices and relations that, as Marx (1852) wrote, weigh "like a nightmare on the brains of the living." Yet it is from existing practices and relations that the new is fabricated, which is to say that the future is already contained as potential within the present. "Fermenting in the process of the real itself" is what Ernst Bloch called "the concrete forward dream: anticipating elements are a component of reality itself" (1986: 197).

Counter-hegemony, as distinct from defensive forms of subaltern resistance, strives to shape those "anticipating elements," so that they may become lasting features of social life. For counter-hegemony, the challenge is to seek out in the present the preconditions for a postcapitalist future and to develop political strategy based on an analysis of those immanent possibilities (Ollman 2003). Gramsci captured this dialectic with the metaphor of welding the present to the future: "How can the present be welded to the future, so that while satisfying the urgent necessities of the one we may work effectively to create and 'anticipate' the other?" (1977: 65).

The new is no mere "fashion," the latter being a preferred trope of modernity (Blumer 1969), closely integrated with consumer-capitalist accumulation strategies, and thus with reproducing the status quo. Often the new reworks the old, with radical effects. Viewed dialectically, the new preserves yet transforms extant reality, as in the incorporation of indigenous ways as alternatives to neoliberal practices that have grown decidedly old (cf. Bahn 2009).

This dialectic between what already exists and what might be constructed out of that is integral to any project of purposeful socio-political change. Movements, as Melucci (1989) has emphasized, are laboratories for social invention. They are carriers of the "new means and values, new practices, new relationships and kinds of relationships" that Williams (1977: 123) identified with cultural emergence; "emergent publics" that create possibilities for a more democratic way of life (Angus 2001). Movements succeed in creating change when political and cultural opportunity structures open up (Tarrow 1998). But which movements, which practices and which alignments of movements and practices, in short which "new combinations" (Dyer-

Witheford 2001) might already carry the new—and under what contemporary conditions might they have efficacy? These are more concrete questions of counter-hegemony. Theorists of agency and structure note that, although social structures are sustained solely through the practices that reproduce them, such practices, precisely because they are structurally reproductive, do not produce much that is new; only transformative practices have that capacity (Bhaskar 1989; Fraser 1995). Indeed, a well-established hegemonic structure naturalizes social cleavages and contradictions, securing the active, agentic consent of subalterns to their subordination (De Leon, Desai and Tuğal 2009: 216; Joseph 2002).

Organic Crisis

Gramsci, following Marx and anticipating Bourdieu, recognized crisis as a necessary condition for undoing the doxa that is perhaps the most salient feature of well-entrenched hegemony. In Gramsci's formulation, *organic crisis* is a crucial element in creating the new. In this kind of crisis, the structures and practices that constitute and reproduce a hegemonic order fall into chronic and visible disrepair, creating a new terrain of political and cultural contention, and the possibility (but only the possibility) of social transformation. Such a situation entails a crisis of authority:

> If the ruling class has lost its consensus, i.e., is no longer 'leading' but only 'dominant', exercising coercive force alone, this means precisely that the great masses have become detached from their traditional ideologies…. The crisis consists precisely in the fact that the old is dying and the new cannot be born; in this interregnum a great variety of morbid symptoms appear. (1971: 275-6)

Gramsci asks whether the interregnum will "be resolved in favour of a restoration of the old" (276), as in an elite-engineered passive revolution that reconstitutes social relations within new forms of a continuing capitalist order (Morton 2007: 150–51). For him, the key instance was the *Risorgimento* that brought to Italy a deeply problematic political unification, over the heads of the masses. In our time, neoliberalism played a similar role in the crisis of Fordism and the welfare state which by the late 1970s registered falling rates of profit and rising state deficits. What was "new" in neoliberalism—a vision reaching back to the late eighteenth-century liberal utopia of perfect competition overseen by a night watchman state—was, historically speaking, archaic. The market-centred practices of neoliberalism did not create the rational, self-equilibrating social order celebrated by neoclassical economics. Capitalism's tendencies toward uneven development—temporally, sectorally, spatially—and toward polarized incomes were exacerbated by deregulation.

In the 1980s, neoliberal austerity succeeded in boosting rates of profit, but by the mid-1990s it was only through financialization and other forms of accumulation by dispossession that high profits demanded by shareholder capitalism could be sustained. Yet these very measures set the table for global crisis.

Parameters of Hegemony

This chapter is mainly about movements from below and counter-hegemony, but these are internally related to movements from above, and hegemony. To view structure as the contingent sedimentation of past practice implies that movements move not in relation to some permanent fixture, as in a reified conception of the state, but in relation to each other (Magnusson 1997). "Social movements emanate from and are grounded in the collective skilled activity of both dominant and subaltern groups" (Nilsen 2009: 115). A movement from above strives to maintain or modify a dominant structure in ways that reproduce and/or extend the power of dominant groups and their hegemonic position within the social formation (115), and in this sense, neoliberalism has been as much movement as policy paradigm. Across three and a half decades, the neoliberal movement has been expertly assembled and led by organic intellectuals that include in their ranks politicians, academics, journalists and business leaders, through densely networked movement organizations both global (e.g., the Mont Pelerin Society, the World Economic Forum) and local (e.g., the Atlantic Institute for Market Studies; Carroll and Shaw 2001; Carroll 2007; Carroll and Sapinski 2010). This is what Stephen Gill (1995) means when he refers to neoliberalism's transnational historical bloc.

Elsewhere (Carroll 2006), I have specified some parameters of hegemony that are central to early twenty-first-century capitalism. At a deep level of the social formation, and most saliently in the global North, these include:

- *postmodern fragmentation*: the commodification of everyday life fragments collective identities and inculcates a depoliticizing fascination with style and spectacle;
- *the neoliberalization of political-economic relations*: deregulation of markets insulates a protected economic realm from popular will while accumulation by dispossession privatizes the public interest and promotes possessive individualism;
- *capitalist globalization*: the densification of transnational economic relations augments the structural power of capital (Gill and Law 1989) and promotes a project of global governance within a neoliberal framework.

John Agnew has identified a parameter of hegemony in this era that includes elements of the first and last of these, namely *the globalization of Americanism* as a way of life. In Agnew's formulation (which is inspired by Gramsci's essay on Americanism and Fordism), the hegemony of marketplace society, achieved within the United States in the first two-thirds of the twentieth century, has been projected into the world at large setting the political basis for a globalization that has had two salient aspects (2005: 100).

> On the one hand, U.S.-based institutions have had the power to enact globally a dominant vision of 'the good society.' On the other hand, this vision has been one of ever-increasing mass consumption. The hegemony of marketplace society is therefore what lies at the centre of contemporary world society. (2005: 8)

As a parameter of hegemony, globalization of Americanism is distinct from notions of American hegemony that centre upon the imperial American state. It is the American way of life, not the fading lustre of American state power that gained global hegemony in the late twentieth century.

The Current Crisis

Although these economic, political and cultural forms have provided a basis for an emergent, transnational hegemony in the post-Cold War era, the hegemony on offer has been a troubled one—fragile and tentative, thin on the ground as it were, in great part because the neoliberal historical bloc is far less inclusive than its Fordist-Keynesian predecessor (Cox 1987). We can understand the current organic crisis as a cumulative decline in the capacity of hegemonic forms to promote accumulation and secure popular consent. In the case of American hegemony, ever-increasing mass consumption on a global scale requires Americanism's epicentre to borrow funds and import vast quantities of goods to fuel domestic spending, in a pattern of asymmetrical accumulation that is probably unsustainable (Agnew 2005: 192–218). In economic terms, as David McNally (2009) has shown, neoliberalism's crisis was already evident in the Asian financial meltdown of 1997. The ensuing decade inflated a bubble economy that burst in the autumn of 2008, putting deregulatory logic into question and also questioning basic premises of Americanism, as endlessly expanding, credit-driven consumption came unstuck in global capitalism's heartland. But this organic crisis has involved more than economic failings and associated crisis management strategies such as the corporate bail-outs and stimulus spending packages of 2008–10. Integral to it have been the challenges from below, from the Zapatistas' declaration of war against neoliberalism in 1994 through the 1999 Battle of Seattle and the various incarnations of social forums to recent general strikes in southern Europe in resistance to the new wave of austerity—in each instance, a critical, collective response to the privations and indignities that are neoliberalism's legacy. Such campaigns and "wars of position" challenge the hegemony of neoliberal globalization, but they also work against the ideological effects of the commodification of everyday life, gesturing however incompletely to another possible world.

Crucially, the economic crisis of neoliberal globalization has been accompanied and amplified by a deepening ecological crisis. In the twentieth century, capitalism "scaled up" from a network of local economies centred in a few regions of the global north (articulated via colonialism with precapitalist modes of production on the periphery) to a system of transnational production and consumption in which most of the world's burgeoning population is ensnared. So did the ecological externalities of accumulation, so that by the late twentieth century capitalism's footprint, evident in species extinction, the thinning of the ozone layer, and global warming, was outgrowing the biosphere. What James O'Connor (1990) has called the second contradiction of capitalism sharpened, as capitalist appropriation of nature cumulatively eroded capital's own conditions for expanded reproduction (Kovel 2006). The economic and ecological moments of crisis are interconnected, but they do not follow a unitary logic. As John Foster (2010) reminds us, in contrast to ecological crisis, economic crises are of their nature cyclical. Short of an exit from capitalism, economic crises eventually resolve themselves, on the backs of workers and other subordinates, as conditions for robust accumulation are re-established or invented; a case in point being neoliberalism's own success in disassembling many of the impediments to accumulation that Fordist regulation and the Keynesian welfare state eventually presented. The deepening ecological crisis, on the other hand, has no bottom, in the sense of an anticipated "recovery." Without timely and radical intervention, ecological overshoot portends only a downward spiral, giving new meaning to the choice Rosa Luxemburg (1970a) posed between humanity's exit from capitalism and its likely descent into barbarism. The global character of ecological crisis, and the growing consciousness of that global character, add a new element to the organic crisis, and to the project of counter-hegemony.

Indeed, the organic crisis of our time needs to be understood as an assemblage of economic, ecological and socio-political moments. It has both a political-economic face and a political-ecological one. But it is the ecological race against time that makes this crisis unprecedented in its challenges and in the morbidity of its symptoms.

Counter-Hegemony in Theory

Against this backdrop of organic crisis, I want to consider the *political challenge for counter-hegemony*, first in a rather formulaic manner, then more concretely.

Let us begin with Gramsci's own formulation of how power works, which recognizes that within advanced capitalism the combination of force and persuasion that comprises hegemonic rule entails a panoply of relations both within the state and throughout civil society that serve to organize subaltern consent. Consent is never total or seamless. Subalternity typically involves episodic, fragmented resistance and a contradictory consciousness whose common sense includes elements of "good sense," and of the new. However, the lack of coherence among various oppressed and subordinated groups enables bourgeois ideology to dominate (Ives 2004: 24). From this general diagnosis of subalternity, which I believe is fully relevant today, Gramsci envisages the constitution of a collective will encompassing a wide range of identities and democratic aspirations, posing an alternative social vision, a socialist way of life—what we now call counter-hegemony. A cultural-material formation of this sort is comprised of several facets:

- The coming-into-being of a collective will requires a process of *catharsis* in which "structure ceases to be an external force which crushes man, assimilates him to itself and makes him passive; and is transformed into a means of freedom, an instrument to create a new ethico-political form and a source of new initiatives" (Gramsci 1971: 367). This remarkable passage describes the transition from an economic-corporate phase in which subordinates define their interests narrowly and in immediately instrumental terms, to an ethico-political project that can bring formerly disparate identities onto common ground. As Ives (2004: 107) and De Sousa Santos (2006) have argued, this involves the work of translation across various cultural domains and contexts, involving organic intellectuals—activists, organizers, "permanent persuaders" (Gramsci 1971: 10) whose practice is rooted in subordinate experiences and resistances.[1]
- Importantly, a counter-hegemonic formation includes both *class forces* directly articulated with the process of accumulation and *popular-democratic currents*—movements and identities that arise through practices centred in civil society (Urry 1981).[2] Without the former, and in particular, broad elements of the working class, a radical challenge to capitalism is strategically unsustainable; without the latter, the collective will fails to encompass the diversity of needs and aspirations that partially constitute Bloch's "concrete forward dream." The welding together of disparate class and popular-democratic interests is not a mechanical assemblage of convenience; rather, "the process of coming together to form a specifically *hegemonic* force involves each group being

partly transformed," as it takes on elements of the identity and agenda of other groups and comes to adopt the interest of others as its own (Purcell 2009: 296–97). The famous slogan from Seattle 1999, "Teamsters and turtles, united at last!" exemplifies this reciprocal process in forming a counter-hegemonic collective will.

- *war of position/war of manoeuver*: in capitalist societies, civil society comprises a strategically important "arena in which capitalist hegemony is secured but also where subaltern classes forge alliances and articulate alternative hegemonic projects" (Munck 2006: 330). Through a war of position, which does not exclude struggles directed at the state (Simon 1982: 75), the balance of power in civil society can be shifted and space won for radical alternatives, unifying dissenting groups into a system of alliances capable of contesting bourgeois hegemony. This prepares subordinate groups for self-governance by creating postcapitalist sensibilities and values, practical democratic capacities, and a belief in the possibility of a radically transformed future (Carroll and Ratner 2010). As Staggenborg and Lecomte (2009) found recently, within particular social movements wars of position and of manoeuver can be mutually reinforcing processes: in the Montreal women's movement community, winning space for an alternative community has created capacity for successful collective campaigns, and vice versa.
- The *national and the inter/transnational*. For Gramsci (1971: 240), writing in the 1930s, "the line of development is towards internationalism, but the point of departure is 'national'." Since the mid-twentieth century, capitalist globalization has created more extensive bases for both hegemonic and counter-hegemonic movements to contend within a global civil society that is itself constantly constructed as contested terrain by diverse social groupings (Munck 2006: 330; Carroll 2007). Nevertheless, one should not impute a "singularly transnational logic" to contemporary struggles for hegemony; national, regional and local dynamics continue to shape the conduct of these struggles (Morton 2007: 199).
- Welding the present to the future. *Prefiguration* was central to Gramsci's conception of counter-hegemonic politics.[3] For Gramsci, inspired by the factory councils' movement to democratize workplaces, prefiguration "meant that politics would be integrated into the everyday social existence of people struggling to change the world, so that the elitism, authoritarianism, and

> impersonal style typical of bureaucracy could be more effectively combated" (Boggs 1976: 100). Indeed, a war of position includes a process of moral and intellectual reform that not only renovates common sense into good sense, but incrementally erodes the distinctions between leaders and led, creating the basis for participatory democracy in a widening sphere of activities (Simon 1982).

- Catharsis, prefiguration, and the articulation of class and popular-democratic forces, of the national and the international, and of wars of position and manoeuver, add up to the construction of a *historical bloc*, around a counter-hegemonic project. Such a bloc combines leadership in civil society with "leadership in the sphere of production" (Simon 1982: 86). Its development expresses movement from subalternity to a counter-hegemonic collective will.

This schematic account gives us a normative-strategic template for considering emergent themes and practices in movement politics and their implication for counter-hegemony today. How might contemporary developments in counter-hegemony yield insights on welding present to future in our times? In the space at hand, I will telegraph seven interrelated themes that stand out in recent work by movement theorists, intellectual historians and social researchers. In reflecting on these themes we can gain perspective on how new sensibilities and practices—often reworked from old sensibilities and practices—provide *resources of hope* (Williams 1989) for counter-hegemonic politics, and twenty-first-century socialism.

Counter-Hegemony in Practice: What's New?

Increased Transnationality

Just as hegemony has been increasingly organized on a transnational basis—through the globalization of Americanism, the construction of global governance institutions, the emergence of a transnational capitalist class and so on (Soederberg 2006; Carroll 2010)—counter-hegemony has also taken on transnational features that go beyond the classic organization of Left parties into internationals. What De Sousa Santos (2006) terms the rise of a global Left is evident in specific movement-based campaigns, such as the successful international effort in 1998 to defeat the Multilateral Agreement on Investment (MAI); in initiatives such as the World Social Forum, to contest the terrain of global civil society; and in the growth of transnational movement organizations and of a "democratic globalization network," counterpoised to neoliberalism's transnational historical bloc, that address issues of North-South solidarity and coordination (Smith 2008: 24).

As I have suggested elsewhere (Carroll 2007), an incipient war of position is at work here—a bloc of oppositional forces to neoliberal globalization encompassing a wide range of movements and identities and that is "global in nature, transcending traditional national boundaries" (Butko 2006: 101). These moments of resistance and transborder activism do not yet combine to form a coherent historical bloc around a counter-hegemonic project. Rather, as Marie-Josée Massicotte suggests, "we are witnessing the emergence and re-making of political imaginaries... which often lead to valuable localized actions as well as greater transborder solidarity" (2009: 424). Indeed, Gramsci's adage that while the line of development is international, the origin point is national, still has currency. Much of the energy of anti-capitalist politics is centred within what Raymond Williams (1989) called militant particularisms—localized struggles that, "left to themselves... are easily dominated by the power of capital to coordinate accumulation across universal but fragmented space" (Harvey 1996: 32). Catharsis, in this context, takes on a spatial character. The scaling up of militant particularisms requires "alliances across interrelated scales to unite a diverse range of social groupings and thereby spatialize a Gramscian war of position to the global scale" (Karriem 2009: 324).

Such alliances, however, must be grounded in local conditions and aspirations. Eli Friedman's (2009) case study of two affiliated movement organizations in Hong Kong and mainland China, respectively, illustrates the limits of transnational activism that radiates from advanced capitalism to exert external pressure on behalf of subalterns in the global South. Friedman recounts how a campaign by the Hong Kong-based group of Students and Scholars Against Corporate Misbehaviour to empower Chinese mainland workers producing goods for Hong Kong Disneyland failed due to the lack of local mobilization by workers themselves. Yet the same group, through its support for its ally, the mainland-based migrant workers' association, has helped facilitate self-organization on the shop floor. In the former case, well-intentioned practices of solidarity reproduced a paternalism that failed to inspire local collective action; in the latter, workers taking direct action on their own behalf, with external support, led to "psychological empowerment" and movement mobilization (Friedman 2009: 212). As a rule, "the more such solidarity work involves grassroots initiatives and participation, the greater is the likelihood that workers from different countries will learn from each other," enabling transnational counter-hegemony to gain a foothold (Rahmon and Langford 2010: 63).

The Political Ecology of Counter-Hegemony
In a context of biospheric crisis, the recent turn to Gramsci in political ecology has great pertinence to our analysis (Mann 2009; Kebede, 2005). As a

"new front" in the analysis of hegemony and counter-hegemony, Gramscian political ecology understands the production of nature as a co-evolution of humans and their environments pointing to "the conditions of possibility for radical change that might emerge through interactions with nature" (Ekers et al. 2009: 288). From this perspective, bourgeois hegemony is achieved though the reification of particular spaces and natures (Wainwright 2005), as in the common sense of a consumerism founded upon industrialized agriculture, automobility and suburban sprawl, and north-south relations that displace ecological costs onto the periphery (Rice 2007). The turn to Gramsci enables us to see the environment as "a socio-natural entity… a particular terrain over which hegemony is consolidated and contested" (Ekers et al. 2009: 289). In an era of deepening ecological crisis and of rising consciousness of that crisis, social groups aspiring to hegemony must demonstrate their ability "to pose solutions to a variety of issues related to nature and the environment" (Ekers et al. 2009: 289).

This insight reconfigures the meaning of counter-hegemony around a vision of eco-socialism. To forge an alternative hegemony, counter-hegemonic movements must go beyond resisting the capitalist growth machine, *into prefiguration*: "they have to develop alternative forms of production and re-production or alternative conceptions of nature-society relations" (Karriem 2009: 318). Abdurazack Karriem's study of the Brazilian landless movement (MST) gives us a case in point. The war of position that MST has waged through a combination of land occupations and popular education has not only moved from local sites to transnational arenas; it has had a strong prefigurative thrust. Besides the ethical-political claim that food and food sovereignty are human rights, the MST has promoted ecological alternatives to corporate agriculture, in alliance with the environmental and indigenous movements—all aspects of "a long, slow process of practical and ideological struggle for an alternative hegemony" (2009: 324) that refuses the regime of "sustainable degradation" on offer from transnational neoliberalism (Luke, 2006).

Reclaiming the Commons
MST exemplifies a third theme in contemporary counter-hegemonic politics. In response to neoliberalism's dynamic of accumulation by dispossession, multifarious movements and campaigns have arisen to protect and reclaim the commons from privatization and commodification (Harvey 2005b: 166–72). Initially reactive and protective, harkening back to much earlier resistances to enclosure (Linebaugh 2008), indigenous struggles for land, agrarian struggles for seeds, crops and biodiversity, political campaigns against privatization and the like open a "political dynamic of social action across the whole spectrum of civil society" (Harvey 2005b: 166, 168, 172) that often (as with

MST) combines struggles for self-determination with ecological sustainability (Klein 2001: 88). In providing a communal way of regulating activity without the state or market, "the commons" presents a rich counter-hegemonic template (Wall 2005), but raises challenges as to how it will articulate with "whatever states also claim authority over the resource or territory in question" (McCarthy 2005: 24).

Notwithstanding such issues, the vision of a global commons "defended by a multiplicity of state and non-state actors in the name of human survival" (Watts 2010: 22)—visible beyond the cabal of hegemonic state, inter-state and NGO actors that dominated formal negotiations at the 2009 Copenhagen Conference on Climate Change (COP15)—offers a radical imaginary for emerging counter-hegemonic sensibilities worldwide. This strong image can be applied not only to political-economic matters, but to ideological struggles against enclosure of the moral field within economistic and legal-bureaucratic frameworks (Smith 1997). On matters ranging from biopiracy and intellectual property rights to the idea of a global commons, "the commons" can work as a unifying signifier—of "resistance, community, collective action and common values" (Holder and Flessas 2008: 299). Indeed, as Bakker (2007) shows in her study of struggles against water privatization in the global South, whereas human rights discourse frames issues individualistically and in ways compatible with commodification, the "commons," in championing a collective property right creates space for radical strategies of ecological democracy to decommodify public services, resource management, and so on. A contemporary reworking of a very old theme, anti-enclosure offers, in response to the "dictatorship of no alternative" (Unger 2009), the germ of a Left response to neoliberalism beyond "narrow (and conservative) social democracy" (Watts 2010: 24). The key is to find, or create, the "organic link" between reclaiming the commons and opposing capital's domination of labour (Harvey 2005a: 203), thereby connecting the struggle to decommodify land, intellectual property, public utilities and the like with the struggle to decommodify labour.

Mediatization and the Struggle to Democratize Communication

Many of the issues at stake in the politics surrounding the form and content of communications media comprise a special instance of the struggle to reclaim the commons. The world of the early twenty-first century is densely networked by virtue of an unprecedented apparatus of communications, which has opened new possibilities both for bourgeois hegemony and for oppositional politics. Media now comprise a vast field of cultural struggle. In a media-saturated world, capitalist organization of communication creates a multifaceted *democratic deficit*, evident for instance in the failure of mainstream media to create a democratic public sphere, the centralization of power in media corporations, inequality in media access, homogenization of media content, the undermining of communities through commodification, and the corporate enclosure of knowledge. "Media activism" can be read as a critical response that takes different forms depending on location in the media field. Media democrats struggle to limit corporate power and commercial logic, to democratize media workplaces and labour processes, to develop alternative media, and to foster more literate and critical readers of media texts. When we look at media activism "on the ground," we find many of the rudiments of counter-hegemonic politics. Activists see the struggle to democratize communication as a multi-frontal war of position that needs to be waged in conjunction with other movements. Communicative democracy comprises a social vision in which the voices of citizens and communities carry into a vibrant and diverse public sphere. In pursuing this social vision on several fronts including those of state, corporate media and lifeworld, media democrats build a new nexus among movements, a place where strategies might converge across issue areas and movement identities (Hackett and Carroll 2006; Downing 2001).

As a political emergent, media activism underlines the importance to counter-hegemony of reclaiming or creating the means and forms of communication necessary for subaltern groups to find their voices and to organize, both locally and translocally. The formation of organic intellectuals is substantially caught up in this struggle to break the dominant class's monopoly within the intellectual field (Thomas 2009: 418–19). Here, the new includes a mediatized politics of everyday life, as in proliferation of alternative media (often via the internet; Atton 2009) and the diffusion of culture jamming and other practices of media literacy, yet also a politics, focused upon state and capital, that presses for limits upon corporate power and for an opening of access to the means of communication (Hackett and Carroll 2006). The politics of media democratization is necessarily multi-frontal and intersectional. All progressive-democratic movements have a stake in these struggles; the extent to which movements take up democratic communication as a general interest is a measure their catharsis from fractured subalternities (with their characteristic foci upon single issues and narrow constituencies) to an ethico-political collective will.

The Question of Autonomy

Autonomy from old-Left parties and unions, and from overweening regulatory states, was cited by NSM theorists of the 1970s and 1980s as a criterial attribute of the emergent movements of late modernity. In Jean Cohen's (1985) classic, and rather Americanized treatment, these movements were viewed as practitioners of a "self-limiting" identity politics that rejected large-scale projects. This stylization was never unproblematic as an empirical account, and several decades later, in the wake of neoliberalism's global triumph and in the midst of its global crisis, the appeal of self-limiting politics is embarrassingly limited. Yet autonomy remains a lasting legacy of the so-called NSMs.

Autonomy informs aspects of contemporary counter-hegemonic politics at the level of everyday life, as shown in Gwyn Williams's (2008) ethnography of alterglobalization activism in the Larzac plateau of southern France. Famous since their dismantling of a McDonald's restaurant in 1999 and for the slogan, "the world is not a commodity," these activists resist the hegemony of global market society "by cultivating themselves as 'autonomous' political subjects and organizing a movement considered to be an 'autonomous' counter-power" (Williams 2008: 63). This has meant not only maintaining independence from political parties and functioning in a "bottom-up" or "horizontal" manner but cultivating in themselves and others an autonomy that partly frees them from neoliberal ideology and the power of consumer society. Here, prefiguration is grounded in a moral imperative to "become aware" and to act "coherently" (2008: 72) by living the ideals to which one aspires.[4]

Becoming aware is both an ongoing aspect of autonomous self-development and a movement-building praxis instantiated in a range of pedagogical activities—forums, information evenings and media actions—designed to provoke public debate and to persuade people join the cause (Williams 2008: 72–73). Although activists can never be fully autonomous from the forms of power to which they are subject, the struggle for autonomy is a crucial element in challenging hegemony and in bringing into existence what Gramsci (1971: 327) called a "new conception of the world… which manifests itself in action."[5]

As a sensibility that holds both visionary and strategic implications, autonomy has roots not only in NSM theory, but in historical materialism. Harry Cleaver, who introduced the notion of autonomist Marxism into English-language academia in the 1970s (Cleaver 2001; Wright 2008: 113), predicated it on an agency-centred analysis of the working class, defining autonomy as:

> the ability of workers to define their own interests and to struggle for them—to go beyond mere reaction to exploitation, or to self defined "leadership" and to take the offensive in ways that shape the class struggle and define the future. (Cleaver 1993)

The key question is how autonomy and other emergent features of activism might figure in a counter-hegemonic historical bloc. Mark Purcell, drawing on Ernesto Laclau and Chantal Mouffe, (1985), suggests that relations between elements of such a formation be conceptualized in terms of *equivalence,* "a concept that evokes relations of simultaneous interdependence and autonomy, obligation and freedom, unity and multiplicity, sameness and difference" (2009: 301). The movements and interests that comprise the bloc do not dissolve completely into it, but they move together and lean into one another.

Intersectionality

In sorting out the nuances of counter-hegemonic unity-in-diversity, what stands out as the complement to autonomy as a cultural emergent is the concern for intersectionality. Arriving in the 1990s as a way of rescuing feminism from the cul-de-sac of identity politics, intersectionality transformed feminist praxis itself. Beginning with the critique in the 1980s by lesbian feminists and women of colour of the exclusionary practices in bourgeois, white, heteronormative feminism, intersectional praxis has unfolded, roughly speaking, in stages. First, a group-centred framework recognized that a more inclusive politics must give voice to the qualitatively distinct experiences of subalternity arising from intersections of class, gender, sexuality, race and other social positionings (Choo and Ferree 2010). A process-centred approach then moved from positional categories to "dynamic forces"—racialization, economic exploitation, gendering—and highlighted the distinctive operations of power across institutional fields (ibid.: 134), as "multiple relations and structures of power interact in context-specific ways" (Eschle 2004: 119; Walby 2009). In this formulation, intersectionality becomes an operating principle for building a historical bloc and conducting a multi-frontal war of position, guided by an understanding of intersecting relations of domination and subalternity and of the need for dialogical efforts to mediate a multiplicity of identities, communities, and contexts (Rice 2010).

Spike Peterson has recently brought poststructural insights to an intersectional perspective that recognizes gender as a governing code which, as it privileges *masculinity*—not necessarily men—also naturalizes the power relations that constitute multiple forms of exploitation and subordination (Peterson 2009). As a hegemonic code, gender interlinks and reifies diverse hierarchies by feminizing those who are subordinated—devaluing "not only women but also sexually, racially, culturally, and economically marginalized men (e.g., 'lazy migrants,' 'primitive native' 'effeminate gays'" (ibid.: 35). The binary code is self-validating in practice, as "common sense becomes a two-sided justification of hierarchy: not only are the subordinated devalorized by feminization but the qualities they lack are typically just what the dominating (masculinized) group has to offer" (ibid.: 36). Peterson's decisive break from identity politics deepens our understanding of how hegemony works through a confluence of discourse and material relations. By implication, she clarifies an aspect of the cathartic passage from the economic-corporate to the ethico-political:

> We are not simply talking about male-female relations or promoting
> the status of "women." We are first addressing the exploitation of
> *all* whose identities, labour, and livelihoods are devalued by being
> feminized and, second, advancing the critical project of theorizing
> *intersections* of devalorization that link hierarchies of race/ethnicity,
> class, gender/sexuality, and nation. (ibid.: 38)

Intersectional analysis is a resource in the struggle for dignity that
has been highlighted in Zapatismo and other autonomous struggles. Yet
it presses toward a unity-in-diversity that challenges both postmodern
fragmentation and the single-issue sectionalism prevalent in many social
movements, including mainstream environmentalism. Recognizing the deep
connections between environmental sustainability and social reproduction,
intersectionality is a tool for political ecology. It asks how the "intersection
of specific economic, social, and environmental conditions" might disable
an individual's or community's ability to survive (Di Chiro 2008: 286)—a
question that motivates the search for alternatives within which individuals,
communities and ecosystems may thrive.

New Organizational Forms

A final theme in recent thinking calls attention to new organizational forms
within which a historical bloc for a just and sustainable alternative to the
current world order might take shape. Different projects "imply different
forms of organisation, which thus require different types of organic intellectuals, whose role it is to elaborate such organisation in both ideological
and practical terms" (Thomas 2009: 416). The activists of the Larzac, struggling for autonomy both in everyday life and in publicly oriented actions,
exemplify this relation between activism and organization. The same might
be said of the Zapatistas, whose campaigns in Mexico and in cyberspace
activated national and global civil society while constructing new forms of
local autonomous governance that validate indigenous tradition and identity
within a contemporary context (Morton 2007: 191; Bahn 2009: 551). Yet such
autonomism, if pursued singularly, undercuts the possibilities for creating a
counter-hegemonic unity in diversity. The Zapatista slogan "one no, many
yeses" creates a unity around a shared rejection of transnational neoliberal
capitalism that resists

> any fixed meaning of the collective subject that undertakes activism.
> The central dilemma for activist life becomes whether the "many
> yeses" arising in its wake can exert counter-hegemonic power in a
> long-term war of position. (Gibson 2008: 256)

Beyond autonomy, beyond pluralism, but not in opposition to them, is the cathartic transition from the many, the sectional, to a "political unity across cultural differences" (Sanbonmatsu 2004: 130). The question is how to construct "forms of political agency that allow for the necessary diversity of a global counter-hegemony while allowing for the necessary commonality of a global counter-hegemony" (Stephen 2009: 494).

Gramsci characterized the historical bloc that might issue from such formative efforts in terms of the "modern prince"—"the fusion of a new type of political party and oppositional culture that would gather together intellectuals (organisers) and the masses in a new political and intellectual practice, 'organising the organisers'" (Thomas 2009: 437). In considering prospects for what Gill (2000) and Sanbonmatsu (2004) have termed a "postmodern prince," adequate to the political task of exiting from today's globalized and crisis-ridden capitalism, the World Social Forum has been said to represent "in organizational terms, the most consistent manifestation of counter-hegemonic globalization" (De Sousa Santos 2008: 249). The WSF contests the claim that capitalism is here to stay while it provincializes conventional, northern-based Left thinking through practices of intercultural dialogue. Convened first in 2001 and proliferating subsequently into regional and national social forums, the Forum has created an "open space" for discussion and a transnational site for organizing concrete collective practices.

In its scale and breadth, the WSF is, indeed, new. Moreover, it has spurred a process of intellectual and moral reform that begins to provide a cultural infrastructure for global counter-hegemony. Within WSF discussions it has become clear that "the global Left is intercultural" (De Sousa Santos 2008: 261); hence the importance of mutual translation, an emergent practice that preserves autonomy while creating common ground. A related contribution that the WSF has made to the global Left is its horizontal, network politics, which enables the work of translation and is further elaborated through that work.

Yet the shape of the network is worth pondering, and on this question of form, the WSF's counter-hegemonic capacities to wage a war of position are doubtful (Gibson 2008; Stephen 2009; Worth and Buckley 2009).[6] Gramsci's modern prince anticipated a relatively centralized network encompassing a dialectical relation between masses and leaders—rather distinct from the rhizomic networks, celebrated by the postmodern Left (Deleuze and Guattari 1987; Hardt and Negri 2004), which lack any central basis for co-ordination. Organizationally, a certain degree of centrality is needed to ensure that "the movement will be able to *move* when the time is right" (Purcell 2009: 304). Alternatively, it is difficult to know how a rhizomic movement "will be able to move at all, much less take coordinated and strategic action that shifting political opportunities demand" (305). On this point, Peter Evans is correct to claim that "the eventual construction of counter-hegemonic globalization

will almost certainly combine 'rhizomic' networks with traditional 'trees'"
(2008: 291), the latter branching out authoritatively from well defined centres
of decisionmaking.

Although the WSF's rhizomic structure has limited its capacity to serve
as much more than an open space for building cultural infrastructure and
launching episodic campaigns, an even more formidable constraint resides
in the neoliberal organization of global governance, in which a Westphalian
state system coexists with international apparatuses like the World Trade
Organization (WTO), in a context of globalizing capitalism. The debacle
that was COP15 (December 2009) illustrates the toxicity of this combination,
wherein the old system of state sovereignty is dying but a new global political
order cannot yet be born. The Westphalian "partitioning of political space
along territorial lines insulates extra- and non-territorial powers from the
reach of justice" (Fraser 2005: 81), offering increased scope to transnational
capital.[7] Progressive politics framed at the "global" level are circumscribed
by the lack of a global state that might be democratically transformed; hence
they take the form of a cultural war of position within global civil society (e.g.,
the WSF) punctuated by occasional defensive wars of manoeuver against such
threats as the MAI (defeated 1998), WTO (stalled in 1999) and Free Trade Area
of the Americas (defeated in 2005). Instructively, defensive campaigns of this
sort are successful only to the extent that the collective action of movements
meshes with actions taken by progressive state actors. The WSF's open space
and the defensive campaigns that have significantly sapped neoliberalism's
momentum cannot in themselves create a global postcapitalist formation; they
only gesture in that direction. Resplendent in its slogan that another world
is possible, the WSF instantiates the not-yet, the concrete forward dream of
a global Left—a counter-hegemonic collective will—not yet the reality. For
now, it is at the national level that system change is feasible (though inherently dependent on transnational alignments of movements and progressive
state actors)—confirming the continuing validity of Gramsci's adage that the
"point of departure" for radical, transformative politics is national.

The hotbed of such politics is contemporary Latin America, where Jerry
Harris (2007: 1) has discerned a developing "democratic dialectic" of state
and civil society. Flowing strongly but not exclusively from the labouring
classes, the new movements of the twenty-first century seek "a novel relation to the formal political realm by fundamentally reworking relations of
power" (Stahler-Sholk et al. 2007: 6). Across much of Latin America, the
project is "to reappropriate democracy from a restricted and statist form by
means of an expanded and participatory model" (Harris 2007: 14). Many of
these movements maintain autonomy from parties and governments, acting
as a *counterbalance* that pressures the state to withstand the demands of global
capitalism (15). Where the Left has formed the government, particularly in

Venezuela and Bolivia, radical forces within the state have united with social movements, giving the state-civil society dialectic "a revolutionary character and expanded potential that is lacking in countries where autonomist power remains isolated from the government" (Harris 2007: 19).

This dialectic animates Marta Harnecker's (2010) analysis of Venezuela's Bolivarian revolution. Noting the transition within the Left from workerism to an understanding that "the new political instrument must respect the plurality of the new subject and take on the defense of all discriminated social sectors" (2010: 5), she emphasizes that at the heart of the revolution, inscribed in Venezuela's constitution, is a conception of *protagonist democracy*—a commitment to popular participation in public affairs that brings with it individual and collective development (2010: 37). Conjoined to protagonism in this counter-hegemonic project is a "socialist conception of decentralization" that reworks Marx's (1871) comments on the Paris Commune—a decentralization "imbued with a spirit of solidarity," which strengthens communities, deepens democracy, and collaborates with the central state as it coordinates society-wide plans (2010: 51). These elements of autonomism and of the commons take concrete shape in Venezuela's co-operatives, now a key economic form for state decentralization and mass participation, and in Community Councils that enact democratic planning for human needs at the local level (Magdoff and Foster 2010; Spronk and Webber 2010). Here we find the "organic link" mentioned earlier, between the emancipation of labour and reclaiming the commons: between building worker control in production and building communal control within places. In the historical bloc prefigured by these forms, activists become *producers* rather than protesters demanding more services, and their alternative economic activity produces new social relations that concretize a social vision of sustainable human development (Harris 2007: 22). Under these nationally-specific conditions, facilitated greatly by emergent intergovernmental alliances such as ALBA (Kellogg 2007), the prospects for twenty-first-century socialism—though circumscribed by legacies of political cronyism and corruption, of charismatic populism as a form of leadership that may reinforce subalternity, and of ecologically problematic "extractivism" as a means of generating wealth (Gudynas 2010)—are real.

The exemplars, however, are not restricted to Latin America. In her ethnographic account of building participatory democracy in Kerala, India, Michelle Williams observes many strikingly similar socio-political inventions. There, the Communist Party of India (Marxist) (CPI(M)) has developed a "counter-hegemonic generative politics that attempts to establish new institutions and practices that extend the role of civil society over the state and the economy" (2008: 9). Operating both arborescently and rhizomically, partly through a succession of coalition governments but especially through organic ties to Kerala's vibrant popular sector, the CPI(M) has coordinated innovative initiatives in participatory democracy and decentralized, self-reliant development. The provisional result of this decades-long war of position is an empowered civil society that enjoys one of the highest levels of human development and quality of life in the majority world. As in Latin America, participatory democracy in Kerala confirms the viability of counter-hegemonic generative politics, but it also suggests that such politics requires "a new type of political party, one that is not afraid to empower civil society" (Williams 2008: 156).

It is these fragile prospects that have propelled the recent effort to create a "Fifth Socialist International"—a space where "socialist-oriented parties, movements and trends of thought" will be able to propose a common strategy for the struggle against imperialism, for transitioning from capitalism to socialism and for international economic integration within a framework of solidarity.[8] Proposed in November 2009 by Hugo Chávez at a meeting of more than 50 parties and movement organizations from 31 countries, the Fifth International may yet grow to complement the World Social Forum, but as a tree-like, arborescent formation, whose project is more action-oriented and whose roots in organized parties and Left governments enable coordinated action in a global field, something the WSF seems incapable of delivering. Significantly, and in contrast to the template for party-based internationals, Chávez's proposal emphasized the inclusion of both movement organizations and parties, and noted that a new international would have to function "without impositions" and would have to respect diversity (Janicke 2009). Subsequent elaboration of the idea (Albert 2010) and debate about its assumptions and entailments (Waterman 2010) help clarify the possibilities for such a new Left formation, based in autonomist and intersectional practice and a thoroughgoing provincialization of Europe. Whether these possibilities will be actualized is at the time of writing entirely undecided.

Conclusions

My point of departure was a meditation on the new, and the problem of welding present to future. Counter-hegemony, however, requires more than a cataloguing of what is new; welding the present to the future has an indelibly *programmatic* aspect, registered in such notions as war of position and historical bloc. As an instrument of transformative politics, the "programmatic imagination" marks a direction and defines the next steps in taking up that trajectory (Unger 2009: xxi). Marking a direction sketches the contours of a counter-hegemonic project—a possible alternative—but it is the choice of next steps that enables motion. In this respect, "the possible that counts is not the fanciful horizon of possibilities but the *adjacent possible*: what is accessible with the materials at hand, deployed in the pursuit of movement in the desired direction" (Unger 2009: xxi, emphasis added). The emergent themes and practices discussed above help mark a direction: toward a post-capitalist way of life that is broadly eco-socialist, that subordinates the state to an empowered civil society structured around practices of participatory democracy, dialogical communicative relations, and autonomous governance of the commons, both physical and informational; that combines, within an ethico-political framework, the autonomy of individuals with an abiding appreciation of the intersecting relations that implicate us in each other's lives. This direction implies a process of democratic globalization that reaches beyond the Westphalian division of humanity into (potentially) warring factions—and well beyond the current state of the world.

The elements of the new I have sketched also illuminate the next steps, toward the adjacent possible. Transnational networks and campaigns, new media and new communicative struggles, initiatives to reclaim the commons, and quotidian practices of becoming aware and acting coherently all mark a cathartic shift from protest to *generative politics*, to *production* of sustainable agriculture, of communications and culture, of collective property, of new social relations and subjectivities. For such generative politics to take root "a synergistic relation between political parties and civil society must be forged in order to ensure that the necessary institutional spaces are created and the capacity for civil society participation is developed" (M. Williams 2008: 156). As for the national and transnational, what seems adjacently possible is an "institutionalization of multilevel contestation," combining rhizomic networks and "traditional" trees, reaching from the local to the global, and including as allies progressive state actors, in "virtuous circles" that strengthen both movements and initiatives by state leaders at the global level (Evans 2008).

These politics must be substantially rooted in local and national contexts: local self-empowerment is a requirement of democratic mobilization, and winning state power is indispensable to transformation at a global level. Counter-hegemonic globalization is sustained by the transnational cultural infrastructures and activist networks that shape global civil society, but also by arborescent formations such as new democratic Left parties in Europe (Rao 2009; Solty 2008), the intergovernmental organizations developing within the Bolivarian process and what may be an emerging Fifth International inclusive of parties and movements. The movement of movements will walk on both legs, creating new relations, practices and subjectivities both on the cultural terrain of civil society and within/against the state, globally and in national and local contexts—or else it will stumble.

These developments portend a global Left, a counter-hegemonic historical bloc organized around a project of sustainable human development and participatory democracy, whose constituents recognize in the intersections of power and oppression an emancipatory collective interest. This project faces great challenges, when placed in the context of the ecological race against time and the continuing hegemony of consumer capitalism. Indeed, in North America, where the marketplace society and postmodern fragmentation discussed earlier are most entrenched—where the Left's marginality contributes to a toxic condition of "dreamlessness," as Bloch put it[9]—it is unlikely that transformative politics will gain traction until consumerism as a way of life that contains its own self-reproducing end values is rejected by (or becomes unviable for) great numbers of people. In practising sustainable consumption in the North, the autonomist politics of the Larzac plateau is exemplary.[10] To break from the hegemony of marketplace society is to endeavour "in the here and now to create in the interstices of the system a new social metabolism rooted in egalitarianism, community, and a sustainable relation to the earth" (Magdoff and Foster 2010).

Globally, pressure for change may arise most urgently from a growing "environmental proletariat" (Foster 2010: 15) in areas of failing habitability, and leadership in counter-hegemonic globalization can be expected to emanate from the South. Yet achieving the global *contraction* in greenhouse gas emissions and *convergence* in emissions per capita necessary to avert the worst ecological scenarios will require a strong ethico-political solidarity of North with South—quite the reverse of what was on display at COP15 in Copenhagen in December 2009, and presently a distant possibility.

Nevertheless, it is the steps taken in that direction that cumulatively might open an exit hatch from capitalism. Such a global transition would require that ecological and social revolutions in the South "be accompanied by, or inspire, universal revolts against imperialism, the destruction of the planet, and the treadmill of accumulation" (Foster 2010: 15). What is particularly *new* in this organic crisis is the entwinement of human survival with democratic socialist construction, the twin exigencies of our time.

Notes

1. To construct a General Will, to raise consciousness and transform ideas into a material force, "movements must continuously form new organic intellectuals" (Karriem 2009: 318); hence the process of translation is not top-down but an active and reciprocal "educative relationship" (Gramsci 1971: 350).

2. Here I use "civil society" in the contemporary sense of that which is neither state nor economy. Gramsci's use of the term is complex, in some contexts contrasting state with a civil society that includes economic relations; in other contexts contrasting capitalist economic relations with an "integral state" ("State = political society + civil society, in other words hegemony protected by the armour of coercion" [Gramsci 1971: 263]). See Anderson's (1976) classic discussion for a critical take.

3. With reference to Marx's Sixth Thesis on Feuerbach, that human "essence" is the *ensemble* of human relations, he identified political activity with the dialectical production of new relations and new subjects: "to transform the external world, the

general system of relations, is to potentiate oneself and to develop oneself" (1971: 360).

4. Since domination dwells within one's own person, since each person's actions reproduce forms of domination, changing the world implies an ongoing process of 'work on oneself' that cultivates autonomy (G. Williams 2008: 75). That activists are thoroughly embedded in the extended relations of global capitalism problematizes the achievement of coherence, yet by living relatively simply, in full respect of the environment and their fellow human beings, the activists of the Larzac "distance themselves from the power of capitalism, consumer society and neoliberalism, they banish it from their lives and thereby partially fulfil their vocation as activists. To banish power is to create an autonomous space in which to live your life, itself an act of resistance. This is something that requires effort, and ongoing attention to the way you act in the world that is a part of the developmental process of becoming aware" (Williams 2008: 77).

5. Gramsci's own commitment to autonomous human development was deeply seated in his conception of counter-hegemony. "Is it better to take part in a conception of the world mechanically imposed by the external environment; i.e., by one of the many social groups in which one is automatically involved from the moment of his entry into the conscious world…? Or, on the other hand, is it better to work out consciously and critically one's own conception of the world and thus, in connection with the labours of one's own brain, choose one's sphere of activity, take an active part in the creation of the history of the world, be one's own guide, refusing to accept passively and supinely from outside the moulding of one's personality?" (1971: 323–24).

6. On this issue, Worth and Buckley are especially caustic. The WSF "has suffered from being a directionless series of events, whereby the working formula of 'open space' has led to the creation of nothing more than a 'talking shop,' rather than any valid construction of counter-hegemony" (2009: 650).

7. This problem is exacerbated by the highly uneven distribution of powers among intergovernmental institutions. Although international agencies like the WTO that enforce the rule of global capital are invested with some degree of state power, other international bodies and sites—such as the Copenhagen conference, the ILO, and the U.N. Declaration on the Rights of Indigenous Peoples—lack state authority and exist only by the good graces of the states that selectively participate. See Clarkson 2010.

8. "Commitment of Caracas." <http://www.psuv.org.ve/files/tcdocumentos/commitment.caracas.pdf> accessed March 7, 2010. See also "The Venezuelan Call for a New International Organization of the Left," *The Bullet*, No. 312, February 15, 2010 <http://www.socialistproject.ca/bullet/312.php>.

9. In contrast to the concrete forward dream that informs prefigurative practice, dreamlessness "which is associated with standing still or with a realism which only appears to be such, even in a state of resignation, is actually the ruling state of mind of many thinking though unperceptive people in a society without perspectives (and with an abundance of inaccuracy)" (Bloch 1971: 31).

10. As Magdoff and Foster (2010) point out, a postcapitalist future generalizable to humanity in its entirety implies a radical shift from the unsustainable consumerism that middle-income North Americans take for granted. "An economic system that is democratic, reasonably egalitarian, and able to set limits on consumption will undoubtedly mean that people will live at a significantly lower level of consumption

than what is sometimes referred to in the wealthy countries as a 'middle class' lifestyle (which has never been universalized even in these societies). A simpler way of life, though 'poorer' in gadgets and ultra-large luxury homes, can be richer culturally and in reconnecting with other people and nature, with people working the shorter hours needed to provide life's essentials."

10

Venezuela under Chávez: The Dialectics of Twenty-First-Century Socialism

Jeffery R. Webber

Elected in late December 1998, Hugo Chávez assumed the presidency of Venezuela in February 1999.[1] A decade into the Bolivarian process of social and political change, it is incumbent upon the international Left to step back and reflect on the images and realities of *Chavismo*. An historical sociological approach is employed in this chapter to analyze the big trends and contradictions characterizing politics, economics and class struggle in Venezuela over the last ten years. Recent processes are considered against the backdrop of the country's earlier social formation, taking the long view of historical and material developments in Venezuelan political economy over the last half century from which the Bolivarian process emerged. The chapter emphasizes a theoretical approach that understands the transition to socialism as: the overturning of still-existing capitalist class rule and the capitalist state in Venezuela through the self-activity and struggle of the popular classes themselves; movement toward democratic social coordination of the economy; communal ownership of economic and natural resources; worker and community control of workplaces and neighbourhoods; the deep expansion of radical democratic rule through all political, social, economic and private spheres of life; and an internationalist socialist orientation which privileges solidarity with emancipatory movements of the oppressed and exploited around the globe. This is quite distinct from versions of socialist theory that privilege merely state ownership of the means of production and state allocation of resources.

Six overarching, interrelated theses are advanced.

First, popular struggles in Venezuela over the last decade have rejuvenated the international critique of neoliberalism and brought socialism back on the Left's agenda, although no socialist revolution has been achieved in Venezuela.[2] *Chavismo* is riddled by profound and abiding contradictions, thus far preventing a revolutionary overturning of capitalist class rule and the capitalist state.

Second, Hugo Chávez was elected president in 1998 because his anti-neoliberal, Left-populist platform filled the void created by the collapse of the traditional political system and the absence of a revolutionary socialist alternative. Modestly reformist at the onset of its first term, the Chávez government was slowly and partially radicalized when faced with a series of imperialist and domestic, legal and (mainly) extra-legal, Right-destabilization campaigns.

Third, the government's radicalizing tendency is a result, more specifically, of counter-revolutionary pressure that spurred a dramatic effervescence of grassroots struggles among the working class and urban poor, a small but important minority of whom are committed socialists, beginning in April 2002 and accelerating during and after the oil lockout of 2002–03. "Revolutionary processes cannot simply be implanted from above," suggests Gonzalo Gómez, co-founder of the radical web-zine aporrea.org and a militant in the Socialist Tide current of the PSUV. "They must come from below. It is all very well and good to have a state that supports the struggle, which backs up the workers against their employer, for example. But the state shouldn't pretend that it is guiding the revolutionary process. Rather, the state should let the revolutionary processes unfold from its own roots."[3] Stalin Pérez Borges, a national co-ordinator of the *Unión Nacional de Trabajadores* (National Union of Workers, UNT) concurs: "The revolutionary elements of this process have always emerged from the base, from the workers, not from legislatures and bureaucrats."[4]

Fourth, against this grassroots, Left-populist, and sometimes socialist struggle from below, conservative, bureaucratic layers within *Chavismo* have taken on an important role within the state apparatus and have hampered a transition to socialism. "Given the fact that we still live in a capitalist society," Gómez argues, "we confront many contradictions in the process. The bureaucratic, bourgeois state gives rise to many of the contradictions. Indeed, one of the largest threats to the revolution is the conservatism of the thick bureaucratic layer of civil servants, who have centralized political power and material benefits and act as a break on the process."[5]

Fifth, the empirical record regarding poverty reduction and social programs in Venezuela suggests both real social progress and serious contradictions. Poverty has been reduced at rates similar to other centre-Left governments in the region during the commodities boom (2003–07). Venezuela's highly unequal income distribution, moreover, makes clear there has been no fundamental shift toward socialism. As Luis Primo, a leader of the *Unión Regional de Trabajadores* (Regional Workers Union, URT) in the state of Bolívar notes:

From my perspective, we are not really in a transition to socialism.

Rather, we have a progressive government that has been promoting important reforms, especially through the social missions, such as in health, education and the provision of subsidized food. These reforms are fundamental—they are needed to resolve the material conditions of the population. But this is not enough. These missions tend to lose their momentum after a number of years. There is a problem with continuity and permanence. And while the progressive government confronts the bourgeoisie on some issues, the state remains totally capitalist because the social relations of production remain capitalist.[6]

Sixth, the global economic crisis creates novel opportunities and challenges for the Bolivarian process, not least as a consequence of the fluctuating international price of oil.

In the conclusion, I consider the impact of the global economic crisis for the Left in Venezuela and Latin America more widely, argue for the necessity of sustained advance toward socialist transformation from below and consider the various implications for solidarity activists outside of Venezuela.

International Images of Venezuela under Chávez

Mainstream punditry in North America and Europe associates Venezuela with the *bad* Left in contemporary Latin America. This Left is "nationalist, strident, and close-minded," "depends on giving away money" and has "no real domestic agenda." For the bad Left, "the fact of power is more important than its responsible exercise," and for its leaders, "economic performance, democratic values, programmatic achievements, and good relations with the United States are not imperatives but bothersome constraints that miss the real point" (Castañeda 2006). George W. Bush's national security strategy documents claimed that Hugo Chávez was a "demagogue awash in oil money," seeking to "undermine democracy" and "destabilize the region." Donald Rumsfeld compared Chávez to Adolf Hitler, reminding us that Hitler, too, had been elected (Grandin 2006).[7] Not much has changed since Barack Obama took over the world's most powerful presidency. The White House message continues to be that Chávez runs a dangerously authoritarian regime in desperate need of "democratization."[8]

Chávez has been a leading opponent of free trade deals between Latin American countries and the United States, instead invoking the memory of independence hero Simón Bolívar with his vision of a united South America to promote a series of trade deals based on principles of solidarity (Chávez 2003; Katz 2008; Kellogg 2007). Chávez is openly inspired by the Cuban revolution and has a warm friendship with Fidel Castro, while stressing Venezuela's independent path towards a less state-centred and more pluaralistic twenty-first-century socialism. Chávez emphasizes the need to forge stronger South-South connections against the imperialism of the core capitalist states of the world system. This explicitly anti-imperialist stance helps to explain U.S. support for reactionary forces in Venezuela, even in the relative absence of direct threats to American corporate interests.[9]

The Bolivarian Alternative for the Americas (ALBA), first imagined by the Venezuelan government in 2001 as a counter to the North American-led Free Trade Area of the Americas (FTAA), is the most important expression of Venezuelan-led regional integration. Formally established in 2004 by Venezuela and Cuba, it expanded to include Bolivia, Nicaragua, Dominican Republic, Honduras, Ecuador, St. Vincent and the Grenadines, and Antigua and Barbuda, with Paraguay scheduled to join later in 2009 (Hart-Landsberg 2009). Moreover, soon after Evo Morales' election in Bolivia in December 2005, Cuba, Venezuela and Bolivia signed what they called a Peoples' Trade Agreement.

Chávez is revered by many on the Left since few leaders of the Global South today openly and regularly denounce the crimes of American imperialism from a Left-wing perspective.[10] Along with its record of poverty reduction and anti-neoliberalism, pursued with popular support in the face of domestic right-wing and imperialist assaults, Venezuela helps to revive the idea of socialism as a viable political choice. This is an important development following the Soviet bloc's collapse and the discrediting of socialism in the wake of Stalinist policies, and explains why Venezuela has inspired so much attention and debate.

From the Right, Chávez has sometimes been crudely lumped in with recent "neopopulist" presidents elsewhere in the region, such as Alberto Fujimori in Peru, and Carlos Menem in Argentina (Weyland 2001). Chávez's neopopulism, on this view, includes a feverishly authoritarian bent, where "political competition" means "[o]pponents must be crushed," and where Chávez employs "hate speech" that sounds "more dictatorial than democratic" (Corrales 2009: 81). More serious discussion is occurring on the Left. There are those who think Chávez is a moderate social democrat and celebrate this stance as a reasonable and realistic response to the current hostile context of neoliberalism and imperialism (Ali 2006). Some social democrats, however, celebrate the perceived social gains of the Bolivarian process, but fear a "regressive evolution" in the "sphere of politics" in which they perceive a "closing of the space for participation and democratic decisionmaking" (López Maya 2007: 175). Other Leftists, while remaining critical of different components of the government's approach, contend that Chávez represents something more radical than social democracy, something even potentially revolutionary and transformative. They tend to stress the social and economic achievements of the regime thus far in the face of daunting odds (Wilpert

2007; Lebowitz 2006; Ellner 2008; Robinson 2007). There are those, finally, who orient themselves toward struggling within and for the socialist advance of the Bolivarian process, but who emphasize the contradictions, obstacles, delays, setbacks and bureaucratization that have thus far stood in the way of genuine socialist transition from below; these obstacles, for the latter set of thinkers, represent the clear and present danger to the possibilities for emancipation of the popular classes from the exploitation of capital and the oppression of imperialism.[11] This chapter situates itself most closely within the last of these sets of Leftist commentaries on the Venezuelan scenario.

Historical Backdrop: From *Puntofijismo* to *Neoliberalismo*, 1958–1998

Between 1945 and 1948 (the *trienio*) a populist-reformist government was led by the *Acción Democratica* (Democratic Action, AD)—Venezuela's social democratic party. The period's economic elite, threatened by the potential deepening of the AD government's modest social reforms, formed the conservative, Christian democratic, *Comité de Organización Política Electoral Independiente* (Committee of Independent Electoral Political Organization, COPEI), and backed a military overthrow of the democratically-elected AD administration. The signing of the Pact of Punto Fijo a decade later was the culmination of a compromised democratic transition out of the authoritarianism following the 1948 coup. The AD moderated its social reformist inclinations and COPEI its overtly authoritarian predilections, agreeing to a range of social, economic and political pacts that shaped the new democratic order.

The series of compromises encompassed in Punto Fijo included power-sharing between the signatory parties—the AD, COPEI and a smallish left-wing party, *Unión Republicana Democrática* (Democratic Republican Union, URD)—and the exclusion of the *Partido Comunista de Venezuela* (Communist Party of Venezuela, PCV) from the legal political system. As the AD and COPEI converged ideologically, and the URD faded, oil money "made it possible to induce business, labor, church, and military co-operation with the democratic regime" (Roberts 2003: 57). Venezuelan democracy "rested upon a material basis: the distribution of international oil rents through a system of clientelism." The oil boom of the 1970s, "and nationalization of the foreign oil companies in 1976 were the culmination of this project associating democracy, oil nationalism, and development" (Hellinger 2003: 27). This nationalization had important consequences, creating a form of national rentier capitalism and attendant fractions of the domestic bourgeoisie whose benefits and interests were tied to its continuation. Protection of these interests helps to explain the origins and intensity of the oil lockout in late 2002 and early 2003.

Between 1970 and 1980 oil prices increased 948 percent (Weisbrot and Sandoval 2007: 5), creating tremendous wealth, most of it captured by the state through oil rents. Capital's continued allegiance to the regime was secured through extremely low domestic tax rates and abundant access to cheap public credit. Meanwhile, a meagre but important part of the rent trickled down to the popular classes, particularly during the first administration of Carlos Andrés Pérez (1974–79). Workers were paid higher wages than in the rest of Latin America and there were price controls and subsidies on basic food goods, transportation, and social services like education and health care (Roberts 2003: 57). Nostalgia for the golden years of the 1970s permeated Venezuelan political and social life for the subsequent two decades as the economy endured a dramatic reversal.

Contrary to many claims, Venezuela's political economy between the 1960s and early 1980s was not exceptional but typical of Latin America. The region's economy grew by 82 percent between 1960 and 1980, the same time that Venezuela experienced its boom. Likewise, when oil prices crashed and Latin America entered the debt crisis of the 1980s—growing only 15 percent in the 26 years between 1980 and 2006—Venezuela also plunged into the abyss—although Venezuela's fall proved longer and deeper than most. Real GDP plummeted by 26 percent between 1978 and 1986, hitting the floor in 2003 at 38 percent below its 1978 high (Weisbrot and Sandoval 2007: 4). The neoliberal economic restructuring initiated in 1989, during Pérez's second administration and consolidated in the mid-to late 1990s under Rafael Caldera, made the crisis particularly intense.

In some other South American nations neoliberals were re-elected in the 1990s—Alberto Fujimori in Peru and Carlos Menem in Argentina, for example. Yet, Venezuelans consistently voted for anti-neoliberal candidates. Pérez, elected in 1989, was identified with the state interventionist policies of his first government. Caldera (1994–99) ran on an explicitly anti-neoliberal platform, unlike his rivals. Likewise, Hugo Chávez was the only anti-neoliberal presidential candidate (Ellner 2008: 89). Pérez and Caldera later revealed themselves devotees of International Monetary Fund (IMF) orthodoxy but both were elected on anti-neoliberal platforms.

In the 1990s there was a rash of privatizations—including the state telephone company, CANTV, the state steel industry, SIDOR, and the social security system. Trade, prices and the financial sector were liberalized. The labour market was made "flexible," and other policies conforming to the so-called "Washington Consensus" were introduced (Gott 2005: 54). Richard Gott writes: "In earlier and happier times, when claiming leadership of the Third World in the 1970s, Pérez had denounced the economists of the IMF as 'genocide workers in the pay of economic totalitarianism.' Now he was having to go on all fours to beg for money from an institution he had once described as 'an economic neutron bomb' that 'killed people but left buildings standing'" (Gott 2005: 54).

The social repercussions were severe. Per capita income by 1998 had declined 34.8 percent from its 1970 level, the worst collapse in the region. Likewise, by 1997, workers' share of the national income was half what it had been in 1970, and the country's Gini coefficient measure of income inequality was worse than in the notoriously unequal Brazil and South Africa (Lander and Navarrete 2007: 9). Cuts to wages and social spending in 1989 precipitated an increase in poverty from 46 to 62 percent (Roberts 2003: 59).

Parallel to trends in inequality and poverty, the rural and urban class underwent profound transformations in the 1980s and 1990s. Employment moved away from agricultural and industrial sectors towards the service sector, and from the formal to informal sector. Precariously constructed shantytowns in major urban centres—particularly Caracas—expanded massively.[12] "Throughout the 1980s," notes historian Greg Grandin, "Caracas grew at a galloping pace, creating combustible concentrations of poor people cut off from municipal services—such as sanitation and safe drinking water—and hence party control" (Grandin 2006). The under- and unemployed workers who populated these Venezuelan slums made 30 percent lower wages in the informal sector compared to the formal sector (Roberts 2003: 60). By the end of the 1990s, the informal economy employed 53 percent of the workforce (Ellner 2003: 19).

The *Caracazo* and Popular Resistance

Venezuela's neoliberalization was contested. Pérez's restructuring plan of 1989, including the end of domestic gasoline subsidies, led to a hike in fuel costs. Drivers of the most common form of working-class transit in urban centres, known as *por puestos*, attempted to transfer costs to passengers by illegally doubling fares, a measure that ignited mass protests and riots, known as the *caracazo*, between February 27 and March 5, 1989. Tens of thousands of the urban poor participated. The army and police violently repressed the protests, leaving an official count of 287 dead, and unofficial counts of between 1,000 and 1,500 killed, according to national medial personnel. The highest, widely-circulated figure is 3,000 dead (Wilpert 2007: 16; Hellinger 2003: 31). Today, the *caracazo* is deeply ingrained in the popular memory of the Venezuelan Left, marking the start of the Bolivarian "revolutionary process."[13] The rebellion and repression had an impact on some officers in the Venezuelan armed forces who "had not assimilated to North American geopolitical doctrines nor been fully integrated into the structures of *punto-fijismo*." Among these was Hugo Chávez, part of the "first cohort of officers to have attended civilian universities and not to have undergone training at U.S. counterinsurgency schools" (Hellinger 2003: 41).

Chávez Fills a Void

In the early 1980s, when Chávez was a sports instructor at the military academy in Caracas, he and other likeminded military critics of the Venezuelan social and political system formed the *Ejército Bolivariano Revolucionario-200* (Bolivarian Revolutionary Army, EBR-200), the "200" representing the anniversary of independence hero Simón Bolívar's birth in 1783 (Wilpert 2007: 16). Following the *caracazo*, the EBR-200 increased contacts with civilian political groups, and changed its name to the *Movimiento Bolivariano Revolucionario-200* (Bolivarian Revolutionary Movement, MBR-200) (Raby 2006: 149). Civilians included Douglas Bravo, a guerrilla leader in Falcón in the 1960s, who collaborated with Chávez in the 1980s "but withdrew after 1992, convinced that civilians were being by-passed and that Chávez's program was insufficiently radical" (Gott 2005: 17–18).

Between 1989 and 1992, Chávez and his co-conspirators planned a military uprising against the Pérez government, launching the rebellion on February 4, 1992. It achieved some early military objectives, but most military insurgents were quickly captured and surrendered.[14] No civilian uprising accompanied the coup attempt. Chávez's conspiratorial effort to challenge neoliberalism through the militant actions of a small group, rather than through the mass mobilization and self-emancipation of the exploited and oppressed themselves, was an inevitable failure.[15] But in the wake of the state murders during the *caracazo*, the attempted coup's bold challenge to the regime was well-received by the popular classes. Chávez was sent to prison for two years and was amnestied in 1994. In November 1992, a second failed coup occurred, but without the progressive veneer of the February attempt. "It was clear that a further uprising would have neither military feasibility nor popular support," notes historian D.L. Raby, "the strategy now had to be political" (Raby 2006: 156).

The Chávez Alternative in Lieu of a Revolutionary Left

The popular narrative of the Venezuelan Left today describes a steadily building wave of popular rebellions from the *caracazo* of 1989 to the two coup attempts of 1992. Yet, the spontaneous and relatively disorganized character of the *caracazo*, and the elitist military strategy of the 1992 events, actually signaled the weakness of the Venezuelan revolutionary Left during this period, and the relatively thin basis for organized, wide-scale, radical popular movements from below, compared to those that swept Bolivia between 2000 and 2005, for example.[16] This is not to suggest the total absence of Left traditions in the Venezuelan context, and their ongoing reverberations in formal and informal politics. While popular struggles from below in Venezuela never reached the historic depths of Bolivia and Ecuador, for example, in the twentieth century, there has been nonetheless an array of social movements and

Left formations active in the country in different periods that have received too little attention in existing historiography (Fernandes 2010: 39–63). As Dario Azzellini points out, eclectic traditions fused together over the course of the 1970s and 1980s:

> Many political, social and cultural movements of the most diverse types influenced the formation of the historical current in the 1970s and 1980s. Many of them were anti-authoritarian, anti-Stalinist, and linked to socialism's council tradition and to dissident voices within "party communism," be it pro-Soviet or pro-Chinese. The influences included Guevarism, Mariateguism, Trotskyism, and European workerism and autonomism. One would read and discuss Anton Pannekoek and Antonio Gramsci; workers' and autonomous popular movements arose. Also present were currents of liberation theology, of national liberation, and of indigenous and Afro-Venezuelan resistance. Insurrectional movements emerged in different social sectors. Over time, the concept of emancipator Bolivarianism was adopted by many organizations and movements with differing origins and histories. (Azzellini 2010: 14)

On an aggregate scale there were, by some accounts, roughly 5,000 protests in the first three years of neoliberal reforms (1989–91), but these were mainly restricted to community-based, localized and defensive strategies of the urban poor (Roberts 2003: 61). Likewise, the visible spread of neighbourhood council movements, some feminist organizing, social justice groups, environmental activism and human rights organizations later in the 1990s did not represent an offensive and organized challenge to capital but rather isolated defensive, local struggles.

The labour movement was also relatively quiescent, suffering structurally from the flexibilization and informalization of work and the dramatic changes to class structure wrought by neoliberal reforms. Politically, the labour movement was still overwhelmingly controlled by the Confederation of Venezuelan Workers (CTV), whose leadership quickly capitulated to the neoliberal regime.

La Causa Radical (The Radical Cause, LCR), with origins in the fledgling independent union movement of the late 1980s, appeared to represent an electoral alternative for the Left in the early 1990s. For example, the party's presidential candidate, Andrés Velásquez, won a surprising 22 percent in the 1993 elections (Ellner 1999). The party initially defended, "grass-roots democracy and bottom-up organizing based on the autonomy of working-class and popular communities." However, beginning in 1994 the party "allowed itself to be drawn into parliamentary horse-trading" with traditional, mainstream political parties, abandoning grass roots organizing and losing its main constituency (Raby 2006: 140, 144). By 1997, the party had split, with the larger contingent forming the *Patria Para Todos* (Fatherland for Everyone, PPT) (Gott 2005: 132). The splintering of the LCR, and the absence of any other serious Left alternative, provided political space for Chávez's *Movimiento Quinta República* (Fifth Republic Movement, MVR), the party that those in and around the MBR-200 had created to participate in the 1998 presidential elections.

Thus, we have a complex conjuncture at the close of the 1990s that is ultimately conducive to Chávez's electoral victory. Chávez won 56 percent of the popular vote in the December 1998 elections, taking office as president in 1999. The urban poor had responded to Chávez's "vitriolic attacks on the political establishment," just as "the middle and upper classes recoiled before the uncertain scope and depth of impending changes" (Roberts 2003: 55).

Class polarization was highly racialized, challenging the long-standing nationalist myth of Venezuelan racial democracy. According to national census figures, 67 percent of Venezuelans are *mestizos*, or mixed race, 10 percent are black, 21 percent are white and 2 percent are indigenous. "The esteem in which Chávez is held by the dark-skinned poor," Grandin suggests, "is amplified by the rage the Venezuelan president provokes among the white and the rich" (Grandin 2006). Chávez's self-identification as "Indian," "black" or "mixed-breed" infuses these terms with a novel sense of pride. When Chávez is critiqued by the Right as "Indian, monkey, and thick-lipped," this racial contempt serves to ally Chávez with the majority of the population that similarly identifies as "mixed breed," "Black," or "Indian" (Herrera Salas 2005). Class and racial identification thus combine in a form or populist support for Chávez.

Anti-Neoliberalism to Twenty-First-Century Socialism? Chávez's Trajectory

The New Constitution and Neoliberalism with a Human Face, 1999–2000
Chávez's 1998 electoral campaign and first two years in office were characterized by moderate socioeconomic proposals that failed to break with the basic neoliberal model.[17] Chávez did take a bold initiative in restoring power to the Organization of Petroleum Exporting Countries (OPEC), with lasting effects on state revenues. During the administration's first months, Alí Rodríguez Araque, the Minister of Oil and Mines, was sent on a series of diplomatic trips to member countries of the cartel, as well as to non-OPEC oil-producing states such as Mexico. An agreement to cut production was reached, and by the end of 1999 the price of oil had increased to $US25 per barrel from the historic low of $US9 per barrel in February of that year (Raby 2006: 161). The revived OPEC quotas for production, in conjunction

with the Iraq war, led to the steady rise of oil prices from that period until the recent global financial crisis.

Politically, the new government was more ambitious, convening a Constituent Assembly and a relatively participatory process of drawing up a new Constitution. The 1999 constitution, approved by a popular referendum, emphasizes that Venezuelan democracy is participatory and protagonistic, not merely representative, and states that human relations should be rooted in "equality of rights and duties, solidarity, common effort, mutual understanding, and reciprocal respect." It views as necessary "the participation of the people in forming, carrying out and controlling the management of public affairs." This participation will "ensure their complete development, both individual and collective" (quoted in Lebowitz 2006: 89).

The Constitution bans the privatization of the state-owned oil company, *Petróleos de Venezuela* (PDVSA) and includes language favourable to various economic, personal, cultural and environmental rights and protections. The state pledges that workers will have sufficient salaries to live dignified lives and explicitly recognizes unpaid work within the home—principally conducted by women—as an economic activity, which, in theory if not yet fully in practice, makes it eligible for social security (Grandin 2006). Additionally, the Bolivarian Constitution recognizes various indigenous rights and forbids foreign troops on Venezuelan soil. At the same time, the constitution does not protect women's right to abortion, nor does it include anti-discrimination on the basis of sexual diversity, although Chávez himself has pledged support for such rights (Webber 2004).

Yet the limitations are most starkly revealed in the economics sphere. The nation's twenty-seventh Constitution remains distant from anti-capitalism, guaranteeing the right of property (Article 115), supporting the role of private initiative in fostering economic growth and employment (Article 299), and promising state support for private initiatives (Article 112). The Constitution entrenches balanced budgets (over several years), and provides for the Venezuelan Central Bank's autonomy in monetary policy (Articles 311 and 318) (Lebowitz 2006: 90), an approach that assumes that bankers, not elected governments, should make critical economic decisions (Lebowitz 2008).

The early Chávez government's limited vision in the socio-economic sphere was evident in its first long-term development plan, published in 2001 as a guide for state policy through to 2007 (MPD 2001). The document presupposed that the best way to transform the Venezuelan economy was to attract "private capital, both domestic and foreign" through state interventions promoting financial stability, the creation of free trade zones, stable exchange rates, and a stock market to "create a growing democratisation of management capitalism," among other measures designed to reassure foreign investors (Lander and Navarrete 2007: 15).

The development plan reflected the neo-structural influence of the United Nations Economic Commission on Latin America and the Caribbean (ECLAC, or CEPAL in its Spanish acronym). Neo-structuralism is the Latin American equivalent of neo-Keynesianism in the advanced capitalist countries, a "third way" road adapting social democracy to the fundamental macroeconomic constraints of neoliberalism (Leiva 2008). At this stage of the Chávez presidency, Venezuela adhered to wider politico-economic developments across Latin America in the wake of the deep regional downturn (1999–2000) and the overwhelming de-legitimization of orthodox neoliberalism. But no real break with neoliberalism had occurred: "Without relinquishing its essential emphasis on the rationality of the market as the foremost organizing principle of social life, contemporary neoliberalism has dramatically broadened the scope of its social engineering in order to address its internal contradictions and attempt to mediate the ensuing social conflicts that have sharpened over the last 3 decades" (Taylor 2009: 23). Thus, targeted anti-poverty programs aimed at the most destitute have been introduced, without challenging neo-liberalism's fundamental ideological premises.

A number of commentaries from the international Left, published in journals like *Green Left Weekly, Venezuela Analysis, Monthly Review* and *Links*, have made bold retroactive assertions about the radicalizing nature of the Chávez regime as early as 1999 and 2000. But such analyses have been rooted in hopes and aspirations of the past few years rather than being based on actual developments of the period in question. Indeed, "Shortly after taking office in 1999, the Venezuelan president traveled to Wall Street to assure the moneymen of the 'credibility' of his government and its aims of a 'diversified' and 'self-sufficient economy,' as well as throwing the first pitch at a New York Yankees baseball game and ringing the bell at the New York Stock Exchange" (Sustar 2007: 19).

Counter-Revolution and the Awakening of Popular Power from Below, 2001–04
Nonetheless, the government's economic policy slowly changed beginning in 2001, with a new package of 49 laws, among them, the Organic Hydrocarbons Law, the Lands Law and the Fisheries Law. The hydrocarbons law re-established majority government ownership in the public-private companies in the principal oil operations of the country. The Lands Law opened idle land up to potential expropriation by the state. The Fisheries Law expanded the area off the shoreline from which major commercial trawlers were forbidden, and explicitly favoured small-scale fishers (Ellner 2008: 113).

All three were seen by Venezuela's right-wing opposition—composed of various political parties, the CTV, the business federation (FEDECAMARAS), the overwhelming majority of private print and TV media, right-wing student groups and the Catholic Church hierarchy, among other minority social forces—as potentially threatening fundamental private property rights. Led by FEDECAMARAS and CTV, the opposition initiated a concerted destabilization campaign with a two-month general strike that began in December 2001, followed shortly thereafter by the April 2002 coup, in which Chávez was temporarily ousted and FEDECAMARAS president Pedro Carmona declared the country's new leader.

All of this transpired with imperial backing (Golinger 2008: 13). Indeed, the United States government supported the coup, seeing Chávez as a threat for his outspoken comments on American imperial interventions in Afghanistan and the broader "war on terror," Chávez's support for a multi-polar world order, and his efforts to foment anti-imperialist consciousness and Latin American independence and solidarity across the region as against the unilateral project of U.S. imperial might. As mentioned above, Chávez did not directly threaten U.S. material interests, but the ideological and political threat of anti-imperialism was sufficient to warrant American support for reactionary forces, including destabilizing, right-wing non-governmental organizations (NGOs) operating within Venezuela.

Yet, as Leon Trotsky's observes, "a revolution needs from time to time the whip of the counter-revolution," which can provide "a powerful impetus to the radicalization of the masses" (Trotsky 2005 [1932]: 774). When word broke of the coup, "hundreds of thousands of poor Venezuelans poured down from the 'ranchos' [shantytowns]," and "surrounded the Presidential Palace, leading to division in the armed forces." A minority of right-wing military officers favoured "a massive bloodbath," whereas a majority rejected such measures, either out of loyalty to Chávez's Left-populist program or out of fear of a class-based civil war (Petras 2007).

The April 2002 mobilizations were of a scale and importance not witnessed since the *Caracazo*. They marked a turning point in which class struggle from below—albeit with a stronger populist than socialist flavour—erupted with new force as a response to right-wing counter-revolution (Robinson 2007). Rather than pushing ahead from this newly mobilized basis of support, however, Chávez moderated his rhetorical flourishes and offered concessions to the opposition in the wake of the coup: the Presidential Commission for a National Dialogue was established, bringing together coupist oppositional forces and the government; more radical officials in the Chávez government were replaced with known moderates; decentralization provisions of the 1999 Constitution that favoured right-wing possibilities in state governorships were brought forward on the agenda, and oil company executives at PDVSA fired prior to the coup were rehired by the President (Ellner 2008: 118).

The opposition proved uninterested in the government's goodwill gestures. The Right clung to the hope of throwing Chávez out altogether. "Following a brief period of uncertain calm," Gregory Wilpert points out, "the opposition interpreted Chávez's retreat as an opportunity for another offensive against him, this time by organizing an indefinite shutdown of the country's all important oil industry in early December 2002" (Wilpert 2007: 25). Rather than a "general strike," as the opposition labeled the actions, "it was actually a combination of management lockout, administrative and professional employee strike, and general sabotage of the oil industry." The business lockout was in part supported by the bourgeois fractions that had been created and sustained by national rentier capitalism following the 1970s nationalization of the oil industry. In solidarity with the rentier element, "[i]t was mostly the U.S. fast food franchises and the upscale shopping malls that were closed for about two months. The rest of the country operated more or less normally during this time, except for food and gasoline shortages throughout Venezuela, mostly because many distribution centers were closed down" (Wilpert 2007: 25).

In the short term, the oil lockout cost the Venezuelan economy $US6 billion (Grandin 2006). In the longer term, it generated new revenue for the Venezuelan government because once the lockout had been defeated, real state control of the oil industry was finally wrested from the hands of the old PDVSA elite: "Due to their subversive and saboteur attitude, around 18,000 upper and middle-level managers who opposed the government—and who actually exercised control of the company—created the conditions in which they could be legally dismissed" (Harnecker 2007: 181).

The defeat of the 2002–03 oil lockout had a major impact on the labour movement. Within the oil industry, skilled and unskilled workers restarted production with the assistance of technical personnel and from surrounding communities, "at a time when most high-ranking PDVSA employees had walked off the job." During the strike the "workers collectively chose their supervisors and took charge of the basic operational facet of the industry," setting "an important precedent" (Ellner 2008: 162, 187). The period of workers' control and self-management did not last long, but its significance is difficult to exaggerate (Sustar 2007: 20). Immediately following this example of workers' power, capacities, and commitment, a section of the labour movement pressured PDVSA for greater workers' control in the industry. However, "PDVSA heads adhered to a view… that the oil industry should avoid the types of worker participation being established in other state-controlled sectors due to its overwhelming importance to the nation's economy" (Ellner 2008: 162). In this they were ultimately backed by the government—one example of unevenness and contradiction in Chávez's commitments to socialism.

Also in this 2002–03 period of heightened class struggle, workers occupied a number of large- and medium sized enterprises claiming that the owners had locked them out without pay or severance benefits. Encapsulating the contradictions of *Chavismo*, "The government refused to dislodge the workers but also refrained from turning the companies over to worker management and instead deferred to the courts" (Ellner 2008: 124). Finally, at the end of these heated months, militant workers formed the National Union of Venezuelan Workers (UNT) as an alternative labour confederation to the Confederation of Venezuelan Workers (CTV). The CTV had collaborated with the state under the Punto Fijo system, capitulated to neoliberalism in the late 1980s and 1990s, and participated directly in the April 2002 coup attempt, and 2002–03 oil lockout. The UNT's formation in May 2003 became a pivotal space for debate around "issues of worker control, their workplaces and the role of unions" (Gindin 2005).

Having failed to depose Chávez through extra-parliamentary channels in 2002 and 2003, the Right exploited a new democratic opening established in the 1999 Bolivarian constitution: the right to force a recall referendum to determine whether or not the President finishes his or her term in office if 20 percent of the population, or 2.4 million people, express their desire to do so through a petition. By November 2003, the opposition had collected 3 million signatures, but the National Electoral Council (CNE) determined that only 1.9 million were valid, leaving the opposition less than a week to meet the deadline for required signatures. The government established a group of loyal militants under the title "*Comando Ayacucho*" to mobilize their base and raise consciousness, in order to prevent the opposition from gathering the necessary remaining signatures. Despite constant reassurances to the contrary, however, the *Comando Ayacucho* failed and a recall referendum was set for August 2004.

The struggle within Venezuelan society in the months leading up to the referendum revealed new strengths in autonomous working-class organization and initiative, this time in the popular *barrios*, or poor neighbourhoods, of the capital city. There is undoubtedly a level of mutually reinforcing synergy between the popular movements in the barrios and the figure of Chávez. Nonetheless, the former have "realized the need to chart an independent trajectory from the Chávez government, of 'oficialismo'… to defend the interests of their community and sustain their projects.'" Indeed, community activists felt "shocked and betrayed by the *Comando Ayacucho*," when they heard the news that a recall referendum would be held. They strategically co-operated with vertically-oriented structures but insisted on the role of autonomous community organizations in mobilizing to defeat the referendum, as this passage describes:

> In a series of local assemblies in La Vega, 23 de Enero, and other barrios, community leaders emphasized the need for self-organization, saying that barrio residents could not rely on the government and officially appointed committees to organize "on their behalf"….

> In the lead up to the referendum, local networks and activists were key in organizing popular sectors in support of the "No" campaign to keep Chávez in office. Chávez replaced the Comando Ayacucho with the Comando Maisanta, and a vertically-organized structure of local units known as Unidades de Batallas Electorales (UBEs). Community groups co-operated with the UBEs and at times even incorporated into them, but for the most part these were tactical and temporary groupings to win the referendum. The driving force behind the "No" campaign came from organized community activists, who launched an aggressive campaign to register and mobilize voters to vote in the referendum. Community organizers set up Voter Registration Centers in all the parishes, and these were staffed around the clock by teams of local activists. Barrio-based radio and television stations and newspapers devoted space to explaining the importance of the referendum and encouraging people to vote for Chávez.... Rather than Chávez's charisma, his subsidized social programs, or the ineptitude of the opposition, the decisive factor in Chávez's ultimate victory was the mobilizing role played by local barrio organizations. (Fernandes 2007a: 18)

In the event, Chávez defeated the opposition by 58 to 42 percent. This result, later combined with the opposition's disastrous boycott of the December 2005 congressional elections, strengthened the government's hand and ushered in a new phase of the administration, characterized by increasingly radical rhetoric, and a series of anti-neoliberal, if not socialist measures.[18]

Where's the Revolutionary Democracy?
The Grassroots and the PSUV

In early 2005 Chávez first declared his commitment to twenty-first-century socialism at the World Social Forum in Brazil. What is meant by that phrase has taken on somewhat more developed programmatic content since, but in 2005 it was especially vague: a new socialism, as distinct from the failed projects of the same name in the twentieth century. It would be more decentralized, more democratic, less state-centred and committed to "establishing liberty, equality, social justice, and solidarity." While a bold move to reclaim the term socialism, its opacity made it "indistinguishable from most other social projects of the twentieth and twenty-first century," that promised the same things (Wilpert 2007: 7).

What is clear is that over the course of 2005 and 2006 the special mission programs in health and education established in 2003—erected parallel to the existing structures of the old state apparatus in these fields—were widened and deepened. Co-management, allowing for workers' representation on state company boards was extended beyond certain aspects of the corporatist structures seen in European social democracies in a limited number of companies. In the state aluminum company, ALCASA, for example, there was labour and community participation in the drawing up of the 2006 budget. Likewise, in early 2005 the state expropriated the paper company VENEPAL, changing its name to the Venezuelan Endogenous Paper Industry, or INVEPAL. Valve and tube companies were also expropriated. By the end of 2005, INVEPAL was a worker-run co-operative.[19] Land reform also advanced in 2005, with the government dividing up some large estates owned by domestic and foreign agro-capitalists. These were distributed to landless peasants.

The existing tax system, long ignored by many businesses, was enforced, generating new revenue for the state outside of oil rents. In urban land reform, the state devolved some power to urban land committees (CTUs) first been established in 2002. By mid-2005, over six thousand CTUs, made up of residents in poor urban neighbourhoods, were in operation. They were authorized to survey their shantytowns, distribute land titles, and collectively generate ideas and designs for public and recreational spaces in their communities.[20]

In 2005 and 2006, the government extended the "social economy," including "redistribution of wealth (via land reform programs and social policies), promotion of co-operatives, creation of nuclei of endogenous development, industrial co-management, and social production enterprises" (Wilpert 2007: 77). By some accounts, the number of co-operatives expanded from 762 in 1998 to more than 100,000 by 2005 (Wilpert 2007: 77). Many of these registered co-operatives however, never actually got up and running, and were a major area of corruption and government revenue loss.[21]

In the December 2006 elections, Chávez was re-elected to another six-year term with 63 percent of the popular vote. With a new mandate and the opposition at its weakest level in years, the President signaled a radicalization of the Bolivarian Process with the announcement of the "five motors" of twenty-first-century socialism in January 2007. These included: an "enabling law" giving the executive new legislative power for a set period of time so as to speed up the transition to socialism; a reform of the 1999 Bolivarian Constitution to amend sections to help establish twenty-first-century socialism; a campaign of political and social education and consciousness-raising called "Morality and Enlightenment," to be carried out by community councils in communities and workplaces; revisions of the country's political and territorial units to redistribute power more equitably on geographic terms throughout the country's cities, states and countryside; and, fifth, what was deemed "the revolutionary explosion of communal power," devolving economic, social, political, and democratic power to the communal councils (Harnecker 2007: 187–88).

Chávez called for the creation of a United Socialist Party of Venezuela (PSUV) as an umbrella for all parties supporting his government—his own MVR, the PPT, Podemos, the PCV and roughly twenty other micro-parties. Further, he promised that key sectors of the Venezuelan economy would be nationalized, beginning with the telecommunications, energy and oil production sectors. The formerly state-owned telephone company CANTV was re-nationalized, as were the regional-based electricity companies throughout the country. Most crucially, the government announced the nationalization of the only oil fields in the country that continued under private control, those of the Orinoco Oil Belt. These nationalizations entailed the movement of state control from minority to majority share-holding status and billions of dollars in compensation to multinational corporations. The nationalizations failed to incorporate the essential socialist ingredient of workers' control, democracy and self-management. A series of new nationalizations since 2009 have once again sparked debate around workers' control, and left-wing trade unions and various workers' collectives began to struggle with renewed intensity for this objective (Touissant 2010). Gustavo Martínez, a union activist in a worker-controlled coffee factory in Caracas remarks:

> My vision of the role of workers' control, essentially, is that in order to push forward the revolution, to advance toward an authentic transition to socialism, the means of production have to be in the hands of the workers. And the chances of our success in achieving this, is going to depend, above all, on the level of consciousness of the workers, and the level of commitment to achieving workers' control among the workers themselves…. Because we've seen what happened elsewhere, when workers' control and workers' democracy were defeated and replaced with bureaucracy. In the Soviet Union a new bureaucracy was created which crushed the soviets themselves. What existed in the Soviet Union wasn't socialism; it was a brutal, Stalinist bureaucracy. And we don't want that to happen here, so we're working very hard to build consciousness around workers' control and workers' democracy.[22]

Gonzalo Gómez also sees workers' control as central to any authentic project of building socialist democracy:

> Workers' control is important from the perspective of democracy. It helps workers overcome their sense of alienation, to be considered a creative person whose opinion matters. Dignity is related to so much more than one's salary; it touches on fundamental aspects of our humanity. Workers' control is about having influence, feeling like

one is more than a machine that simply follows orders. It is about being a member of a collective.[23]

While the nationalizations initiated by the Chávez government in these years were critically excluded the prospect of workers' control in strategic sectors of the economy, they nevertheless signaled a radicalization of government policy (Wilpert 2007: 219–23).

Most important in this radicalization were the proposed amendments to the 1999 Bolivarian Constitution. On December 2, 2007 Venezuelans participated in another referendum, in which they had the opportunity to ratify or reject sixty-nine constitutional changes, thirty-three proposed by Chávez, and 36 drafted by the National Assembly. Among the progressive characteristics of the proposed reforms were the reduction of the work week to thirty-six hours; elimination of the autonomy of the Central Bank; requirement of gender parity in positions of public office; recognition of Afro-Venezuelan groups; reduction of the voting age from eighteen to sixteen; recognition and increased funding for Councils of Popular Power, including student, peasant and workers' councils, as well as co-operatives and community enterprises; state promotion of a new economic model, based in humanism and co-operation, and introducing legal recognition of various forms of social, communal and state property, as well as state promotion of social forms of production and distribution and mixed public-private enterprises (Fernandes 2007b). This conglomeration of amendments still recognized the legality of privately-owned capitalist enterprises but undoubtedly represented an advance on the 1999 scenario.

When the referendum amendments were defeated by a margin of roughly 200,000 votes, with an abstention rate of 45 percent, it represented a major political blow to the Chávez government. The process of change has been insufficiently democratic and top-down, based increasingly on the personification of twenty-first-century socialism in Chávez, rather than in the revolutionary practice, initiative and the popular power of the exploited and oppressed. These fundamental shortcomings in strategy, ideology and orientation—a consequence of both a lack of commitment to revolutionary democracy within the dominant currents of the Chávez government and the simultaneous absence of a sufficiently powerful socialist rather than populist working-class base of support—bled into some ill-considered content in the proposed amendments.

The proposal to extend the presidential term from six to seven years, and the elimination of the two-term limit is an example of the misguided nature of many reforms. This has confused sections of the radical Left. On the one hand, the imperialist and domestic Venezuelan Right is hypocritical when they argue that this amendment signaled the death of democracy in the country and the advance of totalitarian communism. None of these pundits question the democratic character of consecutive terms in office for the executive power in multiple European and North American states (Petras 2007). And clearly, Chávez is no dictator, immediately accepting the referendum defeat in December 2007 and congratulating his opponents.

On the other hand, the "low-level personality cult that exists around Chávez is an obstacle to the full implementation of the Bolivarian project" (Wilpert 2007: 200). As a number of revolutionary socialists inside Venezuela have suggested in relation to the presidential term extension: "The important thing should not be such a possibility, but changes making it possible to advance towards a more democratic regime, which instead of continuing to invent new tasks and responsibilities within the executive power, legitimates the power of the workers' and peoples' organizations, envisages that they should have majority representation in a new Parliament, extends the possibilities of recall by the voters, in an immediate way and for all functions, and defends at all levels of political and economic decision the right of the people to express themselves and to decide" (Peres Borges, García and Vivas 2008).

"At a moment when the context made it possible to go much further, to undertake a reform by establishing spaces of dialogue and power all over the country," Fernando Esteban observes, "Chávez threw down a challenge to the entire Bolivarian and revolutionary movement, forcing it to be with him or against him." The line was: "To vote No is to vote for Bush, to vote Yes is to vote for Chávez" (Esteban 2008). While the content of the reforms was broadly progressive, and threatening to capital and the various right-wing opposition forces, it was developed without participation by the popular classes. Indeed, Chávez drafted the proposals with the participation of a small, select group of advisers personally chosen by him (Fernandes 2007b). "Until the government's defeat in the referendum held in December 2007," Steve Ellner (2010: 83) suggests, "the Chávista movement consistently postponed internal debate and self-criticism."

Since Chávez's reelection in December 2006, the founding of the United Socialist Party of Venezuela (PSUV) and the role of expanding communal councils have been the most important political and organizational questions for the Venezuelan Left. The PSUV is full of internal contradictions, and has developed into the battle ground between the Right and Left *within* the Bolivarian process. On the one hand, there are the radical aspirations and impressive organizational capacities of the grassroots militants of the party, and the fact that the party quickly grew to over four million members soon after its founding July 2007—although clearly with different levels of participation among the membership. A number of revolutionary socialists became delegates to the party's congress in March 2008, while others have played essential roles in the local battalions of the party on an ongoing basis. Activists formerly involved in different revolutionary parties have committed themselves to constructing the PSUV, building Left currents within the party against more bureaucratic, opportunistic and right-wing components. The Assembly of Socialists, for example, managed to congeal more than 20 revolutionary organizations in November 2006. Another revolutionary current within the PSUV is *Marea Socialista*, or Socialist Wave, formed by Leftists of a Trotskyist background who were formerly involved in the Party of Revolution and Socialism, and heavily influential within the UNT (Fuentes 2008).

The party's congress in March 2008 illustrated the depth of seriousness with which conservative and bureaucratic layers within the *Chavismo* sought to domesticate and control the party's formation, program, and trajectory. Fernando Esteban describes some of the early setbacks with regard to electing the party leadership:

> The first stage consisted of designating the members who had the right to vote. Out of 5 million members, only 80,000 could vote, without anyone knowing on what criteria this choice was based. In a second stage, once the 35 members of the national leadership had been elected, Chávez designated on live TV the members of the political bureau. There you can only find members of the government, and there are not representatives of the social or trade union movement. (Esteban 2008)

Yet there continues to be space in the party for the revolutionary Left and its attempts to roll back corruption, bureaucracy and alliances with the so-called national bourgeoisie.

Militants of the Socialist Wave defend their participation within PSUV, refusing to relegate themselves to the extreme margins of the principal popular struggle occurring in the country, a struggle likely to determine the country's trajectory. By actively participating in assemblies, presenting radical proposals, responding to the interests of the rank and file and uniting with other Left currents they hope to contribute to the radicalization of PSUV, turning it in an explicitly anti-capitalist direction and protecting the party against top-down, bureaucratic, and even militaristic, lines of hierarchy and control (Peres Borges, García and Vivas 2008). The ultimate fate of the Venezuelan experiment will be the balance of forces within *chavismo*, between those in favour of democratic revolutionary socialism from below, and those bureaucratizing the process and cementing their privileges from above.

Social Indicators and the Economy

The social advances of the Bolivarian process are important. According to the latest figures from the United Nations Economic Commission for Latin America and the Caribbean, Venezuela reduced its poverty and extreme poverty rates from 48.6 and 22.2 percent of the population respectively in 2002, to 28.5 and 8.5 percent by 2007 (CEPAL 2008: 16). The proportion of people living in poverty fell from 48.6 percent in 2002, to 30.2 percent in 2006, down to 28.5 percent in 2007. In 2006 alone, as a consequence of sharp surges in social spending, the poverty rate fell from 37.1 percent to 30.2 percent (CEPAL 2007: 18).

Yet, these trends are typical advances of centre-left regimes elsewhere in the region over the same period, a consequence of the conjunctural primary commodity boom in Latin America between 2003 and 2007. For example, the urban areas of Argentina under Nestor Kirchner's government registered a decline in poverty and extreme poverty from 45.4 and 20.9 percent respectively in 2002, to 21 and 7.2 percent in 2006. In 2000, Chile had a poverty rate of 20.2 percent, while the extreme poverty level was 5.6 percent. By 2006, those figures had fallen to 13.7 and 3.2 percent respectively. What is more, Venezuela's poverty rate of 28.5 percent in 2007 continues to compare poorly to Chile's 13.7 (2006), Costa Rica's 18.6 (2007), and Uruguay's 18.1 (2007) (CEPAL 2008: 16).

Nonetheless, the Venezuelan figures, because they only measure income poverty, substantially underestimate the Chávez administration's advances in poverty reduction more broadly through large-scale improvements in the social wage of the working class, i.e., social services. And by 2009, some economists argue, poverty had been reduced by 47 percent and extreme poverty by 70 percent (Weisbrot and Ray 2010: 4). Various mission programs that bypass bureaucratic and unco-operative state structures are the principal means of delivering these social services. *Barrio Adentro* provides free health care to the poor through the assistance of tens of thousands of Cuban doctors and the establishment of new community clinics; *Mercal* is a state distributor of food at subsidized prices; *Robinson 1 and 2* are missions focusing on literacy and primary education for adults; *Ribas* and *Sucre* target secondary and university education for individuals who never had the opportunity to attend or those who dropped out; and *Vuelvan Caras* provides state-funded training for employment and the creation of workers' co-operatives (López Maya 2007: 165).

Some results are impressive. In 2005, for example, UNESCO declared that Venezuela was "a territory freed from illiteracy" (Esteban 2008). The figures on health care are also remarkable:

In 1998 there were 1,628 primary care physicians for a population

> of 23.4 million. Today, there are 19,571 for a population of 27 million. In 1998 there were 417 emergency rooms, 74 rehab centers and 1,628 primary care centers compared to 721 emergency rooms, 445 rehab centers, and 8,621 primary care centers (including the 6,500 "check-up points," usually in poor neighbourhoods, and that are in the process of being expanded to more comprehensive care centers) today. Since 2004, 399,662 people have had antiretroviral treatment from the government, compared to 18,538 in 2006. (Weisbrot and Sandoval 2007: 9)

This spending is contingent on massive oil rents unique to Venezuela in the Latin American and Caribbean context. From the first quarter of 2003, following the end of the oil lockout, to the second quarter of 2008, Gross Domestic Product (GDP) grew 94.7 percent, an incredible annual rate of 13.5 percent (Weisbrot, Ray, and Sandoval 2009: 6).

Social democratic commentators emphasize that "in spite of the expansion of government during the Chávez years, the private sector has grown faster than the public sector," with finance and insurance at the leading edge (Weisbrot, Ray and Sandoval 2009: 7). Absolute figures for social spending have been very high, but public social spending as a percentage of gross national product has not been impressive relative to the rest of Latin America. In the year 2004–05, for example, Argentina, Bolivia, Brazil, Chile, Colombia, Costa Rica and Cuba all showed higher rates of public social spending as a percentage of gross national product than Venezuela (CEPAL 2007: 132).

From the time the Chávistas came to power until 2002, the share of national income going to the richest 10 percent of the population fell minimally, while the share going to the bottom 40 percent decreased marginally. In 1999 the richest 10 percent of the population received 31.4 percent of national income and in 2002, 31.3 percent. Meanwhile, the poorest 40 percent received only 14.5 percent of the national income in 1999 and by 2002, just 14.3 percent. "The more than twofold increase in automobile sales in 2007 and the large number of new SUVs visible in middle-class neighbourhoods," Steve Ellner points out, "put in evidence the improved purchasing power of the well-to-do" (Ellner 2010: 90).

This situation has since improved, but there has hardly been a revolutionary wealth transfer. Income inequality as measured by the Gini index fell from 46.96 to 40.99 between 1999 and 2008. As a comparison, between 1980 and 2005 the United States experienced an accelerated concentration of wealth upwards, from 40.3 to 46.9 as measured by the Gini index (Weisbrot, Ray and Sandoval 2009: 10). Between 2002 and 2007 the share of income going to the bottom 40 percent of households rose to 18.4 from 14.3 percent, and the share going to the top 10 percent of households fell from 31.3 to 25.7

(CEPAL 2008: 231). In 2007, across Latin American countries, the poorest 40 percent of households on average received 15 percent of total income, and only in Uruguay did they receive more than 20 percent (CEPAL 2008: 75). Measured by Gini coefficient, today Venezuela has the least unequal distribution of income in Latin America (Weisbrot and Ray 2010: 4).

Huge concentrations of personal wealth and privilege remain untouched by the Bolivarian process. Almost 30 percent of the population live in poverty by ECLAC's measurements, which underestimate poverty. As one analyst suggests, "[a]ny serious attempt to make Venezuelan society more egalitarian—let alone socialist—would begin with a radically progressive tax system aimed at redistributing wealth" (Sustar 2007: 24). How this might be done has become radically more complex in a ravaged global economy. Leading socialist-feminist PSUV member, and president of the Women's Development Bank, Lidice Navas, reflects on the distance left to travel on the road toward socialism:

> There is so much yet to be done. First, we have to strengthen popular power. Only the people can lead the people. We need a public that is organized and prepared. Socialism cannot be based upon exclusion. Everyone needs to be included in all of the plans. Everyone needs to be included as a productive subject, to be capable of improving their quality of life. You can't have socialism if there is hunger. You can't have socialism without health. You can't have socialism without workers, but the form of work has to be transformative and advance the human being…. Second, you can't have socialism without democracy, a democracy in which the people are the protagonists. This implies the participation of the people with everyone organized. We can't solve our problems as individuals. Solutions have to be for all. Since the problems are infinite and the resources are finite, solutions have to be found by coordinating the actions of the state and the community.[24]

The Global Crisis and Venezuela

By April 2008, the International Monetary Fund (IMF) suggested that we were witnessing the largest financial crisis in the United States since the Great Depression. However, as David McNally has observed, this suggestion underestimated the scale of the crisis. First, while originating in the U.S., the crisis is global. Second, the crisis is no longer narrowly financial, but deeply impacting the "real economy." "Having started in the construction-, auto- and electronics-sectors," he observes, "the slump is now sweeping through all manufacturing industries and spilling across the service-sector" (McNally 2009: 36). Bankruptcies, factory closures and layoffs are a response to over-accumulation—over 250,000 jobs have been lost in the North American automobile industry alone. Waves of downsizing in non-financial corporations feed the under-consumption dynamic of this crisis. "As world demand and world-sales dive," McNally points out, "the effects of overcapacity (factories, machines, buildings that cannot be profitably utilized), which have been masked by credit-creation over the past decade, will kick in with a vengeance" (McNally 2009: 37). Typically for the world capitalist system, we are increasingly witnessing the "geographical displacement of crisis: attempting to offload the worst impacts onto those outside the core" (Hanieh 2009: 61).

From the vantage point of late 2010, the suggestion of Luiz Inácio Lula da Silva, President of Brazil, that the crisis would not seriously affect Latin America appears deeply naïve (Cárdenas 2008). The slowdown of the 2003–07 commodity-driven boom deepened in Latin America over the first two quarters of 2008 (Ocampo 2009: 705). The significant accumulation of foreign exchange reserves and reduction of dollar-denominated public debt during the boom years provided a temporary cushioning of the global crisis in Latin America, but this situation is unlikely to matter if the world recession turns into a prolonged slump. "The budget surpluses are temporary stopgaps to finance some stimulus packages," James Petras notes, "but they are totally insufficient to reverse the fall in all export sectors, the drying up of private credit and the drying up of new local/foreign investment. In fact the first sign and substance of growing recessionary tendencies is the large outflows of capital by investors anticipating the crisis" (Petras 2009).

The drop in world trade had already made itself felt by mid-2008; and then commodity prices simply collapsed after September of the same year. Export revenues for the region contracted at an annualized rate of 30 percent in the final quarter of 2008, having a severe impact on GDP growth (Ocampo 2009: 708). The effects of collapsing remittance flows have been uneven across different Latin American countries based on fragmentary evidence, but are likely to inflict increasing pain on the popular classes over time as right-wing fueled xenophobia, "draconian restrictions on the movement of migrant-labour," and "tighter control and regulation of the movement of labour" in the countries of the Global North deepen and expand (McNally 2009: 78; Hanieh 2009: 73).

In Venezuela, the plunge in energy prices has been the most important element of the crisis. Oil accounts for 90 percent of the country's exports and more than half of government revenues (*The Economist* 2008; Mander 2008). In July 2008, crude had reached the remarkable world market price of $US147 per barrel. By December that year it collapsed to just $US32.40. In 2009 it slowly rose back to $US73 in early June 2009 amid mainstream-economist optimism regarding so-called "green shoots" in the world economy, and Chinese strategic stockpiling. As stunningly bad U.S. job figures came out later that month, however, the green shoots wilted, and oil prices fell to $US66 (McCarthy 2009). The immediate fall in revenues for the Venezuelan government potentially threatens many social programs domestically and abroad. Following six years of breakneck growth, the Venezuelan economy sunk into a steep recession in 2009, with the economy shrinking by 3.3 percent over the year (Weisbrot and Ray 2010: 4). Figures available for the second quarter of 2010 suggest that the recession was relatively short-lived, and a modest recovery is afoot (ibid.: 5).

Yet, this is an opportune moment for the Venezuelan process to reconcile its most profound internal contradictions, pushed by organized socialists in the labour movement, radical social movements of the urban poor, and radical currents within the PSUV itself. Until now, oil rents have lubricated a system of moderate redistribution to the popular classes without serious attack on the concentrated assets of a tiny elite and the ongoing expansion of the private sector. To defend and expand social programs, and to move forward with a multifaceted transition to socialism, a radical new wave of class struggle from below will be required. This struggle will face opposition from the Right, which will use the crisis to seek to destabilize the Chávez regime, with the assistance of imperialist powers. Within *Chavismo*, bureaucratic conservative layers will defend a state-capitalist response to exiting the crisis, rather than deepening shifts toward a transition to socialism.

The Venezuelan internal struggles will have repercussions for the Latin American Left. The bold revitalization of ALBA, as a means of deepening South-South links throughout Latin America, will require Venezuela's lead. Whether projects like Banco del Sur (Bank of the South) take on *socialist* forms, such as providing funds to finance land reform and improvements in the lives of the popular classes region-wide, or whether reforms will subsidize the survival of local ruling classes to improve their chances of competing with international rivals, will ultimately depend on the trajectory of class struggle, not least in Venezuela (Katz 2009).

Neoliberal ideology suffered massive setbacks in Latin America during the last major regional recession (1998–2002), and during the uptick in radical popular movements between 2000 and 2005.[25] With the rise of different centre-left governments in much of the region, social movements have subsequently subsided, with some having been co-opted into state machinery. At the same time, the extreme Right holds onto power in countries like Colombia, Mexico and Peru.

The Left internationally has a responsibility to expose the failings of the global capitalist system, but the Latin American Left in particular has the most potential to seize the moment, given the expansion and consolidation of anti-neoliberal and anti-imperialist consciousness among much of the population over the last decade. A subjective shift from anti-neoliberalism and anti-imperialism toward revolutionary socialism from below is the urgent necessity of the day (Katz 2007). "The current gap between favourable objective economic condition," Petras suggests, "and the under-development of (subjective) revolutionary socialist consciousness is probably a temporary phenomena: The 'lag' can be overcome by the direct intervention of conscious socialist political formations deeply inserted in everyday struggles capable of linking economic conditions to political action" (Petras 2009).

The Bolivarian Revolutionary process must be defended against imperialism, particularly through solidarity with independent labour and popular community movements of the urban and rural poor that insist that authentic socialism comes from below, from the exploited and oppressed themselves. Support must be given to those who defend Chávez against each and every imperialist and counter-revolutionary measure, but who never hesitate to organize beyond the horizons of the conservative and bureaucratic layers within *Chavismo*; who denounce government capitulations to the interests of domestic and foreign capital; who insist on the independence of the working class from state control; and who call for a thoroughgoing transition to a profoundly democratic socialism, rooted in the social ownership of the means of production, worker and community control and self-management in all the spheres of social, political and economic life, and the democratic social coordination of the economy.

Notes

1. This chapter is based in part on fieldwork carried out in Venezuela in August and September 2008 and June 2010. All interviews in 2010 were carried out together with Susan Spronk, who also provided valuable insights on the current Venezuelan conjuncture during our many conversations. Chávista government officials and rank-and-file activists were interviewed in Mérida and Caracas, and the author toured two Nuclei of Endogenous Sustainable Development (Nudes) and various radicalized barrios in Caracas, as well as popular community radio stations, and several health and education missions set up by the Chávez government. I presented an early draft of the paper at the International Institute for Research and Education (IIRE) in Amsterdam, as part of the Returns of Marxism Lecture Series. Thanks to everyone who attended the talk for the fruitful discussion and debate, especially Antonio Carmona Báez, Peter Thomas and Sara Farris. David Camfield also provided useful feedback on an earlier draft. Many thanks also to Elaine Coburn for her comments, editing and suggestions on earlier drafts, as well as to Henry Veltmeyer and Tom Brass for their editorial and substantive advice. A shorter version of this chapter was published in 2010 in *Socialist Studies* 6, 1.

2. This thesis needs to be qualified in two respects. First, there were clearly socialist currents and individuals across the world for which socialism did not fade from the agenda after 1989. In other words, it did not require the election of Chávez to rekindle their commitment to socialism. Nonetheless, the wider ideological impact of the rise of Chávez on opening up new discussions of socialism to wider layers of people internationally must be recognized. Second, signalling the importance of

Chávez's election in 1998 should not be taken to mean that there was no preceding opposition to neoliberalism. In the Latin American context, the Zapatista uprising in Mexico in 1994, and the growth of the Landless Rural Workers Movement (MST) in Brazil throughout the 1990s, are two important examples of such resistance predating the Chávez phenomenon.

3. Personal interview, Caracas, June 15, 2010.

4. Ibid.

5. Ibid.

6. Ibid.

7. On U.S. imperialism in Venezuela over the course of the Bush presidency, see Golinger 2006, 2007.

8. For exemplary commentary from Secretary of State Hilary Clinton, see Henao 2009 and Suggett 2009.

9. Thanks to an anonymous reviewer for calling my attention to this point.

10. Iran's Mahmoud Ahmadinejad is an example of a reactionary government opposed to U.S. power. Chávez's unconditional support for Ahmadinejad's regime as it ferociously repressed mass demonstrations in the streets of Tehran and elsewhere in June and July 2009 was a travesty that revealed the deeply flawed understandings of socialist internationalism within his government.

11. See, especially, the Venezuelan magazine *Marea Socialista*.

12. This process was not unique to Venezuela. Mike Davis (2006) charts trends of accelerated proletarianization of the peasantry throughout the Third World in the neoliberal age, as well as the rise of an "informal proletariat" and the proliferation of shantytowns in his book, *Planet of Slums*.

13. Personal interview, Oscar González, coordinator of the Organization of Social Movements for Popular Power, in the Mérida branch of the new *Partido Socialista Unido de Venezuela* (United Socialist Party of Venezuela, PSUV), September 5, 2008, Mérida, Venezuela.

14. For one account, see Gott 2005: 63–70.

15. As Rosa Luxemburg argued in the course of the revolutionary events in Germany in 1918 and 1919, "The socialist revolution is the first which is in the interests of the great majority and can be brought to victory only by the great majority of the working people themselves." And elsewhere: "Socialism will not and cannot be created by decrees; nor can it be created by any government, however socialistic. Socialism must be created by the masses, by every proletarian. Where the chains of capitalism are forged, there they must be broken. Only that is socialism, and only thus can socialism be created" (quoted in McNally 2006: 348).

16. On Bolivia, see, in particular Hylton and Thomson 2007, Webber 2010 and Gutiérrez Aguilar 2008.

17. The periodization, if not always the characterization, of the different stages of the Chávez government in this section corresponds closely to Ellner 2008 and Lander and Navarrete 2007.

18. Here I concur with Susan Spronk: "While Chávez—arguably the one of the most radical leaders of the 'Pink Tide'—speaks passionately about alternatives to capitalism, his actions in the first ten years of the Bolivarian Revolution have indicated that the primary goal of his 'twenty-first century socialism' has been the construction of a capitalist welfare state with pockets of co-operativism on the margins of the economy." See Spronk 2011.

19. Kiraz Janicke explains how "Venezuela's recovered factories, despite having the

support of the Chávez government, are in essence faced with the same problems of the recovered factories in Argentina: how to survive in a sea of capitalist economic relations, how to ensure supply of raw materials, how to ensure a buyer for the finished product. INVEPAL is suffering from both of these problems" (Janicke 2007).

20. This section draws heavily from Ellner 2008: 121–26.

21. This is clear, for example, in the following assessment: "The failure of mass numbers of state-financed co-operatives—due to improvisation or, worse yet, misuse of government funds—has translated into the loss of tens or hundreds of millions of dollars. While many co-operatives never got off the ground, in other cases co-operative members ended up pocketing the money received from loans or the down payments for contracts prior to the initiation of work" (Ellner 2008: 130).

22. Personal interview, Caracas, June 10, 2010.

23. Personal interview, Caracas, June 15, 2010.

24. Personal interview, June 18, 2010.

25. See, among many others, Robinson 2008.

11

Socialism or Barbarism?

James Petras and Henry Veltmeyer

The fundamental issue addressed by this book is the problem of building socialism in the 21st century under the conditions and growing barbarism of a system in crisis. Historically this dichotomy (barbarism or socialism) was resolved via: (1) the conquest of the state and (2) the socialist transformation of the economy and the society by means of state power and the active mobilization of the working classes. The form that socialism subsequently took—and it took various forms, some actualized, others not—and the successful transition from capitalism to socialism in some contexts and the failure in others, were contingent on changing conditions. Material and objective conditions and their effects on subjective and political consciousness as well as the correlation of class forces and the particular conjuncture of these conditions effected the transition to socialism. Today, the problem of building socialism is very different, particularly the changed conditions of capitalist development (neoliberal globalization) and the added dimension of having to rebuild it under conditions of the collapse, some two decades ago, of a particular form of socialism. Because conditions today are manifestly different than they were in the twentieth century this complicates the terms for bringing about socialism—the question of "what can be done" under these conditions?

Because the fundamental problem of building socialism today under existing conditions of capitalist development is different than it was in the twentieth century, the challenge is to determine the particular mix and precise conjuncture of objective and subjective conditions that permit or facilitate actions that might lead towards socialism. In terms of this problematic, the fundamental issue remains the same: do socialists wait upon the maturation of objective conditions created by the inherent contradictions of the system—its "eternal verities" (propensity towards crisis, etc.)—to bring about the transition towards socialism? Or do they determine what "needs to be done" under available conditions, and create the necessary conditions.[1]

In this chapter we reflect on this question, taking particular account of recent and current developments in North America and Latin America. The conclusion that we come to and the argument advanced is that the world faces—the dilemma and fundamental choice identified by Rosa Luxemburg some 95 years ago in conditions of another class war: *socialism or barbarism*. The barbaric conditions of capitalist development, advanced in the form of imperialist militarism and neoliberal globalization, by no means make socialism inevitable but they do make it possible and urgent.

There is much talk and writing these days about the "global financial crisis" notwithstanding the fact that the crisis is neither global in scope nor financial in nature. The "financialization" of capitalist development and the deregulation of the global movement of capital, together with an enormous expansion of fictitious and speculative forms of capital, have brought about belated but apparently fruitless efforts by the guardians of the imperial world order to discipline the excessive greed and overweening search for profit by the financial elite that dominates the global economy. However, if the system is in crisis it is not because of the instability of capital markets or the lack of liquidity and credit, but because of the incapacity of the imperialist system in meeting the basic needs of more than a billion people worldwide exploited and dispossessed by the system, and in securing the legitimacy of its governing myths. In this connection we argue that imperialist development is pushing the system to its limits, creating barbaric social conditions and the emergence of diverse forces on the Left, while encouraging a regrouping on the Right.

The correlation of these forces need to be assessed. But it is safe to assert that they cut both to the Left, in different albeit unorchestrated efforts to overthrow the system, and to the Right, in a concerted effort to intensify the power and concentrate wealth in the capitalist class. The political centre here is concerned to stave of pressures on the Left for positive changes and unbridled capitalism and blind reaction to the Right.

This project of the "political centre" is to save capitalism from itself, from the barbarism of a system pushed to its extreme limits. This relates to and is based on a "post-Washington Consensus" on the need to "create a better balance between the market and the state" (Ocampo 2006, 2007) and to bring about a more "inclusive form of development" (Sunkel and Infante 2010) via the agency of what is perceived as "global social democracy."

A System in Crisis

One of the verities of capitalism (see Veltmeyer 2010) is a propensity towards crisis, which inevitably leads to a weakening of the ruling class and the emergence of mass movements and the opportunity to transform the capitalist system. The most recent manifestation of capitalist crises is the so-called "global financial meltdown," which by some accounts was triggered by the sub-prime mortgage debacle in the United States. A closer look at this crisis, however, reveals, first of all, that it is not at all global. Second, its roots are located in the production crisis of the early 1970s, and in the financialization of the economies of the U.S., U.K. and E.U. in the 1980s, conditions in which the doctrines of "economic freedom" released the capitalist class from the regulatory constraints of the welfare-development state. The crisis extends beyond the speculative economy resulting from the process of deregulated capitalist development. The result is a multifaceted production crisis, with permutations in different parts of the world effecting diverse dimensions—including the socioeconomic structures, food insecurity and hunger and the environment.

The crisis has exacerbated the deterioration of socioeconomic conditions, both in the post colonial and imperial countries, and most especially the very heartland of the U.S. empire. As a result an array of strategic and political responses have emerged against and in support of the system. These responses and forces will be identified and briefly analyzed below.

The Rising Tide of Barbarism

Western societies and imperial states, in the throes of a multifaceted crisis of significant regional proportions, are moving inexorably toward policies that can be described as barbaric in their effects. These policies are reversing decades of social welfare and subjecting nations, labour, natural resources and the wealth of entire populations to raw exploitation, pillage and plunder, destroying civilized lives, driving living standards downward and provoking, in some countries, unprecedented levels of discontent and anger.

In the ancient world, the cradle of Western civilization, "barbarism" was seen as a threat from the outside—from uncivilized invaders in outlying regions of the Roman Empire. In the contemporary world, the barbarians come from within. An elite group of powerful and wealth members of the ruling classes of the U.S., U.K. and the E.U. are intent on imposing a world order that is destroying the social fabric and foundation of secular and Islamic societies and undermining the livelihoods of millions across the world. Imperial wars and exploitation are pushing large and growing numbers of people into poverty and misery, conditions that are accurately described as "barbaric."

We need only look at conditions within the U.S. itself, the heartland of the empire. The degree of deterioration over the past two decades resulting from imperial wars and neoliberal policies affecting social conditions of most U.S. workers, especially those of colour (Blacks and Latinos), is staggering in its enormity and scope. It is estimated that up to one-third of all children in the U.S., across different categories of race and class, depend on food stamps in order to stave off hunger and other social conditions of poverty. Unemployment and underemployment rates of 20 percent, which in some segments of the population, especially in the eighteen to twenty-five age category, reaches 75 percent, and dispossession of homes, of one out of ten mortgage holders resulting from the sub-prime mortgage debacle, are symptomatic of the deepening social crises.

According to the *Financial Times* (September 17, 2010), "poverty among the working-age population of the United States rose to the highest level for almost fifty years in 2009.... The overall poverty rate rose to 14.3 percent." According to the Census Bureau 43.6 million people were living in poverty; by race the poverty rate was 25 percent for Blacks and Hispanics. The Census report also shows that the number of Americans without health insurance rose to a record 50.7 million as unemployed workers lost health coverage and capitalists shifted the payment of health insurance onto workers who cannot afford it. In reality the poverty line set by Washington is totally inadequate because it does not include the cost of basic items growing at double the average rate of inflation such as healthcare and education. As a result, poor workers are more susceptible of dying from curable diseases.

The processes of capitalist development, neoliberal globalization and empire-building have produced conditions of an extreme class polarization between a small stratum of super-rich, less than 1 percent of the population, and an impoverished working class that according to official statistics encompasses some 13 to 14 percent of all families and individuals but in reality reaches well into the so-called "middle class," which, by diverse accounts is being "hollowed out" in the process of capitalist development in the era of neoliberal globalization. The form and extreme conditions of this "development" can best be traced out in the extreme concentration of the wealth generated over this period (the 1980s to date) but even at the level of income distribution—the distribution of wealth is much more unequal than income in its different forms (investment based, earned, etc.) the pattern is clear. For example, the share of national income received by the richest 1 percent of Americans from 1972 to 2001 (already 57.5 percent of total income in 2003) increased by 7 percent, while the share of the richest .01 increased by 12.4 percent. As for the poorest 50 percent of households, the value of their share of national income fell by 12 percent.[2] This means that the share of national income of the richest 1 percent of all income recipients increased by a factor of 25 times the share of the remaining 99 percent. We do not have to look too far to find the detritus of this enormous wealth grab. It can be found in the deteriorating socioeconomic situation of the U.S. working class and the barbarism of the worsening conditions that afflict the poorest elements of this class, already some 25 percent of the population.

The key to barbarism today is found in the social structure of the imperial state and economy, in the conditions generated by this structure. These include an economic system in which the forces of production, wealth and income, are highly concentrated, a social system characterized by dramatic and growing inequalities in the distribution of income and associated conditions, and more broadly the genocidal wars organized and directed by American and European imperial forces in the quest for political and military domination, goals which have prejudiced the U.S. economic empire but favoured Israel colonial interests, especially in the Middle East.

Studies by U.N. agencies charged with the responsibility of protecting the most vulnerable members of society tell the tale: in countries under U.S. imperial domination an enormous global development divide exists between a small powerful elite and a vast mass (some three billion by conservative estimates) of people immersed in poverty. And in the Middle East, on the front lines of imperial colonial wars led and directed by U.S. militarists and Zionists, we have the destruction of entire societies, a frontal assault on diverse forces of resistance, accompanied by the disarticulation of the forces of independent national development, and the murder and exile of skilled workers, scientists, professors and entrepreneurs and the total destruction of organized production of basic infrastructure.

The economists and sociologists who prepared UNDP's 2010 *Report on Latin America* attribute the global development divide and the polarization of world society between the wealth of the few and the poverty of the many to the starkly inequitable social structure of capitalism and the neoliberal policies that have reinforced it over the past two decades. According to this U.N. report—a very belated recognition to be sure—the fundamental source of global poverty (immiseration on a global scale) and its diverse conditions that afflict billions of working people and classes across the world is in the "structures" (institutionalized practices) brought about and protected by powerful economic interests that have advanced under the cover of the Washington Consensus. In the words of the Report there is a "direct correspondence between the advance of neoliberal globalization and the spread of poverty." "The most explosive contradictions," the report notes, "are given because the advance of [neoliberal] globalization marches hand in hand with the advance of poverty and social polarization. It is undeniable," the authors add, "that the 1980s and 1990s [were] the creation of an abysmal gap between wealth and poverty" (UNDP 2010: xv).

A key source of contemporary barbarism can be found in the financial institutions and agencies of an ascendant class of finance capitalists who have pillaged the productive and financial resources of the middle and working classes of societies across the world. The scale of the pillage is reflected in the enormous fortunes acquired by the billionaires listed by Forbes as well as the enormous volume of capital destroyed in the vortex of the "global financial crisis"—some $10 trillion, by some estimates—which is essentially a crisis of the "centre" of capitalist development (the U.S. and Europe), a crisis that will no doubt require and result in a major restructuring of the global economy and the emergence of new centres of capital accumulation and "economic growth," and the ascension of China.

It is estimated (Saxe-Fernandez and Nuñez 2001) that in Latin America alone over the past two decades of capitalist development in neoliberal form that the regional economy lost some $140 billion to the financial institutions, corporations and financiers of Wall Street and the City. It is true that this destruction relates to capital is largely fictitious in the sense that it has no productive base, and it affects primarily a relatively small group of investors but in many countries the pensions of the middle and working classes (and in some contexts their jobs and mortgages) are also negatively impacted, indeed disproportionately so because the big investors are invariably bailed out.

Conditions of the global resource grab and pillage, if not the crisis where it manifests itself, include the destruction of the livelihoods of hundreds of millions of workers, unemployment and precarious forms of employment and work conditions. The conditions also include the pillage of trillions of dollars from middle- and working-class savers and small investors, mortgage carriers, consumers and the state treasury, siphoning enormous resources from the productive economy into the hands of a parasitic elite of financial capitalists and financiers, a key and powerful element of the dominant class that emerged with the "financialization" of production and the bifurcation of the real economy and the money economy in the 1980s (Bello 2009).

It is estimated by ECLAC economists that in 2008, in the throes of the "global financial crisis" that in Latin America up to 40 billion dollars were "lost"—evaporated—in the process, and this in a region where some have questioned whether there ever was a crisis (see Porzecanski 2009 on "the missing crisis"). In any case, the assets of the large investors and financiers—even the salaries and bonuses of the CEOs and biggest bankers responsible for the debacle—were protected and as it turns out not at risk. What was not protected, however, with the measures adopted by the governments in response to what they saw as simply a financial crisis were the savings, pension funds, mortgages and other assets of the middle class and the jobs of the working class. What insulated the majority of workers in the region from the crisis as it manifested itself in the real economy is the fact that well over 50 percent of all workers do not exchange their labour power against capital but work "on their own account" on the streets, selling what little they have, offering their "services" for direct pay, employing themselves or setting up micro-enterprises.

Notwithstanding the subsequent recovery from the short-lived "crisis" the consequences for the working class of the capitalist rape and pillage of resources, the sacking of the public treasury, and the assault on private savings, are staggering. Also staggering, or at least surprising and difficult to understand, is the relative quiescence of the working class in its myriad old and new forms in the face of this massive assault on the conditions of its social existence. Also surprising in this context is the apparent failure of the Left to mobilize the forces of social discontent that are inevitably brewing under these conditions. An explanation of this quiescence and failure await a closer look and further study of the dynamics involved but we can draw several conclusions from our limited observations and study of the issue. It seems to us that the major reason that workers across the world, and other elements of the popular sector of society, have not revolted is the combined effect of the decline of mass organizations, trade unions and class consciousness resulting from a prolonged capitalist offensive and the power of the dominant ideology (which does not allow for, and let people imagine an alternative system). The decline and weakness of the Left in its diverse permutations and divisions undermines its capacity to respond to the challenge—to understand what needs to be done and to act on this understanding.

A critical social and political pillar of the imperial state and economy is the militaristic political elite that emerged in the wake of the transition from Pax Britannica to Pax Americana in the 1940s. In order to secure the emerging American empire, Washington assumed the responsibility for overseeing a state of virtually permanent warfare within the world order set up at Bretton Woods. Over subsequent years this military caste of politicians and ideologues secured a major voice in the policies of the imperial state and its budget, and with the ascension of George W. Bush total control over foreign policy. Another component of this imperial world order was the U.N. system, designed to prevent any one state from succumbing to the imperial dream of omnipotent power and hegemony. In practice the system constituted an adjunct to the economic development apparatus of the OECD and the security apparatus of NATO, both of which were dominated by the U.S. and its allies in the project of maintaining "order."

Endless wars, cross-border assassinations, military interventions and state terror and the suspension of traditional constitutional guarantees have led to the concentration of dictatorial powers, arbitrary jailing, torture and the denial of habeas corpus—and the institutionalized power of capital and money, hidden behind or disguised as democracy, development and globalization.

Behind the lines of the national and class struggle brought about by the concentration and projection of economic and military power, conditions are deteriorating. In the midst of a deep economic recession and stagnation, high levels of state spending on bailing out financial institutions, military empire-building at the expense of the domestic economy and living standards, reflects the subordination of the local economy to the concerns and dictates of the imperial state.

Corruption at the top in all aspects of state and business activity—from state procurement to privatization to subsidies for the super-rich—encourages the growth of crime worldwide from top to bottom, the *lumpenization* of the capitalist class and a state where *law and order* have fallen into disrepute. The lumpenization process, manifest most clearly in the spread of narco-trafficking throughout Mexico, has profoundly affected the financial system of both Mexico and the United States. For example, Mexico's Financial Intelligence Unit reported that during the first half of 2010 they detected 24,449 suspected cases of money laundering, including a 105 percent increase between the first and second semester. International financial organizations estimate that Mexico's "financial circuit" launders from $15 to 25 billion dollars of drug money annually (*La Jornada*, September 19, 2010). It turns out that major U.S., U.K., E.U., Swiss and Israeli banks are active collaborators. The *London Observer* in this connection quotes the head of the U.N.'s drug and crime division as saying that most of the $352 billion of annual global drug profits were absorbed into the banking system during the crisis (*Financial Times*, September 18–19, 2010). In other words, *lumpen drug capitalism* played a major role in saving the world financial system from collapse, highlighting the ties between lumpen capital and barbaric imperialism not merely in regard to Mexico but also to major countries of the Western world.

The growth of narco-power in the post-colonial countries of the global south as growers, processors and distributors is matched by the distributors, consumers and financiers in the imperial countries, "the final market" of the drug chain. Experts claim that over 60 percent of the profits of the international narco-business are retained and recycled in the U.S., E.U. and the U.K., indicating the degree to which the "respectable bourgeoisie" is embedded in the international circuits of lumpen capital.

One particularly disturbing manifestation of this lumpenization is in Mexico, a major outpost of the U.S. empire where the trafficking of drugs by criminal organizations, it is estimated, now actively engages some 25,000 members. They have spawned an unprecedented wave of diverse forms of criminal activity that is estimated to have a black market value of some $60 billion, most of which is laundered by U.S., Swiss and U.K. banks. According to a legislative report filed in Mexico (*La Jornada*, August 29, 2010), the trafficking of migrant workers nets the narco-capitalists some $3 billion a year.

One group of narco-capitalists, the Zetas, has responded to the ethos of capitalist development by seeking out diverse opportunities to make money, investing capital in the expansion of its original service function as an armed enforcer for the drug-trafficking Gulf Cartel into other informal sectors of the capitalist economy as opportunities arise. Using the recipe for modern capitalist corporate enterprise, the directors of Mexico's most powerful murder-for-hire firm, the Zetas, have begun to diversify from the company's original and principal activity into the lucrative business of stealing and selling contraband gasoline. It now steals hundreds of thousands of barrels from Mexico's nationalized petroleum company PEMEX, and resells the oil to Texas oil companies, including one run by a former Bush administration insider.

Were the group not known for countless brutal murders in Mexico's endless and ever-more violent drug war, it might be considered the poster child of the North American Free Trade Agreement (NAFTA), able to see a business opportunity when there is one, and to cut through trade barriers like a specialized drill cuts into a highly pressurized steel pipe carrying oil. This is not only an example of criminals tapping savvy entrepreneurial skills to make another few million bucks. It is also an example of U.S. policy blowback: the perversely unintended result of a failed policy. On the one hand the Zetas have been able to take advantage of NAFTA partly because of the "two way overland highway of contraband," so aptly described by political economist Jeff Faux. The construction and paving of this highway has been greatly facilitated by the agreement, which has led to and includes not a few companies that now cook deals with organized crime.

The real power of the Zetas, which sets them apart from Mexico's other hit squads, comes from their roots. Before the founding members of the Zetas deserted an elite unit of the Mexican army, they received highly sophisticated training by U.S. Special Forces in anti-narcotic operations. The tale of oil thievery thus takes on added significance, especially in the context of a tenfold increase in "drug war" aid to Mexico under the Merida Initiative. Since 2008 Washington has pumped over a billion dollars into Mexico for drug trafficking control and security operations, with millions designated to military and police training. The U.S. arms industry profits both ways as the main supplier of guns to both the gangs and the Mexican army and the police.

Mexico's biggest drug lord has now entered the ledgers of *Fortune* as one of the ten richest individuals in the world, to the chagrin of the country's president, who is ostensibly engaging in a war against these criminal gangs with the resulting death of several thousand members of the security forces of the state. Of course, significant elements of these security forces, and other parts of the state apparatus, have been corrupted and are in the pay of the druglords. In this connection, an interesting if unexplained statistic is that the operations of the government's security apparatus against one of the most powerful gangs of organized criminals have netted eight times more arrests than the case of the second largest gang, suggesting that the state is not totally neutral in this war.

Most significant and most disturbing about this lumpenization of capitalist enterprise is the incredible degree of insecurity that it generates for most of the working population, not to mention new forms of exploitation sustained by a campaign of shooting, assassination and acts of violence that include the beheading of victims and the dumping of bodies in mass graves. These "developments," which are spreading across the country, are associated with the efforts of the criminal gangs of lumpen-capitalists to diversify their activities from the drug trade into the trafficking of people as well as drugs, and the extortion of small business owners as well as migrant workers. The statistics on this development are horrendous: 28,000 killed between 2006 and 2010, thousands of kidnappings, hundreds of thousands of businesses subject to extortion, the length and breadth of the country "covered" by gangs.

As a result of the exceedingly high costs of capitalist development and empire-building under these worsening conditions, not to mention the pillage by the financial oligarchy and the formal capitalist class, the socioeconomic burden of capitalist development has been placed directly on the backs of waged and unwaged workers, pensioners and the self-employed, as well as members of the middle class, resulting in a long-term, large-scale downward trajectory. With job losses and the disappearance of well-paying jobs, home foreclosures have skyrocketed and the erstwhile stable middle and working classes—the backbone of the productive economy—are shrinking, their members forced to extend their hours of labour and years of work. Some economists and sociologists in the U.S. have conceptualized this development as the "hollowing out of the middle class" in a context of a society increasingly polarized between the well-off (some extremely well-off) and the not so well off, indeed very badly off.

Barbarism via Imperial War

As imperial wars spread across the world targeting entire populations, via sustained bombings and clandestine terror operations, they generate opposing terrorist networks, which also target civilians in markets, transport and public spaces. The world resembles a Hobbesian world of *"all against all."* Rising *ethno-religious extremism linked to militarism* is found among Christians, Jews, Moslems, Hindus, replacing international class solidarity with doctrines of racial supremacy and penetrating the deep structures of states and societies.

The demise of European and Asian welfare collectivism—in the ex-U.S.S.R. and China—has lifted the competitive pressures on Western capitalists and encouraged them to revoke all the welfare concessions conceded to labour in the post World War II period.

The demise of "communism" or "actually existing socialism," and the integration of social democracy into the capitalist system, has led to a severe weakening of the Left, which the sporadic protests of the social movements have failed to replace.

In the face of the current large-scale assault on workers' and middle class living standards, there are only sporadic general strikes in a few countries (France, Greece, Spain, Italy) at best and political impotence at worst. Massive exploitation of labour in post-revolutionary capitalist societies, such as China and Vietnam, includes the exclusion of hundreds of millions of migrant workers from elementary public educational and health services. The unprecedented pillage and seizure by domestic oligarchs and foreign multinationals of thousands of lucrative strategic public enterprises in Russia, the ex-Soviet republics, eastern Europe, the Balkans and Baltic countries was the greatest transfer of public to private wealth in the shortest time in all of history.

In short, "barbarism" has emerged as a defining reality, a product of the ascendancy of a militarist and parasitic financial ruling class. The barbarians are here and now, present within the frontiers of Western societies and states. They are dominant and aggressively pursuing an agenda which is continually reducing living standards, transferring public wealth to their private coffers, pillaging public resources, savaging constitutional rights in their pursuit of imperial wars, segregating and persecuting millions of immigrant workers and promoting the disintegration and diminution of the stable working and middle class. More than at any time in recent history, the super-billionaires found at the top of the heap of global capital, making up less than 0.1 percent of the population, have appropriated an incredibly large and increasing share of global wealth and income.

Popular Responses to the Rise of Barbarism

Capitalism as a system is not only rife with class conflict but also has a propensity towards crisis, which came to the surface in North America and western Europe in 2008, giving rise to a major financial crisis that in some parts of the system turned into a production and consumption crisis in terms of the ability of growing numbers of the poor to afford the market prices of food and other commodified necessities of life. The typical capitalist economic crisis disrupts and weakens, existing institutions, giving rise to movements demanding change which can be mobilized by both the Left and Right.

The dominant response to the so-called "global financial crisis" brought into play the agencies of the capital-controlled international organizations and the imperial state. The response of the guardians of the imperial world order has been to consolidate the system with some feeble efforts to re-establish some regulatory control over capital and a big push to impose austerity programs onto labour. As a result the living standards of the popular sector of society sharply declines, while the financiers and bankers of Wall Street and the City in London have recouped their losses and regrouped in support of the capitalist state stripped of its welfare provisions and resorting to barbaric practices.

The rise of barbarism in our midst has provoked public revulsion against its principal practitioners. Surveys and several studies have found and documented profound and widespread—virtually system-wide—disgust and revulsion against all political parties; that huge majorities harbour profound distrust of the corporate and political elite; that majorities reject the concentration of corporate power and the abuse of that power, especially among bankers and financiers; the existence of widespread questioning of the democratic credentials of political leaders who act at the behest of the corporate elite and promote the repressive policies of the national security state. Even in the U.S., the U.K. and other centres of capitalist development, a large majority rejects the pillage of the state treasury to bail out banks and the financial elite, while imposing regressive austerity programs on the working and middle class. In a few imperial countries and in some post-colonial nations, widespread discontent and general strikes and deep anger, frustration and disgust is growing with politicians, parties and governments both on the Left and the Right.

The question is whether capitalist barbarism can possibly generate a revolutionary situation. The unsettled question has to do with the "subjective" conditions of this possible social transformation. Can the diverse and multiplying forces of resistance and opposition be mobilized and channelled in the direction of revolutionary change?

Building Socialism in an Era of Neoliberal Decline and Barbaric Capitalism

The capitalist offensive under conditions of a financial, production and consumer crisis at the centre of the system has had a major impact on the objective and, to a far lesser degree, subjective conditions of the working and middle classes. Immiseration has provoked a rising tide of social discontent albeit no mass organized political movements. In Latin America radical mass movements in the 1990s were better organized and more powerful then they are today. In fact, the relative quiescence of the working class and other groups in the popular sector is a disquieting feature of the current phase of capitalist development, a problem that requires very close examination. Major capitalist-imposed structural changes eroding collective power demands a coming-to-terms with the current adverse circumstances and barbaric conditions that are emerging throughout the system. A major problem is the identification of new agencies and modes of class struggle and transformation. Proposals for rebuilding a socialist alternative include:

The need to (1) recreate a productive economy and to reconstruct a new industrial working class in the face of years of financial plunder and de-industrialization, not necessarily the "dirty" industries of the past, but certainly new industries using and inventing clean energy sources; (2) dismantle the highly indebted capitalist economies via a fundamental shift from high-cost militarism and empire-building toward a kind of class-based austerity that imposes sacrifice and structural reforms on the banking, financial and big retail commercial sectors, substituting local production for cheap consumer imports; (3) downsize the financial and retail sector, which requires the upgrading of skills of the displaced workers and employees as well as changes in the IT sector to accommodate shifts in the economy; and (4) shift from the money wage to the social wage, in which free public education to the highest levels and universal healthcare and comprehensive pensions replace debt-financed consumerism. This can become the basis for strengthening class-consciousness against individual consumerism.

The question is how to move from weakened, fragmented labour and social movements in retreat or on the defensive, to a position capable of launching an anti-capitalist offensive? Several subjective and objective factors are possibly working in this direction. First, there is the growing negativity of vast majorities to political incumbents and, in particular, to the financial and economic elites who are clearly identified as responsible for the decline in living standards. Second, there is the popular view shared by millions that the current austerity programs are clearly unjust—having the workers pay for the crises that the capitalist class brought forth. As yet these majorities are more "*anti*" status quo than "*pro*" transformation. The transition from private discontent to collective action is an open question as to who and how, but the opportunity exists.

Several objective factors could trigger a qualitative shift from passive angry discontent to a massive anti-capitalist movement. First, a "double dip" recession, the end of the present anemic recovery and the onset of a more profound and prolonged recession could further discredit current rulers and their economic backers. Second, a period of unending and deepening austerity could discredit the current ruling class notion of *"necessary pain for future gain"* and open minds and move bodies to seek political solutions to achieve current gains by inflicting pain on the economic elites. Unending and unwinnable imperial wars that bleed the economy and working class could ultimately create a consciousness that the ruling class has "sacrificed the nation" for "no useful purpose." Likely the combination of a new phase or a deepening of the recession in the world's largest economy, the ramification of this recession in other parts of the world economy, a further dismantling of the welfare state in Europe, growing unemployment and continuing austerity and endless imperial wars can turn the current mass malaise and diffuse hostility against the economic and political elite toward socialism. The problem is what agencies of socialist development are able to respond to the challenge. Is there an effective socialist movement in existence or in the offing? Are the socialist parties that were formed within and have been shaped by the institutional framework of liberal social democracy possible agents of revolutionary change?

If the answer to the above is negative, what is the social base and organizational form of new socialist movements and parties? What would be the most effective strategy for bringing about socialism? Under what conditions could this strategy be implemented? Are these conditions at hand, and if not how could they be brought about?

We have no formulaic "answers" to these questions, but certain basic propositions can be established on the basis of lessons drawn from diverse experiments with, and experiences of, socialism in the twentieth century.

Learning from the Past:
The Cuban Revolutionary Experience

The Cuban revolution has much to teach us about the successes and failures of socialist political and economic development. Cuba provides ample proof of the possibility to carry out and defend a social revolution despite 50 years of imperialist assaults. It also demonstrates the superiority of socialism in implementing and sustaining advanced social programs and constructing security systems capable of defending the integrity of the revolution in the face of imperial backed terrorist warfare.

But in the realm of economic development, egregious economic errors illustrate policies that have to be avoided. They include:

- Reliance on "monocultural"-based economic strategies (sugar exports, tourism) instead of diversified production and export markets leads to greater vulnerability and inefficient use of skilled labour.
- The mistaken notion that the bigger the state sector, the bigger the enterprise and the smaller the private sector the speedier the transition to socialism. Hence, the abolition of 100,000 small and medium size manufacturing and service enterprises (Castro's "Revolutionary Offensive" in 1968). The result was the irrational expansion of public employment and the absence of vital services for the Cuban people. Unless the state can perform the same function as small business it is best to regulate and even encourage it, while tending to the serious business of managing the strategic sectors of the economy.
- The mistaken notion that an aging charismatic leader can combine executive and legislative power for forty-six years via a bureaucratic apparatus in place of the collective wisdom and practical knowledge of workers and farmers organized to propose and implement development policies. The result has been historic economic mistakes and failures, including the policy calling for Cuba to double its sugar production to 10 million tons (1969–70), dislocating the economy; the decision to spe-

cialize in sugar exports (1970–89), creating enormous dependence and vulnerability, instead of becoming food self-sufficient, processing sugar into ethanol (like Brazil), becoming energy independent and developing diverse agro-exports (like citrus products) to ready and available markets; launching costly international military missions in support of reactionary regimes (Ethiopia in the 1980s), and humanitarian programs to countries run by pro-imperialist regimes (Pakistan, Guatemala), which absorb state revenues better spent in diversifying the Cuban economy. A developing country in need of raising national personal consumption cannot afford the expenditures involved in securing international prestige.

- Abrupt shifts in policy to "correct past errors" can lead to new and equally negative consequences. After overloading the state with unproductive employees, the Cuban regime announces the firing of one million functionaries (one-tenth of the labour force), 500,000 in six months, proposing they become "self-employed" or form co-operatives. The "announcement" takes place with no prior discussion among workers and employees affected; no planning or allocation of credits, market research, facilities, tools, training or development of entrepreneurial skills. In taking forty years to correct Fidel's egregious blunder in eliminating the private small business service and manufacturing sector, the regime proposes to convert a half-million unemployed functionaries into productive producers and vendors in six months!

The lessons from Cuba are clear: workers' democracy can lead to mistakes but the possibility of self-correction and rational choice exists in a way that it did not under the most dynamic longstanding leader. Short-term economic polices based on orthodox "comparative advantages" (sugar, tourism) always result in vulnerabilities and crises, in a way that diverse exports and markets, food self-sufficiency, efficient links between education and economy, and productivity-based rewards and incentives do not.

Conclusion

The most elementary starting point in building socialism in the twenty-first century is that class consciousness as it was historically manifested in past struggles has sharply diminished. Any discussion of a socialist revival must identify the points of conflict and contradictions and struggle which lead to heightened class consciousness. It is evident today that the existing centre-left labour and social democratic parties and trade unions are the very executors of some of the most barbarous austerity programs in the U.S., U.K., Spain, Greece and Portugal, among other countries, North and South. Class consciousness is most evident in southern Europe, especially France, and least present in the U.S., northern Europe and Scandinavia, where anti-immigrant

Rightists have taken the lead in creating "racialist consciousness."

The cutting edge of socialist struggle today is found mostly in Venezuela among the urban poor and sectors of the working class in nationalized industries and in Asia among impoverished peasants, tribal peoples and displaced farmers. In wide swaths of northeastern India, revolutionary armed struggles are gaining terrain. In southern Africa, public sector employees and workers have taken the lead in calling for the nationalization of strategic economic sectors against the corrupt and gluttonous black bourgeoisie and their Western corporate "mentors."

Workers in China and Vietnam ruled and brutally exploited by a new class of economic and political oligarchs, under the façade of socialism, draw on their revolutionary past to initiate a "first wave" of mass struggles based on economic demands.

The first point to make is that it is evident that "class consciousness" as a social and political force is developing unevenly within and between regions. Second, class organization has grown in dynamic industrializing countries in which high rates of exploitation, deepening inequality and dispossession of small property holders has led to mass collective class action. Third, class mobilizations have taken place in a regional context, based on local leaders and in many cases without the leadership of an organized working class movement or party.

The current record demonstrates that workers can play a leading role in China, and that poor residents in communal organizations are leading backers of socialist initiatives in Venezuela. Displaced tribal peoples provide the cadres of revolutionary movements in India. Hyper-exploited female textile and garment workers provide the mass base in Bangladesh, India and China. The mass movements in Haiti and Thailand make their demands via populist leaders. In a word, class consciousness in a traditional working class context is the exception and not the rule. How far and how deep these movements will move toward a socialist transformation will depend on the internal ideological dynamics and struggle between varying competing ideological tendencies.

Given the importance of ideology as well as struggle in the making of class consciousness, the role of class-conscious workers, public employees, peasant leaders and intellectuals in the formulation of theoretical, historical and empirical critiques and socialist strategies and alternatives becomes central to a socialist project. Written and oral presentations to class organizations in action are essential and should be the principal basis for "political education." The amorphous "social forums" that eschew political definitions and depend on imperialist foundations for funding have demonstrated their irrelevance compared to class-based uprisings taking place from Nepal to Argentina and to national liberation struggles from Venezuela to Palestine.

Let us be clear—academic Leftist gatherings from New York to London and beyond, despite their claims of "furthering the struggle," have had little measurable impact beyond organizing their next encounter.

The broad scope of popular and class struggles across the world and the different social settings strongly suggest several conclusions. First, potential movements toward socialism are developing in a highly uneven pattern within the imperial and post-colonial states: the highly organized general strikes in France contrast with the moribund trade unions of the U.S. The advance of socialist legislation and worker self-managed industries in Venezuela contrast with Mexico's lumpenized economy and decimated trade union movement.

Second, the intensity and scope of the class struggle over time is uneven: uprisings of workers and the unemployed in some countries and indigenous peoples in others which were prominent in the early part of the decade in Argentina, Bolivia and Ecuador have lost momentum and have been "incorporated" or marginalized at the end of the decade.

Third, long-term, large-scale class warfare has consolidated and expanded over the decade in India's tribal areas, Nepal's cities and countryside as well as in the urban slums of Venezuela and South Africa.

Finally the different socioeconomic settings in which class struggle is taking place and the "ambiguous leadership" and eclectic ideology which informs these radical movements means that the social outcome is likely to take very distinct forms, some of which may have little relation to advanced forms of producer/worker controlled states and productive systems. Class movements rooted in integrated industrialized economies, where the key contradictions are found in social production and private appropriation of profit, are more likely to lead to social ownership of the commanding heights of the economy. This development would be more likely in China, France, South Africa, Venezuela or Bolivia then in petty-commodity Nepal, the tribal regions of India or where ethno-religious movements dominate the national liberation struggles such as in Afghanistan, Iraq and Palestine.

In summary, while the spread of barbarous imperialism erodes the social bases of U.S. and E.U. rule both at home and overseas, class polarization has favoured the advance of the far Right as well as mass workers' movements in exceptional circumstances in southern Europe (Greece, Spain). In contrast, the centres of revolutionary movements are found in post-colonial societies, but in regions and classes not clearly identified with socialist goals, with the notable exception of Venezuela.

If it is true that the onset of barbarism in conditions of capitalist development, neoliberal globalization and imperialism, and the retreat of the workers' movement in many countries, is a valid observation it is well to keep in mind that during several previous historical moments, socialism appeared to be a "utopian" goal. For example, during the global slaughter of World

War I the vast majority of workers' parties and trade unions surrendered to a militarist chauvinist frenzy, leaving in their wake small isolated groups of militants. Likewise in 1939 on the eve of World War II, the fascist juggernaut advanced in Europe, Asia and beyond destroying and decimating all instances of independent class organization. Subsequent events proved the prophets of the "inevitable end of socialism" wrong. Let us hope that history repeats itself.

Notes

1. In the study of social change and development this problem is posed as a question of determining the relative weight of the "structural" and "strategic" factors in the process of change—the former conceived of in terms of the workings of the system, the latter, as the result of actions taken consciously towards a predetermined or defined goal.

2. <http://beatthepress.blogspot.com/2006/06/minimum-wage-and-doctors-pay.html> <http://faculty web.at.northwestern.edu/economics /Gordon/BPEA_Meetingdraft_Complete_051118.pdf>.

Bibliography

Agnew, J. 2005. *Hegemony: The New Shape of Global Power*. Philadelphia: Temple University Press.

Albert, M. 2004. *Parecon: Life after Capitalism*. London: Verso.

______. 2010. "Fifth International?!" *ZNet* January 21 <http://www.zcommunications. org/fifth international-by-michael-albert> (October 10).

Albo, Greg, Sam Gindin and Leo Panitch. 2010. *In and Out of Crisis: The Global Financial Meltdown and Left Alternatives*. Halifax & Winnipeg: Fernwood Publishing/Oakland: PM Press.

Albo, Greg, and Herman Rosenfeld. 2009. "What Should We Do to Help Build a New Left?" *Relay* 28.

Ali, Tariq. 2006. *Pirates of the Caribbean: Axis of Hope*. London: Verso.

Anderson, P. 1976. "The Antinomies of Antonio Gramsci." *New Left Review* I/100: 5–78.

Angus, I. 2001. *Emergent Publics: An Essay on Social Movements and Democracy*. Winnipeg: Arbeiter Ring.

______. 2010. "If Socialism Fails: The Spectre of 20th Century Barbarism." In I. Angus (ed.), *The Global Fight for Climate Justice*. Halifax & Winnipeg: Fernwood Publishing.

Arlacchi, Pino. 1986. *Mafia Business: The Mafia Ethic and the Spirit of Capitalism*. London: Verso.

Atton, Chris. 2004. *An Alternative Internet: Radical Media, Politics and Creativity*. Edinburgh: Edinburgh University Press.

______. 2009. "Understanding Alternative Media." *Media Culture & Society* 31: 683–84.

Autonomia. 1980. "Italy: Post-Political Politics." *Semiotext(e)* III (3).

Azzellini, Dario. 2010. "Constituent Power in Motion: Ten Years of Transformation in Venezuela." *Socialism and Democracy* 24 (2): 8–31.

Badiou, Alain. 2010. *The Communist Hypothesis*. London: Verso.

Bahn, J. 2009. "Marxism in a Snail Shell: Making History in Chiapas." *Rethinking History* 13: 541–60.

Bakker, K. 2007. "The 'Commons' Versus the 'Commodity': Alter-Globalization, Anti-Privatization and the Human Right to Water in the Global South." *Antipode* 39: 430–55.

Barthes, Roland. 1977. *Image, Music, Text*. London: Fontana.

Bello, Walden. 2009. "The Global Collapse: A Non-Orthodox View." *Mrzine* February 20 <http://mrzine.monthlyreview.org/2009/bello200209.html>.

Bhaskar, Roy. 1989. *Reclaiming Reality*. London: Verso.

Billig, Michael. 1993. "Nationalism and Richard Rorty: The Text as Flag for *Pax Americana*." *New Left Review* 202: 69–83.

Bloch, E. 1971. *On Karl Marx*. New York: Herder & Herder.

______. 1986. *The Principle of Hope*. Cambridge: MIT Press.

Blok, Anto. 1974. *The Mafia of a Sicilian Village 1860–1960: A Study of Violent Peasant Entrepreneurs*. New York: Harper and Row.

Bloom, Harold, Paul de Man, Jacques Derrida, Geoffrey Hartman and J. Hillis Miller. 1979. *Deconstruction and Criticism*. London: Routledge & Kegan Paul.

Blumer, H. 1969. "Fashion: From Class Differentiation to Collective Selection." *Sociological Quarterly* 10: 275–91.

Boggs, C. 1976. *Gramsci's Marxism*. London: Pluto Press.

Bibliography

Bragg, Billy. 2006. *Progressive Patriot*. London: Bantam Press.

Brass, Tom. 1991. "Moral Economists, Subalterns, New Social Movements and the (Re-) Emergence of a (Post-) Modernized (Middle) Peasant." *The Journal of Peasant Studies* 18: 173–205.

______ (ed.). 1995. *New Farmers Movements in India*. London: Frank Cass Publishers.

______. 1999. *Towards a Comparative Political Economy of Unfree Labour: Case Studies and Debates*. London & Portland: Frank Cass Publishers.

______. 2000. *Peasants. Populism and Postmodernism: The Return of the Agrarian Myth*. London & Portland: Frank Cass Publishers.

Brittain, Samuel. 2005. *Against the Flow: Reflections of an Individualist*. London: Atlantic Books.

Broad, Robin (ed.). 2002. *Global Backlash: Citizen Initiatives for a Just World Economy*. Boulder, CO: Rowan & Littlefield.

Bukharin, N., and E. Preobrazhensky. 1922. *The ABC of Communism* (translated from the Russian by Eden and Cedar Paul). London: The Communist Party of Great Britain.

Bull, Anna, and Paul Corner. 1993. *From Peasant to Entrepreneur: The Survival of the Family Economy in Italy*. Oxford: Berg.

Burns, Emile. 1935. *Abyssinia and Italy*. London: Victor Gollancz.

Butko, T.J. 2006. "Gramsci and the 'Anti-Globalization' Movement: Think before You Act." *Socialism and Democracy* 20: 79–102.

Butovsky, Jonah, and Murray E.G. Smith. 2007. "Beyond Social Unionism: Farm Workers in Ontario and Some Lessons from Labour History." *Labour/Le Travail* 57 (Spring). <http://www.historycooperative.org/journals/llt/59/butovsky.html>.

Callinicos, Alex. 1994. *Against Post-Modernism: A Marxist Critique*. St. Martin's Press.

______. 2008. "Where Is the Radical Left Going?" *International Socialism* 120 (Autumn).

Cárdenas, Mauricio. 2008. "Global Financial Crisis: Is Brazil a Bystander?" Brookings Institution, Latin America Initiative. October 15 <http://www.brookings.edu/opinions/2008/1015_financial_crisis_cardenas.aspx> (accessed September 7, 2009).

Carroll, W.K. 2006. "Hegemony, Counter-Hegemony, Anti-Hegemony." *Social Studies* 2: 9–43.

______. 2007. "Hegemony and Counter-Hegemony in a Global Field." *Studies in Social Justice* 1: 36–66.

______. 2010. *The Making of a Transnational Capitalist Class: Corporate Power in the Twenty-First Century*. London: Zed Books.

Carroll, W.K., and R.S. Ratner. 2010. "Social Movements and Counter-Hegemony: Lessons from the Field." *New Proposals: Journal of Marxism and Interdisciplinary Inquiry* 4, 1: 7–22.

Carroll, W.K., and J.P. Sapinski. 2010. "The Global Corporate Elite and Transnational Policy Planning Network, 1996–2006: A Structural Analysis." *International Sociology* 25: 501–38.

Carroll, W.K., and Murray Shaw. 2001. "Consolidating a Neoliberal Policy Bloc in Canada, 1976 to 1996." *Canadian Public Policy* 27: 195–216.

Cassirer. 1955. "The Technique of Modern Political Myths." In *The Myth of the State*. New York: Anchor Books.

Castañeda, Jorge G. 2006. "Latin America's Left Turn." *Foreign Affairs* (May–June) <http://www.foreignaffairs.org/20060501faessay85302/jorge-g-castaneda/latin-america-s-left-turn.html> (accessed August 4, 2009).

CEPAL. 2007. *Social Panorama of Latin America 2007*. Santiago, Chile: Comisión Económica para América Latina y el Caribe.

______. 2008. *Panorama Social de América Latina*. Santiago, Chile: Comisión Económica para

América Latina y el Caribe.

Chaturvedi, Vinayak (ed.). 2000, *Mapping Subaltern Studies and the Postcolonial*. London: Verso.

Chávez, Hugo. 2003. *Discursos fundamentales: Ideología y acción política*. Caracas: Foro Bolivariano de Nuestra América.

Choo, H.Y., and M.M. Ferree. 2010. "Practicing Intersectionality in Sociological Research: A Critical Analysis of Inclusions, Interactions, and Institutions in the Study of Inequalities." *Sociological Theory* 28: 129–49.

Clarkson, S. 2010. "The Unbalanced World of Global Governance." Toronto: *Globe and Mail* p. A17.

Cleaver, H. 1993. "An Interview with Harry Cleaver." *Libcom* <http://libcom.org/library/interview-cleaver> (accessed September 2010).

______. 2001. "Reading Capital Politically." <http://www.infoshop.org/texts/cleaver_rcp.pdf> (accessed September 10, 2010).

Cohen, J.L. 1985. "Strategy or Identity: New Theoretical Paradigms and Contemporary Social Movements." *Social Research* 52: 663–716.

Colley, Linda. 1992. *Britons: Forging the Nation, 1707–1837*. London: Pimlico.

Corrales, Javier. 2009. "For Chávez, Still More Discontent." *Current History* 108, 715: 77–82.

Cox, Robert W. 1987. *Production, Power and World Order*. New York: Columbia University.

Crouch, Colin, and Alessandro Pizzorno (eds.). 1978. *The Resurgence of Class Conflict in Western Europe Since 1968: Volume 1: National Studies*. London: Macmillan.

Davis, Mike. 1984. "The Political Economy of Late-Imperial America." *New Left Review* 143 (Jan.–Feb).

______. 2006. *Planet of Slums*. London: Verso.

Day, R. 2006. *Gramsci Is Dead: Anarchist Currents in the Newest Social Movements*. Toronto: Between the Lines.

______. 2007. "Walking Away from Failure." *Upping the Anti* 4: 77–87.

De Leon, C., M. Desai and C. Tuğal. 2009. "Political Articulation: Parties and the Constitution of Cleavages in the United States, India, and Turkeys." *Sociological Theory* 27: 193–219.

De Oliveira, Francisco. 2009. "La Eeorganización del Capitalismo Brasileño." IHU Online, 11 de noviembre <www.ihu.unisinos.br>.

De Sousa Santos, B. 2006. *The Rise of the Global Left: the World Social Forum and Beyond*. London: Zed Books.

______. 2008. "The World Social Forum and the Global Left." *Politics & Society* 36: 247–70.

De Tocqueville, Alexis. 1850. *On the State of Society in France before the Revolution of 1789 and on the Causes which Led to that Event*. London: John Murray.

Debray, Régis. 1981. *Teachers, Writers, Celebrities: The Intellectuals of Modern France* (translated by David Macey). London: Verso.

Deleuze, G., and F. Guattaari. 1987. *A Thousand Plateaus*. Minneapolis: University of Minnesota Press.

Dempsey, Jessica, and James K. Rowe. 2004. "Why Poststructuralism Is a Live War for the Left." *Praxis (e)Press* <www.praxis-epress.org>.

Denis, A. 2008. "Intersectional Analysis: A Contribution of Feminism to Sociology." *International Sociology* 23: 677–94.

Di Chiro, G. 2008. "Living Environmentalisms: Coalition Politics, Social Reproduction, and Environmental Justice." *Environmental Politics* 17: 276–98.

Downing, J. 2001. *Radical Media: Rebellious Communication and Social Movements*. Thousand Oaks, CA: Sage.

Drainville, A.C. 2008. "Present in the World Economy: The Coalition of Immokalee Workers (1996–2007)." *Globalizations* 5: 357–77.

Dyer-Witheford, N. 2001. "The New Combinations: Revolt of the Global Value-Subjects." *New Centennial Review* 1: 155–200.

ECLAC (Economic Commission for Latin America and the Caribbean). 2010. *Time for Equality: Closing Gaps, Opening Trails*. Santiago de Chile: ECLAC.

Economist. 2008. "An Axis in Need of Oiling." October 23.

Ekers, M., A. Loftus and G. Mann. 2009. "Gramsci Lives!" *Geoforum* 40: 287–91.

Ellner, Steve. 1999. "The Impact of Privatization on Labor in Venezuela: Radical Reorganization or Moderate Adjustment?" *Political Power and Social Theory* 13: 109–45.

______. 2003. "Introduction: The Search for Explanations." In Steve Ellner and Daniel Hellinger (eds.), *Venezuelan Politics in the Chávez Era: Class, Polarization, and Conflict*. Boulder, CO: Lynne Rienner.

______. 2008. *Rethinking Venezuelan Politics: Class, Conflict, and the Chávez Phenomenon*. Boulder, CO: Lynne Rienner.

______. 2010. "Hugo Chavez' First Decade in Office: Breakthroughs and Shortcomings." *Latin American Perspectives* 37, 1: 77–96.

Engels, F. 1885 [1967]. "Preface." In K. Marx, *Capital: A Critique of Political Economy* Volume II. Moscow: Progress Publishers.

Epstein, Barbara. 1995. "Why Post-Structuralism Is a Dead End for Progressive Thought." *Socialist Review* 25, 2: 83–119.

Eschle, C. 2004. "Feminist Studies of Globalisation: Beyond Gender, Beyond Economism?" *Global Society* 18: 97–125.

Esteban, Fernando. 2008. "The Bolivarian Revolution at the Crossroads." *International Viewpoint* 403 <http://www.internationalviewpoint.org/spip.php?article1504> (accessed September 4, 2009).

Evans, P. 2008. "Is an Alternative Globalization Possible?" *Politics & Society* 36: 271–305.

Farías, Eduardo Arcila. 1957. *El Régimen de la Encomienda en Venezuela*. Sevilla: Escuela de Estudios Hispano-Americanos.

Faux, Jeffrey. 2005. *The Global Class War*. New York: Wiley & Sons.

Fay, Brian. 1987. *Critical Social Science: Liberation and its Limits*. Ithica, NY: Cornell University Press.

Fernandes, Sujatha. 2007a. "A View from the Barrios: Hugo Chávez as an Expression of Urban Popular Movements." *LASA Forum* 28 (1): 17–19.

______. 2007b. "What Is at Stake in Venezuela's Reform Referendum?" *Znet* November 11 <http://www.zcommunications.org/znet/viewArticle/17429> (accessed November 15, 2009).

______. 2010. *Who Can Stop the Drums? Urban Social Movements in Chávez's Venezuela*. Durham, NC: Duke University Press.

Fioravanti, Eduardo. 1973. *L'esperienza della Assemblea popolare in Bolivia*. Milano: Jaca Book.

Foster, J. 2010. "Why Ecological Revolution?" *Monthly Review* 61, 8 (January): 1–64.

Fraser, N. 1995. "From Redistribution to Recognition: Dilemmas of Justice in a Post-Socialist Age." *New Left Review* 212: 68–93.

______. 2005. "Reframing Justice in a Globalizing World." *New Left Review* 36: 69–88.

Freire, P. 1970. *Pedagogy of the Oppressed*, New York: Seabury Press.

Friedman, E. 2009. "External Pressure and Local Mobilization: Transnational Activism and the Emergence of the Chinese Labor Movement." *Mobilization* 14: 199–218.

Fuentes, F. 2008. "Venezuelan Socialists Discuss the Struggle for a Revolutionary Party." *Green Left Weekly* <http://www.greenleft.org.au/2008/740/38297> (accessed

November 4, 2009).

Fukuyama, Francis. 1992. *The End of History and the Last Man*. London: Hamish Hamilton.

Gates, L.C. 2010. *Electing Chávez: The Business of Anti-Neoliberal Politics in Venezuela*. Pittsburgh, PA: University of Pittsburgh Press.

Geras, Norman. 1990. *Discourses of Extremity: Radical Ethics and Post-Marxist Extravagances*. London: Verso Books.

Gerassi, John (ed.). 1968. *Venceremos! The Speeches and Writings of Ernesto Che Guevara*. London: Weidenfeld and Nicolson.

Gibson, J. 2008. "The Myth of the Multitude: The Endogenous Demise of Alter-Globalist Politics." *Global Society* 22: 253–75.

Gill, S. 1995. "Theorizing the Interregnum: The Double Movement of Global Politics in the 1990s." In B. Hettne (ed.), *International Political Economy: Understanding Global Disorder*. Halifax & Winnipeg: Fernwood Publishing.

______. 2000. "Toward a Postmodern Prince? The Battle in Seattle as a Moment in the New Politics of Globalisation." *Millennium-Journal of International Studies* 29: 131–40.

Gill, S., and D. Law. 1989. "Global Hegemony and the Structural Power of Capital." *International Studies Quarterly* 33: 475–99.

Gillborn, D. 2010. "The White Working Class, Racism and Respectability: Victims, Degenerates and Interest-Convergence." *British Journal of Educational Studies* 58: 3–25.

Gindin, Jonah. 2005. "Made in Venezuela: The Struggle to Reinvent Venezuelan Labor." *Monthly Review* 57, 2 <http://www.monthlyreview.org/0605gindin.htm> (accessed August 24, 2009).

Ginsborg, Paul. 1990. *A History of Contemporary Italy: Society and Politics 1943–1988*. London: Penguin Books.

______. 2003. *Italy and Its Discontents: Family, Civil Society, State, 1980–2001*. New York: Palgrave Macmillan.

______. 2004. *Silvio Berlusconi: Television, Power and Patrimony*. London: Verso.

Golinger, Eva. 2006. *The Chávez: Cracking US Intervention in Venezuela*. New York: Monthly Review Press.

______. 2007. *Bush Versus Chávez: Washington's War on Venezuela*. New York: Monthly Review Press.

Gott, Richard. 2005. *Hugo Chávez and the Bolivarian Revolution*. London: Verso.

Gramsci, A. 1971. *Selections from the Prison Notebooks of Antonio Gramsci*. Edited by Q. Hoare and G. Nowell Smith. London: Lawrence & Wishart.

______. 1977. *Selections from Political Writings, 1910–1920*. New York: International Publishers.

Grandin, Greg. 2006. "The Rebel and Mr. Danger: Is Bush's Nightmare Venezuela's Salvation?" *Boston Review* May–June <http://www.bostonreview.net/BR31.3/grandin.html> (accessed August 17, 2009).

Gudynas, Eduardo. 2010. "The New Extractivism in South America: Ten Urgent Theses about Extractivism in Relation to Current South American Progressivism." Bank Information Center <http://www.bicusa.org/en/Article.11769.aspx> (accessed October 14, 2010).

Guha, Ranajit (ed.). 1982–89. *Subaltern Studies I-VI: Writings on South Asian History*. Delhi: Oxford University Press.

Gutiérrez Aguilar, Raquel. 2008. *Los ritmos del pachakuti*. La Paz: Textos Rebeldes.

Hackett, R.A., and W.K. Carroll. 2006. *Remaking Media: The Struggle to Democratize Public Communication*. London: Routledge.

Hanieh, Adam. 2009. "Hierarchies of a Global Market: The South and the Economic

Crisis." *Studies in Political Economy* 83: 61–84.

Hardt, Michael, and Antonio Negri. 2001. *Empire.* Cambridge, MA: Harvard University Press.

______. 2004. *Multitude.* New York: Penguin Press.

Harnecker, Marta. 2007. "Blows and Counterblows in Venezuela." In Leo Panitch and Colin Leys (eds.), *Socialist Register 2008: Global Flashpoints, Reactions to Imperialism and Neoliberalism.* London: Merlin Press.

______. 2010. "Latin America and Twenty-First Century Socialism: Inventing to Avoid Mistakes." *Monthly Review* 62, 3 (July/August): 3–86.

Harris, J. 2007. "Bolivia and Venezuela: The Democratic Dialectic in New Revolutionary Movements." *Race & Class* 49: 1–24.

Hart, Keith, Anthony Cohen, Anthony Good and Judith Okely. 1989. "Social Anthropology Is a Generalizing Science or It Is Nothing." *Group Debates in Anthropological Theory.* Manchester: Department of Social Anthropology.

Hart-Landsberg, Martin. 2009. "Learning from ALBA and the Bank of the South: Challenges and Possibilities." *Monthly Review* 61, 4: 1–18.

Harvey, David. 1991. *The Condition of Post-Modernity: An Enquiry into the Origins of Cultural Change.* New York: John Wiley and Sons.

______. 1996. *Justice, Nature and the Geography of Difference.* Cambridge, MA: Blackwell.

______. 2003. *The New Imperialism.* Oxford: Oxford University Press.

______. 2004. "The 'New' Imperialism: Accumulation by Dispossession." In Leo Panitch and Colin Leys (eds.), *Socialist Register 2004: The New Imperial Challenge.* London: Merlin Press.

______. 2005. *The New Imperialism.* New York: Oxford University Press.

Hawkins, Kirk A. 2010. *Venezuela's Chavismo and Populism in Comparative Perspective.* Cambridge: Cambridge University Press.

Hegel, G.W.F. 1967. *The Phenomenology of Mind.* New York: Harper Torchbooks.

______. 1975. *Logic.* Oxford University Press.

Hellinger, Daniel. 2003. "Political Overview: The Breakdown of *Puntofijismo* and the Rise of *Chavismo.*" In Steve Ellner and Daniel Hellinger (eds.), *Venezuelan Politics in the Chávez Era: Class Polarization, and Conflict.* Boulder, CO: Lynne Rienner.

Henao, Luis Andres. 2009. "Venezuelan TV Officials: Hillary Clinton Backs Us." *The Miami Herald* July 9.

Herrera Salas, Jesús María. 2005. "Ethnicity and Revolution: The Political Economy of Racism in Venezuela." *Latin American Perspectives* 32, 2: 72–91.

Hobsbawm, E.J. 1969. *Bandits.* London: Weidenfeld and Nicolson.

______. 1994. *Age of Extremes: The Short Twentieth Century, 1914–1991.* London: Michael Joseph.

Hofstadter, Richard, and Seymour Martin Lipset (eds.). 1968. *Turner and the Sociology of the Frontier.* New York: Basic Books.

Holder, J.B., and T. Flessas. 2008. "Emerging Commons." *Social & Legal Studies* 17: 299–310.

Hoy, David, and Thomas McCarthy. 1994. *Critical Theory.* Blackwell Publishers.

Hylton, Forrest, and Sinclair Thomson. 2007. *Revolutionary Horizons: Past and Present in Bolivian Politics.* London: Verso.

Ives, C. 2004. *Gramsci's Politics of Language.* Toronto: University of Toronto Press.

Jameson, Frederic. 1992. *Post-Modernism: Or, the Cultural Logic of Late Capitalism.* London: Verso.

Janicke, Kiraz. 2007. "Venezuela's Co-Managed Inveval: Surviving in a Sea of

Capitalism." <*Venezuelanalysis.com*> July 27 <http://www.venezuelanalysis.com/analysis/2520> (accessed November 14, 2009).

______. 2009. "Venezuela: Chávez calls for New International Organisation of Left Parties." *Links: International Journal of Socialist Renewal* <http://links.org.au/node/1372> (accessed August 2010).

Jones, Bart. 2008. *¡Hugo! The Hugo Chávez Story*. London: Bodley Head.

Joseph, J. 2002. *Hegemony: A Realist Analysis*. London: Routledge.

Karriem, A. 2009. "The Rise and Transformation of the Brazilian Landless Movement into a Counter-Hegemonic Political Actor: A Gramscian Analysis." *Geoforum* 40: 316–25.

Katz, Claudio. 2007. "Socialist Strategies in Latin America." *Monthly Review* 59, 4 <http://monthlyreview.org/0907katz.php> (accessed August 23, 2009).

______. 2008. *Las disyuntivas de la izquierda en América Latina*. Buenos Aires: Ediciones Luxemburg.

______. 2009. "América Latina frente a la crisis global." <http://katz.lahaine.org/> (accessed November 15, 2009).

Keane, John. 2003. *Global Civil Society?* Cambridge: Cambridge University Press.

Kebede, A.S. 2005. "Grassroots Environmental Organizations in the United States: A Gramscian Analysis." *Sociological Inquiry* 75: 81–108.

Kellogg, Paul. 2007. "Regional Integration in Latin America: Dawn of an Alternative to Neo-Liberalism?" *New Political Science* 29, 2: 187–210.

Knox, Chris. 1998. "Revolutionary Work in the American Labor Movement: 1920s to 1950s." In Leon Trotsky, *The Transitional Program*. London: Bolshevik Publications.

Konings, Martijn (ed.). 2010. *Beyond the Subprime Headlines: Critical Perspectives on the Financial Crisis*. London: Verso.

Kovel, J. 2006. *The Enemy of Nature*. New York: Zed Books.

Kozloff, Nikolas. 2006. *Hugo Chávez: Oil, Politics and the Challenge to the US*. New York: Palgrave Macmillan.

Kuczynski, J., and M. Witt. 1942. *The Economics of Barbarism: Hitler's New Economic Order in Europe*. London: Frederick Muller.

Kuhn, Thomas S. 1962. *The Structure of Scientific Revolutions*. University of Chicago Press.

Kumar, Krishan, 2003. *The Making of English National Identity*. Cambridge: Cambridge University Press.

La Blanc, Paul, and Helen C. Scott. (eds.). 2010. *Socialism or Barbarsim: Selected Writings of Rosa Luxemburg*. London & New York: Pluto Press.

Laboratorio Europeo per la Critica Sociale. 2008. "*The Centrality of Theory for the Class Struggle*." *Working Paper* No. 4. Rome.

Laclau, Ernesto, and Chantal Mouffe. 1985. *Hegemony and Socialist Strategy*. London: Verso.

Lafargue, Paul. 1883. *The Right to Be Lazy, and Other Studies* (translated by Charles H. Kerr). Chicago, IL: Charles H. Kerr & Company.

Lamont, Michelle. 1987. "How to Become a Dominant French Philosopher: The Case of Jacques Derrida." *American Journal of Sociology* 93, 3 (November): 584–622.

Lander, Edgardo, and Pablo Navarrete. 2007. *The Economic Policy of the Latin American Left in Government: Venezuela*. Amsterdam: Transnational Institute.

Larsen, Neil. 1993. "Postmodernism and Imperialism: Theory and Politics in Latin America." In Eyal Amiran and John Unsworth (eds.), *Essays in Postmodern Culture*. New York: Oxford University Press.

Lebowitz, Michael A. 1992. *Beyond Capital: Marx's Political Economy of the Working Class*. London: Macmillan.

______. 2003. "El Pueblo y la propiedad en la construccion del comunismo," *Marx Ahora* 16, (Havana).

______. 2006. *Build It Now: Socialism for the Twenty-First Century*. New York: Monthly Review Press.

______. 2007. "Venezuela: A Good Example of the Bad Left of Latin America." *Monthly Review* 59, 3 (July–August).

______. 2008. "The Only Road Is Practice." *Monthly Review* 60, 2 <http://monthlyreview.org/080601lebowitz.php> (accessed September 2, 2009).

______. 2010a. *The Socialist Alternative: Real Human Development*. New York: Monthly Review Press.

______. 2010b. "21st Century Socialism: The Strategy of the Left and the Latin American Experience." <http://www.socialistproject.ca/leftstreamed/ls83.php>.

Lecourt, Dominique. 2001. *The Mediocracy: French Philosophy since the Mid-1970s* (translated by Gregory Elliott). London: Verso.

Leiva, Fernando Ignacio. 2008. *Latin American Neostructuralism: The Contradictions of Post-Neoliberal Development*. Minneapolis: University of Minnesota Press.

Lenin, V.I. 1914. "Unity." *Lenin Collected Works* Vol. 20.

______. 1915a. "The Collapse of the Second International." *Lenin Collected Works* Vol. 21.

______. 1915b "Socialism and War: The Attitude of the R.S.D.L.P. towards the War." *Lenin Collected Works* Vol. 21.

______. 1965. *The State and Revolution*. Peking: Foreign Languages Press.

______. 1970. *What Is to Be Done?* London: Panther Books.

Linebaugh, P. 2008. *The Magna Carta Manifesto*. Berkeley: University of California Press.

López Maya, Margarita. 2007. "Venezuela Today: A 'Participative and Protagonistic' Democracy?" In Leo Panitch and Colin Leys (eds.), *Socialist Register 2008: Global Flashpoints, Reactions to Imperialism and Neoliberalism*. London: Merlin Press

Lopreato, Joseph. 1967. *Peasants No More: Social Class and Social Change in an Underdeveloped Society*. San Francisco, CA: Chandler Publishing Company.

Lowy, Michael. 1973. *The Marxism of Che Guevara: Philosophy, Economics, Revolutionary Warfare* (translated by Brian Pearce). New York: Monthly Review Press.

Lukács, Georg. 1971. "Social Reform or Revolution." In D. Howard (ed.), *Selected Political Writings of Rosa Luxemburg*. New York and London: Monthly Review Press.

______. 1972. *Lenin: A Study in the Unity of His Thought*. London: NLB.

Luke, T. 2006. "The System of Sustainable Degradation." *Capitalism Nature Socialism* 17: 99–117.

Lumley, Robert. 1990. *States of Emergency: Cultures of Revolt in Italy from 1968 to 1978*. London: Verso.

Luxemburg, Rosa. 1951 [1913]. *The Accumulation of Capital* (translated from the German by Agnes Schwarzschild). London: Faber & Faber.

______. 1970a [1915]. "The Junius Pamphlet: The Crisis in the German Social Democracy." In *Rosa Luxemburg Speaks* (edited with an introduction by Mary-Alice Waters). New York: Pathfinder Press.

______. 1970b. "Speech to the Founding Convention of the German Communist Party." In M. Waters (ed.), *Rosa Luxemburg Speaks*. New York: Pathfinder Press.

______. 1971. "Social Reform or Revolution." In D. Howard (ed.), *Selected Political Writings of Rosa Luxemburg*. New York and London: Monthly Review Press.

Lynd, Staughton, and Andrej Grubacic. 2008. *Wobblies & Zapatistas: Conversations on Anarchism, Marxism and Radical History*. Oakland: PM Press.

Lyotard. 1984. *The Post-Modern Condition: A Report on Knowledge*. Minneapolis: University of Minnesota Press.

Magdoff, F., and J.B. Foster. 2010. "What Every Environmentalist Needs to Know about Capitalism." *Monthly Review* 61, 2: 1–30.

Magnusson, W. 1997. "Globalization, Movements, and the Decentred State." In W.K. Carroll (ed.), *Organizing Dissent: Contemporary Social Movements in Theory and Practice.* Toronto: Garamond Press.

Mander, Benedict. 2008. "Venezuela: Chávez Vulnerable." *Financial Times*. October 22.

Mann, G. 2009. "Should Political Ecology Be Marxist? A Case for Gramsci's Historical Materialism." *Geoforum* 40: 335–44.

Mannin, Ethel. 1938. *Women and Revolution*. London: Secker and Warburg.

Marx, Karl. 1844 [1975]. "Economic and Philosophical Manuscripts of 1844." In Marx and Engels, *Collected Works* Vol. 3. New York: International Publishers.

_____. 1844a [1975]. "Comments on James Mill." In Marx and Engels, *Collected Works* Vol. 3. New York: International Publishers.

_____. 1845 [1987]. "Theses on Feuerbach." In K. Marx and F. Engels, *The German Ideology* (edited by C.J. Arthur). London: Lawrence & Wishart.

_____. 1847 [1976]. "The Poverty of Philosophy." In Marx and Engels, *Collected Works* Vol. 6. New York: International Publishers.

_____. 1852. "The Eighteenth Brumaire of Louis Bonaparte." *Marxists.org*. <http://www.marxists.org/archive/marx/works/1852/18th-brumaire/ch01.htm> (accessed August 30, 2010).

_____. 1857–8 [1973]. *Grundrisse* (translated by Martin Nicolaus). London: Penguin Books.

_____. 1867 [1970]. *Capital: a Critique of Political Economy* Vol. I. London: Lawrence and Wishart.

_____. 1871. "The Civil War in France." *Marxists.org*. <http://www.marxists.org/archive/marx/iwma/documents/1871/commune-may30.htm> (accessed August 30, 2010).

_____. 1962. "Critique of the Gotha Programme." In Marx and Engels, *Selected Works* Vol. II. Moscow: Foreign Languages Publishing House.

_____. 1974. "The Civil War in France: Address of the General Council." In *Karl Marx: The First International and After.* London: Penguin Books

_____. 1975. "Critique of Hegel's Philosophy of Right. Introduction." In *Karl Marx: Early Writings*. New York: Vintage Books.

_____. 1976. *The German Ideology*. Progress Publishers.

_____. 1977. *Capital* Vol. I. New York: Vintage Books.

Marx, Karl, and Engels, Frederick. 1846 [1976]. "The German Ideology." In Marx and Engels, *Collected Works* Vol. 5. New York: International Publishers.

_____. 1848 [1976]. "The Communist Manifesto." In Marx and Engels, *Collected Works* Vol. 6. New York: International Publishers.

_____. 1973. "Address of the Central Committee to the Communist League." In *Karl Marx: The Revolutions of 1848*. London: Penguin Books.

_____. 1975. *Selected Correspondence*. Third edition. Moscow: Progress Publishers.

Massicotte, M.J. 2009. "Transborder Activism in the Americas: Exploring Ways to Better Assess and Learn from Less Powerful Forces, Towards Other Possible Worlds." *Globalizations* 6: 411–31.

Mattick, Paul. 1971. *Marx and Keynes: The Limits of the Mixed Economy*. London: Merlin Press.

_____. 1978. *Anti-Bolshevik Communism*. London: Merlin Press.

_____. 1981. *Economic Crisis and Crisis Theory,*. London: Merlin Press.

_____. 1983. *Marxism: Last Refuge of the Bourgeoisie?* (Edited by Paul Mattick Jr.) London: Merlin Press.

Maybury-Lewis, Biorn. 1994. *The Politics of the Possible*. Philadelphia, PA: Temple University Press.

McBride, Stephen, and Heather Whiteside. 2011. *Private Affluence/Public Austerity: Economic Crisis and Political Malaise in Canada*. Halifax & Winnipeg: Fernwood Publishing.

McCarney, J. 2005. "Ideology and False Consciousness." <http://marxmyths.org/joseph-mccarney/article.htm> (accessed January 25, 2011).

McCarthy, J. 2005. "Commons as Counterhegemonic Projects." *Capitalism Nature Socialism* 16: 9–24.

McCarthy, Shawn. 2009. "Oil, Metals Pull Back as China Slows Buying." *Globe and Mail* July 6.

McKay, I. 2009. "O Dark Dark Dark. They All Go into the Dark: The Many Deaths of Antonio Gramsci." *Capital & Class* 98: 131–40.

McNally, David. 2006. *Another World Is Possible: Globalization and Anti-Capitalism*. Winnipeg: Arbeiter Ring Press.

______. 2009. "From Financial Crisis to World-Slump: Accumulation, Financialisation, and the Global Slowdown." *Historical Materialism* 17, 2: 35–83.

______. 2011. *Global Slump: The Economics and Politics of Crisis and Resistance*. Oakland: PM Press/Halifax & Winnipeg: Fernwood Publishing.

Melucci, Alberto. 1989. *Nomads of the Present*. Philadelphia, PA: Temple University Press.

Miliband, Ralph. 1994. *Socialism for a Sceptical Age*. London: Verso.

Morton, A.D. 2007. *Unravelling Gramsci*. London: Pluto Press.

MPD. 2001. *Líneas Generales del Plan de Desarrollo Económico y Social de la Nación 2001–2007*. Caracas: Ministerio de Planificación y Desarrollo. <http://www.mpd.gov.ve> (accessed August 17, 2009).

Munck, R. 2006. "Global Civil Society: Royal Road or Slippery Slope?" *Voluntus* 17: 325–32.

Negri, Antonio. 2008, *Goodbye Mr Socialism: Radical Politics in the 21st Century*. London: Serpent's Tail.

Nilsen, A.G. 2009. "'The Authors and the Actors of Their Own Drama': Towards a Marxist Theory of Social Movements." *Capital & Class*: 109–39.

Nooteboom, C. 2001. *All Souls' Day* (translated by S. Massotty). London: Picador.

O'Connor, J. 1990. "On the Two Contradictions of Capitalism." *Capitalism Nature Socialism* 2: 107–109.

Ocampo, José Antonio. 2007. "Markets: Social Cohesion and Democracy." In J.A. Ocampo, K.S. Jomo and S. Kahn (eds.), *Policy Matters: Economic and Social Policies to Sustain Equitable Development*. London: Zed Books.

______. 2009. "Latin America and the Global Financial Crisis." *Cambridge Journal of Economics* 33, 4 (1): 703–24.

Ollman, B. 2003. *Dance of the Dialectic: Steps in Marx's Method*. Urbana: University of Illinois Press.

Panitch, Leo. 2008. *Renewing Socialism*. Pontypool Wales: Merlin Press.

Panitch, Leo, and Sam Gindin. 2004. *Global Capitalism and American Empire*. Halifax & Winnipeg: Fernwood Publishing/London: Merlin Press.

Paulson, Beldon, 1966, *The Searchers: Conflict and Communism in an Italian Town*. Chicago: Quadrangle Books.

Paxman, Jeremy. 1999. *The English: A Portrait of a People*. London: Penguin.

Peres Borges, Stalin, Sergio García and Vilma Vivas. 2008. "The Bolivarian Revolution at the Crossroads between Imperialism, Constitutional Reform and the Socialist Discourse." *International Viewpoint* 397 <http://www.internationalviewpoint.org/

spip.php?article1428> (accessed August 18, 2009).

Peterson, V.S. 2005. "How (the Meaning of) Gender Matters in Political Economy." *New Political Economy* 10: 499–521.

______. 2009. "Interactive and Intersectional Analytics of Globalization." *Frontiers: A Journal of Women Studies* 30: 31–40.

Petras, James. 1990. "Retreat of the Intellectuals." *Economic and Political Weekly* 25: 2143–56.

______. 2007. "Venezuela: Between Ballots and Bullets." *Global Research* <http://www.globalresearch.ca/index.php?context_va&aid=7543> (accessed September 6, 2009).

______. 2009. "Latin America: Perspectives for Socialism in a Time of a World Capitalist Recession/Depression." <http://www.lahaine.org/petrasb2-img/petras_dec08.pdf> (accessed November 14, 2009).

Petras, James, and Henry Veltmeyer. 2001. *Unmasking Globalization: The New Face of Imperialism.* Halifax & Winnipeg: Fernwood Publishing/London: Zed Books.

______. 2003. "The Peasantry and the State in Latin America: A Troubled Past, an Uncertain Future." In Tom Brass (ed.), *Latin American Peasants.* London: Frank Cass Publishers.

______. 2007. "The 'Development State' in Latin America: Whose Development, Whose State?" *The Journal of Peasant Studies* 34: 371–407.

______. 2009. *What's Left in Latin America.* Ashgate Publishing.

______. 2011. *Social Movements in Latin America: Neoliberalism and Popular Resistance.* New York: Palgrave Macmillan.

Pontusson, J. 1980. "Gramsci and Eurocommunism: A Comparative Analysis of Conceptions of Class Rule And Socialist Transition." *Berkeley Journal of Sociology* 25: 185–248.

Porzecanski, Arturo C. 2009. *Latin America: The Missing Financial Crisis.* Washington, DC: ECLAC.

Powell, John Duncan. 1971. *Political Mobilization of the Venezuelan Peasant.* Cambridge, MA: Harvard University Press.

Purcell, M. 2009. "Hegemony and Difference in Political Movements: Articulating Networks of Equivalence." *New Political Science* 31: 291–317.

Raby, D.L. 2006. *Democracy and Revolution: Latin America and Socialism Today.* London: Pluto Press.

Rahman, Z., and T. Langford. 2010. "The Limitations of Global Social Movement Unionism as an Emancipatory Labour Strategy in Majority World Countries." *Socialist Studies* 6: 45–64.

Rao, N. 2009. "Another Left Is Possible: The Protests in France and the New Anti-Capitalist Party." *The Bullet.* Toronto: Socialist Project. <http://www.socialistproject.ca/bullet/bullet198.html> (accessed August 30, 2010).

Red Notes. 1978. *Italy 1977–78: Living with an Earthquake.* London: Red Notes.

Reed, John. 1926. *Ten Days that Shook the World.* London: Communist Party of Great Britain.

Regalia, Ida, Marino Regini and Emilio Reyneri. 1978. "Labour Conflicts and Industrial Relations in Italy." In Colin Crouch and Alessandro Pizzorno (eds.), *The Resurgence of Class Conflict in Western Europe Since 1968: Volume 1: National Studies.* London: Macmillan

Rice, J.S. 2007. "Ecological Unequal Exchange: International Trade and Uneven Utilization of Environmental Space in the World System." *Social Forces* 85: 1369–92.

______. 2010. "Viewing Trade Liberalization through a Feminist Lens: A Content Analysis of the Counterhegemonic Discourse of Gender and Trade Advocacy Groups." *Sociological Spectrum* 30: 289–316.

Roberts, Kenneth. 2003. "Social Polarization and the Populist Resurgence in Venezuela."

In Steve Ellner and Daniel Hellinger (eds.), *Venezuelan Politics in the Chávez Era: Class, Polarization, and Conflict*. Boulder, CO: Lynne Rienner.

Robinson, William I. 2007. "Transformative Possibilities in Latin America." In Leo Panitch and Colin Leys (eds.), *Socialist Register 2008: Global Flashpoints, Reactions to Imperialism and Neoliberalism*. London: Merlin Press.

______. 2008. *Latin America and Global Capitalism: A Critical Globalization Perspective*. Baltimore, MD: Johns Hopkins University Press.

Rorty, R. 1991. *Objectivity, Relativism, and Truth: Philosophical Papers*. Cambridge: Cambridge University Press.

______. 2007. "Cultural Politics and the Question of the Existence of God." In *Philosophy as Cultural Politics: Philosophical Papers*. Cambridge: Cambridge University Press.

______. 1989. *Contingency, Irony and Solidarity*. Cambridge: Cambridge University Press.

______. 1998. "The End of Leninism, Havel, and Social Hope." *Truth and Progress: Philosophical Papers*. Cambridge: Cambridge University Press.

______. 1999. *Philosophy and Social Hope*. London: Penguin Books.

Roseberry, William. 1983. *Coffee and Capitalism in the Venezuelan Andes*, Austin: University of Texas Press.

Roth, K.H. 1997. "Unfree Labour in the Area under German Hegemony, 1930–45." In Tom Brass and M. van der Linden (eds.), *Free and Unfree Labour: The Debate Continues*. Bern: Peter Lang AG.

Said, Edward W. 1978. *Orientalism*. London: Routledge & Kegan Paul.

Samuel, Raphael (ed.). 1989. *Patriotism: The Making and Unmaking of British National Identity* Vol. I (History and Politics). London: Routledge.

Sanbonmatsu, John. 2004. *The Postmodern Prince*. New York: Monthly Review Press.

______. 2006. "Post-Modernism and the Corruption of the Academic Intelligentsia." *Socialist Register* 42: 196–227.

Saxe-Fernández, John, and Omar Núñez. 2001. "Globalización e Imperialismo: La transferencia de Excedentes de América Latina." In Saxe-Fernández et al., *Globalización, Imperialismo y Clase Social*. Buenos Aires/México: Editorial Lúmen.

Schlesinger, Rudolf. 1953. *Central European Democracy and Its Background*. London: Routledge & Kegan Paul.

Shutt, Harry. 2010. *Beyond the Profits System: Possibilities for a Post-Capitalist Era*. London & New York: Zed Books.

Simon, R. 1982. *Gramsci's Political Thought*. London: Lawrence & Wishart.

Smith, Jackie. 2008. *Social Movements for Global Democracy*. Baltimore, MD: Johns Hopkins University Press.

Smith, Mick. 1997. "Against the Enclosure of the Ethical Commons: Radical Environmentalism as an Ethics of Place." *Environmental Ethics* 19: 339–53.

Smith, Murray E.G. 1996–97. "Revisiting Trotsky: Reflections on the Stalinist Debacle and Trotskyism as Alternative." *Rethinking Marxism* 9, 3.

______. 2010. *Global Capitalism in Crisis: Karl Marx and the Decay of the Profit System*. Halifax & Winnipeg: Fernwood Publishing.

Soederberg, Susanne 2006. *Global Governance in Question*. Winnipeg: Arbeiter Ring Publishing.

Sokal, Alan. 2008. *Beyond the Hoax: Science, Philosophy and Culture*. Oxford: Oxford University Press.

Solty, Ingar. 2008. "The Historical Significance of the New German Left Party." Toronto: Socialist Project. <http://www.socialistproject.ca/theory/Solty-en-Nov17.pdf> (accessed October 14, 2010).

Spriano, Paulo. 1975. *The Occupation of the Factories: Italy 1920* (translated and introduced by Gwyn A. Williams). London: Pluto Press.

Spronk, Susan. 2011. "Neoliberal Class Formation(s): The Informal Proletariat and 'New' Workers' Organizations in Latin America." In J.R. Webber and B. Carr (eds.), *The Resurgence of Latin American Radicalism: Between an Izquierda Permitdia and Cracks in the Empire*. Lanham, MD: Rowman and Littlefield.

Spronk, Susan, and Jeffery R. Webber. 2010. "Communal Power in Caracas: An Interview with Wilder Marcano." *The Bullet*. Toronto: Socialist Project. <http://www.socialistproject.ca/bullet/382.php#continue> (accessed September 15, 2010).

Staggenborg, S., and J. Lecomte. 2009. "Social Movement Campaigns: Mobilizations and Outcomes in the Montreal Women's Movement Community." *Mobilization* 14: 163–80.

Stahler-Sholk, R., H.E. Vanden and G.D. Kuecker. 2007. "Globalizing Resistance: The New Politics of Social Movements in Latin America." *Latin American Perspectives* 34: 5–16.

Stephen, M.D. 2009. "Alter-Globalism as Counter-Hegemony: Evaluating the 'Postmodern Prince.'" *Globalizations* 6: 483–98.

Suggett, James. 2009. "Venezuela Says Clinton's Remarks Reflect 'Profound Lack of Knowledge of Our Reality'." *Venezuelanalysis.com*. <http://www.venezuelanalysis.com/news/4609> (accessed July 9, 2010).

Sunkel, Osvaldo, and Ricardo Infante. 2009. *Hacia un desarrollo inclusivo: El caso de Chile*. Santiago: CEPAL.

Sustar, Lee. 2007. "Where Is Venezuela Going? Chávez and the Meaning of Twenty-First Century Socialism." *International Socialist Review* 54: 14–29.

Tablada, Carlos. 1989. *Che Guevara: Economics and Politics in the Transition to Socialism*. Sydney, Aus: Pathfinder.

Tarrow, S.G. 1998. *Power in Movement*. New York: Cambridge University Press.

Taylor, Marcus. 2009. "The Contradictions and Transformations of Neoliberalism in Latin America: From Structural Adjustment to "Empowering the Poor." In Laura Macdonald and Arne Ruckert (eds.), *Post-Neoliberalism in the Americas*. New York: Palgrave.

Thomas, P.D. 2009. *The Gramscian Moment: Philosophy, Hegemony and Marxism*. Leiden: Brill.

Thompson, E.P. 1981. "The Politics of Theory." In R.Samuel (ed.), *People's History and Socialist Theory*. London: Routledge and Kegan Paul.

Touissant, Eric. 2010. "Venezuela's Bolivarian Revolution at the Crossroads?'" *Links* <http://links.org/au/node/1760>.

Trotsky, Leon. 1970. *The Revolution Betrayed*. New York: Pathfinder Press.

_____. 1970b. *In Defense of Marxism*. New York: Pathfinder Press.

_____. 1971. *The Struggle Against Fascism in Germany*. New York: Pathfinder Press.

_____. 1998. *The Transitional Program*. London: Bolshevik Publications <http://www.bolshevik.org/>.

_____. 2005 [1932]. *History of the Russian Revolution*. New York: Pathfinder Press.

UNDP. 2010. "Informe Regional Sobre Desarrollo Humano para América Latina y el Caribe2010." New York.

Unger, R.M. 2009. *The Left Alternative*. London: Verso.

Urry, J. 1981. *The Anatomy of Capitalist Societies*. London: Macmillan.

Various authors. 2009. *Development Dialogue* 51 (January).

Vasapollo, Lucioano. 2011. *The Crisis of Capitalism*. Leiden: Brill.

Veltmeyer, Henry. 2002. "The Politics of Language: Deconstructing Post-Development Discourse." *Canadian Journal of Development Studies* XX11, 3: 597–624.

______ (ed.). 2010. *Imperialism, Crisis and Class Struggle: The Verities of Capitalism*. Leiden: Brill.

______ (ed.). 2011. The *Critical Development Studies Handbook: Tools for Change*. Halifax & Winnipeg: Fernwood Publishing.

Volkov, Vadim. 2002. *Violent Entrepreneurs: The Use of Force in the Making of Russian Capitalism*. Ithaca, NY: Cornell University Press.

Wainwright, J. 2005. "The Geographies of Political Ecology: After Edward Said." *Environment and Planning A* 37: 1033–43.

Walby, S. 2009. *Globalization and Inequalities: Complexity and Contested Modernities*. London: Sage.

Walker, Kathy Le Mons. 2006. "Gangster Capitalism and Peasant Protests in China: The Last Twenty Years." *The Journal of Peasant Studies* 33, 1.

Wall, Derek. 2005. *Babylon and Beyond: The Economics of Anti-Capitalist, Anti-Globalist, and Radical Green Movements*. London: Pluto Press.

Washbrook, Sarah (ed.). 2007. *Rural Chiapas Ten Years after the Zapatista Uprising*. London: Routledge.

Waterman, P. 2010. "Five, Six, Many New Internationalisms! (Nine Reflections on a Fifth International)." <http://blog.choike.org/eng/category/peter-waterman> (accessed October 10, 2010).

Watts, M.J. 2010. "Now and Then." *Antipode* 41: 10–26.

Webber, Jeffery R. 2004. "*Chavismo*: More than a Personality Less Than a Revolution" *New Socialist* 49 <http://newsocialist.org/newsite/index.php?id=71> (accessed August 17, 2009).

______. 2010. *Red October: Left-Indigenous Struggles in Modern Bolivia*. Leiden: Brill Academic Publishers.

Weisbrot, Mark, and Rebecca Ray. 2010. *Update on the Venezuelan Economy*. Washington, DC: Center for Economic and Policy Research.

Weisbrot, Mark, Rebecca Ray and Luis Sandoval. 2009. *The Chávez Administration at 10 Years: The Economy and Social Indicators*. Washington, DC: Center for Economic and Policy Research.

Weisbrot, Mark, and Luis Sandoval. 2007. *The Venezuelan Economy in the Chávez Years*. Washington, DC: Center for Economic and Policy Research.

Weyland, Kurt. 2001. "Will Chávez Lose His Luster?" *Foreign Affairs* 80, 6: 73–87.

White, Caroline. 1980. *Patrons and Partisans: A Study of Politics in Two Southern Italian Comunities*. Cambridge: Cambridge University Press.

Williams, Gwyn. 2008. "Cultivating Autonomy: Power, Resistance and the French Alterglobalization Movement." *Critique of Anthropology* 28: 63–86.

Williams, Michelle. 2008. *The Roots of Participatory Democracy: Democratic Communists in South Africa and Kerala, India*. New York: Palgrave Macmillan.

Williams, R. 1977. *Marxism and Literature*. Oxford: Oxford University Press.

______. 1989. *Resources of Hope*. London: Verso.

Wilpert, Gregory. 2007. *Changing Venezuela by Taking Power: The History and Policies of the Chávez Government*. London: Verso.

Workman, Thom. 2009a. *If You're in My Way, I'm Walking: The Assault on Working People since 1970*. Halifax & Winnipeg: Fernwood Publishing.

______. 2009b. Personal correspondence with Errol Sharpe.

World Bank. 1995. *World Development Report: Workers in an Integrating World*. Oxford: Oxford University Press.

______. 2008. *Agriculture for Development: World Development Report*. Oxford: Oxford University Press.

Worth, O., and K. Buckley. 2009. "The World Social Forum: Postmodern Prince or Court Jester?" *Third World Quarterly* 30: 649–61.

Wright, Erik Olin. 2010. *Envisioning Real Utopias*. London: Verso.

Wright, S. 2008. "Mapping Pathways within Italian Autonomist Marxism: A Preliminary Survey." *Historical Materialism* 16: 111–40.

Young, T. 2008. "Lulled by the Celebritariat." *Prospect* 153, December.

Zerowork. 1975. *Political Materials 1*. New York

______. 1977. *Political Materials 2*. New York.

Zibechi, Raúl. 2011. "The Decade that Transformed a Continent." January 11. <http://www.cipamericas.org/archives/3841>.

Žižek, Slavoj. 2010. *Living in the End of Times*. London: Verso.

About the Authors

Michael Lebowitz is professor emeritus of economics at Simon Fraser University in Vancouver, Canada, and the author of *Beyond Capital: Marx's Political Economy of the Working Class*, winner of the Isaac Deutscher Memorial Prize for 2004, and *Build It Now: Socialism for the Twenty-First Century*. He is Director of the Program in Transformative Practice and Human Development at the Centro Internacional Miranda, in Caracas, Venezuela.

Marta Harnecker is a sociologist, political scientist, journalist and activist. After studying with Louis Althusser in Paris she returned to her native Chile, but was forced into exile following the military coup against Salvador Allende's government. In Cuba she ran the research institute Memoria Popular Latinoamerica (MEPLA) and continues to write. She has published over sixty books to date, from her classic *The Basic Concepts of Historical Materialism* to the more recent *The Left after Seattle*. An ardent defender of the Bolivarian revolution, Her most recent books are *Hugo Chávez Frias: Un hombre, un pueblo; Venezuela: Militares junto al pueblo*; and *Venezuela: una revolución sui generis*.

Bill Carroll teaches Sociology and is founding director of the Social Justice Studies Program at the University of Victoria. His books include *Organizing Dissent: Contemporary Social Movements in Theory and Practice, Remaking Media: The Struggle to Democratize Public Communication, Challenges and Perils: Social Democracy in Neo-Liberal Times, Critical Strategies for Social Research,* and *The Making of a Transnational Capitalist Class*. He is Research Associate with the Canadian Centre for Policy Alternatives, associate editor of the journal *Socialist Studies*, and a member of Sociologists Without Borders.

Luciano Vasapollo is Professor of applied economics in the Department of economic and social analysis of the University Sapienza of Rome Italy. He is also Professor of Applied Economics at the University of Havana and is Director of the research Centre CESTES and the journals *Proteo* and *Nuestra América*. He is the recipient of numerous awards and distinctions awarded by the Cuba's Ministry of National Culture and the Ministry of Economic Planning, as well as SEPLA (the Society of Latin American political economy and critical Thought). In 2006 he was the winner of an international competition in the writing of alternative economic and social thought. He is author and co-author of more than 40 books published in Italian, English and Spanish.

Mauro Casadio is Director of *Rete dei Comunisti* (The Communist Challenge), independent sociopolitical researcher and committee/board member of *Critica Sociale* (LCS) and *Rete dei Comunisti*. He has authored numerous articles in diverse international journals and has contributed to books such as *No/Made Italy Eurobang*; and *Competizione globale*.

Joshua Dumont is a PhD candidate in the Department of Political Science at York University (Toronto). His doctoral dissertation is a study of the role of the workers' movement in the pension restructuring process in France from 1993 to 2003. His academic interests include organized labour, the history of working-class struggles, political economy, racism and social theory. Josh has been active in socialist politics since the late 1990s.

Murray E.G. Smith is Professor of Sociology and Labour Studies at Brock University, St. Catharines, Canada. He is the author of several books, including *Invisible Leviathan* (1994), *Culture of Prejudice* (2003) and *Global Capitalism in Crisis: Karl Marx and the Decay of the Profit System* (2010), as well as dozens of journal articles, book chapters and encyclopedia entries in the areas of social and political theory, political economy and revolutionary movements. He has been active on the socialist left since the 1970s.

James Petras is Professor Emeritus of Sociology and Adjunct professor in International Development Studies at Saint Mary's University (Halifax, Nova Scotia). He is the author and co-author of over sixty books and numerous other writings on the dynamics of world and Latin American developments, including *Unmasking Globalization*; *Social Movements and the State*; *Multinationals on Trial*; *What's Left in Latin America*; and *Social Movements in Latin America: Neoliberalism and Popular Resistance*. A list and an actual file of his periodical writings and journal articles are maintained and can be accessed at <Rebelión, com>.

Hugo Radice is a political economist working on international issues, especially transnational corporations and development, on Marxist theory, and on East-Central Europe. After teaching economics for many years, latterly at Leeds University Business School, he joined POLIS in 1999 and was Head of the School from 2004 to 2007. In 2008 he retired from his full-time post to concentrate on his main research interests, which are on trends in global capitalist development and the role of the state. He is currently working on the reconstruction of Marx's critique of political economy in the light of the collapse of Soviet-style communism, with a particular focus on labour. Recent publications include 'The Idea of Socialism: from 1968 to the Present-day Crisis," *Antipode*, 41/S1; "The Developmental State under Global

Neoliberalism," *Third World Quarterly* 29/6; and, with B. Dunn, *100 Years of Permanent Revolution: Results and Prospects.*

Errol Sharpe is the founder of Fernwood Books (1978) and Fernwood Publishing (1991) where he is presently hold the position of Publisher. For twenty-five years he taught Political Economy and Sociology of Education, first at Atkinson College, York University in Toronto and later at Saint Mary's University in Halifax. He holds a BA from St. Dunstan's (now University of Prince Edward Island) in Charlottetown and a MA in Atlantic Canada Studies from Saint Mary's. He is author of *A People's History of P.E.I.*

Henry Veltmeyer is Professor of Development Studies at the Universidad Autónoma de Zacatecas (UAZ) in Mexico and Professor of Sociology and International Development Studies at Saint Mary's University (Halifax, Nova Scotia Canada). He is author, coauthor and editor of over forty books on issues of Latin American and world development, including *Dynamics of Social Change in Latin America*; and *Critical Development Studies: Tools for Change.* Books coauthored with James Petras include *Unmasking Globalization*; *System in Crisis*; *Social Movements and the State*; *Empire with Imperialism*; *What's Left in Latin America*; and *Social Movements in Latin America: Neoliberalism and Popular Resistance.*

Thom Workman is Professor of Political Science at the University of New Brunswick in Fredericton. His research interests include political and social thought, critical political discourses, Marxism and labour history. He is currently involved in research projects on the political and social thought of A.N. Whitehead, ancient Greek thought on war and empire, and imperialism and Canada. He teaches courses on literature and politics, alternative political communities, alienation, modern political theory, political leadership, and conflict studies. Recent publications include Social Torment: *Atlantic Canada in the New World Order*; *If You're in My Way, I'm Walking: The Assault on Working People Since 1970*; and *Banking on Deception: The Discourse of the Fiscal Crisis.*